Kirtley Library
Columbia College
8th and Rogers
Columbia, MO. 65201

WITHDRAWN

ACCULTURATION

STANFORD ANTHROPOLOGICAL SERIES
NUMBER TWO

ACCULTURATION

Critical Abstracts, North America

Bernard J. Siegel, *Editor*

Assisted by Rose Wax

Committee for Anthropological Research
Department of Sociology and Anthropology
Stanford University

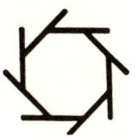

OCTAGON BOOKS

A DIVISION OF FARRAR, STRAUS AND GIROUX

New York   1975

© 1955 by the Board of Trustees of the
Leland Stanford Junior University

Reprinted 1975
by special arrangement with Stanford University Press

OCTAGON BOOKS
A DIVISION OF FARRAR, STRAUS & GIROUX, INC.
19 Union Square West
New York, N. Y. 10003

Library of Congress Cataloging in Publication Data

Siegel, Bernard Joseph, 1913- ed.
    Acculturation: critical abstracts, North America.

    Reprint of the ed. published by Stanford University Press, Stanford, Calif., which was issued as no. 2 of Stanford anthropological series.

    1. Indians of North America—Social conditions—Abstracts. 2. Acculturation—Abstracts. 3. Minorities—North America—Abstracts. I. Title. II. Series: Stanford anthropological series; no. 2.

[E98.S67S55   1975]   301.24'1   75-15397
ISBN 0-374-97433-0

Manufactured by Braun-Brumfield, Inc.
Ann Arbor, Michigan

Printed in the United States of America

PREFACE

In this volume an effort is made to abstract all the major empirical studies reported by anthropologists in the setting of North America which are of importance in analyzing the processes of sociocultural change under conditions of cultures in contact.* The form of the abstracts was suggested by the nature of the project to which they were geared. In addition, however, they should have value for other social scientists working with related phenomena, as well as for the historian and the philosopher interested in culture change and value studies, for they make possible rapid survey and comparison of special fact and interpretations in this field. In all, ninety-four abstracts are presented. It is planned to publish similar materials from studies undertaken in Middle and South America, Africa, the Middle East, Asia, and the Pacific. To the extent that funds are forthcoming, all of these series will be periodically supplemented by publication of subsequent reporting on research. Abstract files of current work will at any event be maintained at Stanford.

Abstractors working under the direction of the editor were Mr. Roland Force, Mrs. Margaret Sumner, and Miss Rose Wax, graduate students in the Department of Anthropology. Thanks are especially due to Miss Wax, who has contributed most extensively to preparing the manuscript for publication. I should like to thank my colleagues, Drs. Felix M. Keesing and George D. Spindler, for their reading and helpful criticism of the introductory discussion. Finally, I am indebted to Marie Keesing for her editorial comments and suggestions. The writer is, of course, responsible for the contents and mode of presentation of the volume in its present form.

Bernard J. Siegel

Stanford University
Stanford, California
   August 2, 1955

---

* The abstracted studies included run through the year 1951.

TABLE OF CONTENTS

PART ONE

INTRODUCTION. Bernard J. Siegel 3

PART TWO

MONOGRAPH ABSTRACTS

1. Adair, John J. A STUDY OF CULTURE RESISTANCE: THE VETERANS OF WORLD WAR II AT ZUNI PUEBLO. 1948, Ph.D. dissertation Univ. of New Mexico....................... 19

2. Barnouw, Victor. ACCULTURATION AND PERSONALITY AMONG THE WISCONSIN CHIPPEWA. 1950. American Anthropological Association, Memoirs, No. 72.................... 24

3. Caudill, William. JAPANESE AMERICAN PERSONALITY AND ACCULTURATION. 1952. Genetic Psychology Monographs, Vol. 45, 3-102........................ 26

4. Cheng, David Te-ch'ao. ACCULTURATION OF THE CHINESE IN THE UNITED STATES; 1948. Fukien Christian University Press, Foochow, China....................... 30

5. Codere, Helen. FIGHTING WITH PROPERTY: A STUDY OF KWAKIUTL POTLATCHING AND WARFARE. 1950. American Ethnological Society, Monographs, No. 18 35

6. Dollard, John. CASTE AND CLASS IN A SOUTHERN TOWN. 1937. Institute of Human Relations, Yale Univ. Press............ 37

7. Du Bois, Cora. THE 1870 GHOST DANCE. Univ. of California Pubs. in Anthropological Records, Vol. III, 1939, 1-152...... 41

8. Elkin, Henry. THE NORTHERN ARAPAHO OF WYOMING. 1940. In Linton, 207-58; see Sec. 25..................... 45

9. Embree, John F. ACCULTURATION AMONG THE JAPANESE OF KONA, HAWAII. 1941. American Anthropological Association, Memoirs, No. 59...................... 47

10. Fauset, Arthur Huff. BLACK GODS OF THE METROPOLIS: NEGRO RELIGIOUS CULTS OF THE URBAN NORTH. 1944. Pub. of the Philadelphia Anthropological Society. Vol. III...... 51

11. French, David H. FACTIONALISM IN ISLETA PUEBLO. 1948. American Ethnological Society, Monographs, No. XIV......... 54

12. Goldfrank, Esther S. CHANGING CONFIGURATIONS IN THE SOCIAL ORGANIZATION OF A BLACKFOOT TRIBE DURING THE RESERVE PERIOD. 1945. American Ethnological Society, Monographs, No. VIII. 57

13. Goldman, Irving. THE ALKATCHO CARRIER OF BRITISH COLUMBIA. 1940. In Linton, 333-89; see Sec. 25. 60

14. Hanks, Lucien M. and Jane. TRIBE UNDER TRUST, A STUDY OF THE BLACKFOOT RESERVE OF ALBERTA. 1950. Univ. of Toronto Press. 62

15. Harris, Jack S. THE WHITE KNIFE SHOSHONI OF NEVADA. 1940. In Linton, 39-118; see Sec. 25 69

16. Honigmann, John J. ETHNOGRAPHY AND ACCULTURATION OF THE FORT NELSON SLAVE. 1941. Yale Univ. Pub. in Anthropology, No. 33. 71

17. Joffe, Natalie F. THE FOX OF IOWA. 1940. In Linton, 259-332; see Sec. 25 73

18. Joseph, A., Spicer, R. B., and Chesky, J. THE DESERT PEOPLE: A STUDY OF THE PAPAGO INDIANS OF ARIZONA. 1949. Univ. of Chicago Press 75

19. Keesing, F. M. THE MENOMINI INDIANS OF WISCONSIN: A STUDY OF THREE CENTURIES OF CULTURAL CHANGE. 1939. American Philosophical Society 80

20. Kluckhohn, C., and Leighton, D. C. THE NAVAHO. 1946. Harvard Univ. Press 83

21. La Violette, Forrest E. AMERICANS OF JAPANESE ANCESTRY: A STUDY OF ASSIMILATION IN THE AMERICAN COMMUNITY. 1946. Toronto. Canadian Institute of International Affairs 87

22. Leighton, Alexander H. THE GOVERNING OF MEN. 1945. Princeton Univ. Press 92

23. Lesser, Alexander. THE PAWNEE GHOST DANCE HAND GAME: A STUDY OF CULTURAL CHANGE. 1933. Columbia Univ. Press. 96

24. Lewis, Oscar. THE EFFECTS OF WHITE CONTACT UPON BLACKFOOT CULTURE WITH SPECIAL REFERENCE TO THE ROLE OF THE FUR TRADE. 1942. American Ethnological Society, Monographs, No. VI 101

25. Linton, Ralph. (ed.) ACCULTURATION IN SEVEN AMERICAN INDIAN TRIBES. 1940. New York: Appleton, Century. 103

TABLE OF CONTENTS ix

26. Macgregor, Gordon. WARRIORS WITHOUT WEAPONS: A STUDY OF THE SOCIETY AND PERSONALITY DEVELOPMENT OF THE PINE RIDGE SIOUX. 1946. Univ. of Chicago Press 105

27. Mead, Margaret. THE CHANGING CULTURE OF AN INDIAN TRIBE. 1932. Columbia Univ. Press. 108

28. Mekeel, Haviland Scudder. A MODERN AMERICAN INDIAN COMMUNITY IN THE LIGHT OF ITS PAST: A STUDY IN CULTURE CHANGE. 1932. Ph.D. dissertation, Yale Univ. 112

29. Miner, Horace. ST. DENIS: A FRENCH-CANADIAN PARISH; 1939. Univ. of Chicago Press 116

30. Nash, Philleo. THE PLACE OF RELIGIOUS REVIVALISM IN THE FORMATION OF THE INTERCULTURAL COMMUNITY ON KLAMATH RESERVATION. 1937. Social Anthropology of North American Tribes, 377-442. 120

31. Opler, Marvin K. THE SOUTHERN UTE OF COLORADO. 1940. In Linton, 119-206; see Sec. 25 .124

32. Powdermaker, Hortense. AFTER FREEDOM: A CULTURAL STUDY OF THE DEEP SOUTH. 1939. New York: Viking Press . .125

33. Smith, Marian W. THE PUYALLUP OF WASHINGTON. 1940. In Linton, 3-38; see Sec. 25. 133

34. Spicer, Edward H. PASCUA: A YAQUI VILLAGE IN ARIZONA. 1940. Univ. of Chicago Press .134

35. Spier, Leslie. THE GHOST DANCE OF 1870 AMONG THE KLAMATH OF OREGON. Univ. of Washington Pubs. in Anthropology, Vol. II, 1927-29, 39-56. 137

36. Spier, Leslie. THE PROPHET DANCE OF THE NORTHWEST AND ITS DERIVATIVES: THE SOURCE OF THE GHOST DANCE. 1935. General Series in Anthropology, No. 1. 139

37. Thompson, Laura. CULTURE IN CRISIS: A STUDY OF THE HOPI INDIANS. (With a chapter, "Time, Space and Language," by Benjamin Lee Whorf). 1950. New York: Harper 141

38. Vogt, Evon Z. NAVAHO VETERANS, A STUDY OF CHANGING VALUES. 1951. Papers of the Peabody Museum of American Archaeology and Ethnology, Harvard Univ., Vol. XLI, No. 1; Reports of the Rimrock Project Values Series, No. 1 145

39. Whitman, William. THE SAN ILDEFONSO OF NEW MEXICO. 1940. In Linton, 390-462; see Sec. 25. 153

x ACCULTURATION ABSTRACTS: NORTH AMERICA

PART THREE

JOURNAL ARTICLE ABSTRACTS

1. Adair, John J., and Vogt, Evon Z. NAVAHO AND ZUNI VETERANS: A STUDY OF CONTRASTING MODES OF CULTURE CHANGE. American Anthropologist 51, 1949, 547-61 159

2. Aginsky, Burt W. and Ethel G. THE PROCESS OF CHANGE IN FAMILY TYPES: A CASE STUDY. American Anthropologist 51, 1949, 611-14 160

3. Albrecht, Andrew C. INDIAN-FRENCH RELATIONS AT NATCHEZ. American Anthropologist 48, 1946, 321-53 161

4. Altus, William D. AMERICAN MEXICAN: THE SURVIVAL OF A CULTURE. Journal of Social Psychology 29, 1949, 211-20 162

• 5. Barber, Bernard. ACCULTURATION AND MESSIANIC MOVEMENTS. American Sociological Review 6, 1941, 663-69 163

6. Barker, George C. SOCIAL FUNCTIONS OF LANGUAGE IN A MEXICAN-AMERICAN COMMUNITY. Acta Americana 5, 1947, 185-202 164

• 7. Barnett, H. G. PERSONAL CONFLICTS AND CULTURAL CHANGE. Social Forces 20, 1941, 160-71 166

8. Caudill, William. PSYCHOLOGICAL CHARACTERISTICS OF ACCULTURATED WISCONSIN OJIBWA CHILDREN. American Anthropologist 51, 1949, 409-27 167

9. Collins, June McCormick. THE INDIAN SHAKER CHURCH: A STUDY OF CONTINUITY AND CHANGE IN RELIGION. Southwestern Journal of Anthropology 6, 1950, 399-411 169

10. Collins, June McCormick. GROWTH OF CLASS DISTINCTIONS AND POLITICAL AUTHORITY AMONG THE SKAGIT INDIANS DURING THE CONTACT PERIOD. American Anthropologist 52, 1950, 331-42 170

11. Dozier, Edward P. RESISTANCE TO ACCULTURATION AND ASSIMILATION IN AN INDIAN PUEBLO. American Anthropologist 53, 1951, 56-66 172

12. Eaton, Joseph W. CONTROLLED ACCULTURATION: A SURVIVAL TECHNIQUE OF THE HUTTERITES. American Sociological Review 17, 1952, 331-40 173

• 13. Gillin, John, and Raimy, Victor. ACCULTURATION AND PERSONALITY. American Sociological Review 5, 1940, 371-80. . . .175

14. Gillin, John. ACQUIRED DRIVES IN CULTURE CONTACT. American Anthropologist 44, 1942, 545-54 177

15. Goldfrank, Esther S. HISTORIC CHANGE AND SOCIAL CHARACTER: STUDY OF THE TETON DAKOTA. American Anthropologist 45, 1943, 67-83 178

16. Goldfrank, Esther S. THE DIFFERENT PATTERNS OF BLACKFOOT AND PUEBLO ADAPTATION TO WHITE AUTHORITY. International Congress of Americanists, Proceedings 29th, 1952, 74-79 179

17. Hallowell, A. Irving. ACCULTURATION PROCESSES AND PERSONALITY CHANGES AS INDICATED BY THE RORSCHACH TECHNIQUE. Rorschach Research Exchange, VI, 1942, 42-50 . .181

18. Hallowell, A. Irving. VALUES, ACCULTURATION, AND MENTAL HEALTH. American Journal of Orthopsychiatry 20, 1950, 732-43 182

19. Hallowell, A. Irving. OJIBWA PERSONALITY AND ACCULTURATION. International Congress of Americanists, Proceedings 29th, 1952, 105-12 183

20. Hawley, Florence, and Senter, Donovan. GROUP-DESIGNED BEHAVIOR PATTERNS IN TWO ACCULTURATING GROUPS. Southwestern Journal of Anthropology 2, 1946, 133-51 186

21. Hawley, Florence. AN EXAMINATION OF PROBLEMS BASIC TO ACCULTURATION IN THE RIO GRANDE PUEBLOS. American Anthropologist 50, 1948, 612-24. 187

22. Heinrich, Albert. SOME PRESENT-DAY ACCULTURATIVE INNOVATIONS IN A NONLITERATE SOCIETY. American Anthropologist 52, 1950, 235-42. 188

• 23. Herskovits, Melville J. THE SIGNIFICANCE OF THE STUDY OF ACCULTURATION FOR ANTHROPOLOGY. American Anthropologist 39, 1937, 259-64 189

24. Herzog, George. PLAINS GHOST DANCE AND GREAT BASIN MUSIC. American Anthropolist 37, 1935, 403-19 190

25. Hill, W. W. THE NAVAHO INDIANS AND THE GHOST DANCE OF 1890. American Anthropologist 46, 1944, 523-27 191

26. Humphreys, Norman D. THE CHANGING STRUCTURE OF THE DETROIT MEXICAN FAMILY: AN INDEX OF ACCULTURATION. American Sociological Review 9, 1944, 622-26 192

xii ACCULTURATION ABSTRACTS: NORTH AMERICA

27. Kinietz, Vernon. EUROPEAN CIVILIZATION AS A DETERMINANT OF NATIVE INDIAN CUSTOMS: THE DELAWARE INDIAN BIG HOUSE CEREMONY. American Anthropologist 42, 1940, 116-21 .194

28. Kraus, Bertram S. ACCULTURATION, A NEW APPROACH TO THE IROQUOIAN PROBLEM. American Antiquity 9, 1944, 302-18 .195

29. Lee, D. D. THE LINGUISTIC ASPECT OF WINTU ACCULTURATION. American Anthropologist 45, 1943, 435-40 .196

30. Malouf, Carling, and Arline A. THE EFFECTS OF SPANISH SLAVERY ON THE INDIANS OF THE INTERMOUNTAIN WEST. Southwestern Journal of Anthropology 1, 1945, 378-91 .197

31. Mekeel, Scudder. A DISCUSSION OF CULTURAL CHANGE AS ILLUSTRATED BY MATERIAL FROM A TETON-DAKOTA COMMUNITY. American Anthropologist 34, 1932, 274-85. .198

32. Mekeel, Scudder. THE ECONOMY OF A MODERN TETON DAKOTA COMMUNITY. Yale University Publications in Anthropology 6, 1936, 3-14 .199

33. Opler, Marvin K. THE INTEGRATION OF THE SUN DANCE IN UTE RELIGION. American Anthropologist 43, 1941, 550-72 .201

34. Pritchett, John Perry. HISTORICAL ASPECTS OF THE CANADIAN MÉTIS. International Congress of Americanists, Proceedings 29th, 1952, 249-55 .202

35. Quimby, George I., and Spoehr, Alexander. ACCULTURATION AND MATERIAL CULTURE. Fieldiana: Anthropology 36, 1951, 107-47 .203

36. Ransom, Jay Ellis. WRITING AS A MEDIUM OF ACCULTURATION AMONG THE ALEUT. Southwestern Journal of Anthropology 1, 1945, 333-44 .205

37. Reichard, Gladys A. THE NAVAHO AND CHRISTIANITY. American Anthropologist 51, 1949, 66-71 .206

38. Rhodes, Willard. ACCULTURATION IN NORTH AMERICAN INDIAN MUSIC. International Congress of Americanists, Proceedings 29th, 1952, 127-32 .207

39. Richardson, Stephen A. TECHNOLOGICAL CHANGE: SOME EFFECTS ON THREE CANADIAN FISHING VILLAGES. Human Organization 11, No. 3, 1952, 17-27 .209

40. Rousseau, Madeleine and Jacques. LE DUALISME RELIGIEUX DES PEUPLADES DE LA FORÊT BORÉALE. International Congress of Americanists, Proceedings 29th, 1952, 118-26 210

41. Senter, Donovan. ACCULTURATION AMONG NEW MEXICAN VILLAGERS IN COMPARISON TO ADJUSTMENT PATTERNS OF OTHER SPANISH-SPEAKING AMERICANS. Rural Sociology 10, 1945, 31-47. 211

42. Shimkin, D. B. DYNAMICS OF RECENT WIND RIVER SHOSHONE HISTORY. American Anthropologist 44, 1942, 451-61 213

43. Siegel, Bernard J. SOME OBSERVATIONS ON THE PUEBLO PATTERN AT TAOS. American Anthropologist 51, 1949, 562-77. 215

44. Slotkin, J. S. JAZZ AND ITS FORERUNNERS AS AN EXAMPLE OF ACCULTURATION. American Sociological Review 8, 1943, 570-75. 216

45. Speck, F. G. ALGONKIAN INFLUENCE UPON IROQUOIS SOCIAL ORGANIZATION. American Anthropologist 25, 1923, 219-27 . . .217

46. Spindler, George Dearborn. PERSONALITY AND PEYOTISM IN MENOMINI INDIAN ACCULTURATION. Psychiatry 15, 1952, 151-59. 217

47. Stewart, Omer C. SOUTHERN UTE ADJUSTMENT TO MODERN LIVING. International Congress of Americanists, Proceedings 29th, 1952, 80-87. 219

48. Thompson, Laura. ATTITUDES AND ACCULTURATION. American Anthropologist 50, 1948, 200-215. 220

49. Tschopik, Harry. NAVAHO BASKETRY: A STUDY OF CULTURE CHANGE. American Anthropologist 42, 1940, 444-62. 221

50. Voget, Fred. INDIVIDUAL MOTIVATION IN THE DIFFUSION OF THE WIND RIVER SHOSHONE SUN DANCE TO THE CROW INDIANS. American Anthropologist 50, 1948, 634-46. 223

51. Voget, Fred. A SHOSHONE INNOVATOR. American Anthropologist 52, 1950, 53-63. 224

52. Voget, Fred. ACCULTURATION AT CAUGHNAWAGA: A NOTE ON THE NATIVE-MODIFIED GROUP. American Anthropologist 53, 1951, 220-31 225

53. Voget, Fred. CROW SOCIO-CULTURAL GROUPS. International Congress of Americanists, Proceedings 29th, 1952, 88-93 226

54. Wallace, Anthony F. C. SOME PSYCHOLOGICAL DETERMINANTS OF CULTURE CHANGE IN AN IROQUOIAN COMMUNITY. Symposium on Local Diversity in Iroquois Culture, Smithsonian Institution, Bureau of American Ethnology, Bulletins 149, 1951, 55-76 228

55. Waterman, Richard Alan. AFRICAN INFLUENCE ON THE MUSIC OF THE AMERICAS. International Congress of Americanists, Proceedings 29th, 1952, 207-18 230

Part One
INTRODUCTION

INTRODUCTION

Bernard J. Siegel

Aims of the Project. — The developing interests of ethnologists in processes of cultural change have mounted steadily over the past two decades and more. By far the greatest amount of empirical data collated on the subject has been done in the context of contact relations effected between the expanding carriers of western European and American cultures and peoples of most of the rest of the world. Motivations for these studies were diverse. Among them were (1) a desire to facilitate the administration of "natives" in colonial areas and of other dependents or semidependents in noncolonial areas (viz., the American Indian); (2) the pursuit of historical interests in the analysis of contemporary events; and (3) the discernment of regularities in short-range changes and of cycles or stages of such changes. Whatever the particular orientation of field workers, the body of empirical observations amassed to the present time is sufficiently impressive to encourage the development of some coherent theory of cultural change.

As a beginning in this direction the writer and one of his colleagues have begun a study designed, in Merton's terms, to codify what is known about the dynamics of acculturation and related phenomena.[1] The object of this phase of our work consists ultimately of drawing all possible theoretical insights and understandings from available empirical research on the subject of change, and to use them as a basis for orienting future research. Specifically this means rephrasing descriptive statements of a text in terms (1) of more general variables stated or implied; (2) of significant relationships that appear to exist between them; and (3) of interpretive variables whose function is that of conceptualizing why a given relationship holds between any two (or more) variables.

A second phase of the project, which must in fact go on simultaneously, involves a reorganization of phenomena studied and of propositions about them into classes or types of understandings. In some cases this is a relatively easy thing to do. Considerable investigation, for example, deals with problems of factionalism in acculturative contexts, others with nativistic reactions, etc. In other cases meaningful classification requires more detailed examination of materials.

Nature of the Critical Abstracts.— The compilation of critical abstracts, of which this is the first volume, was undertaken in order to facili-

---

[1]See R. K. Merton, Social Theory and Social Structure, Columbia University, 1939, especially Chapters 1 and 3. Collaborator on this project is Dr. Felix M. Keesing. The reader is also referred to the latter's publication, Culture Change Stanford Anthropological Series, Number One, Stanford University Press, 1953.

tate analysis and codification. The abstracts are carefully prepared digests of most available sources on American materials.[2] These are recorded in terms of several categories of information considered to be especially relevant to the research aims of this project. In making the breakdown, attention was focused upon what we considered to be an ideal scientific organization of studies, namely: (1) statement of the problem; (2) hypotheses or propositions advanced; (3) methods and techniques used in securing and describing data; (4) basic data; and (5) conclusions reached.[3]

Only a small fraction of the works considered began to live up to this formulation.[4] In all other cases, however, it has been possible to fit statements into this framework, and incidentally to appreciate the astonishingly unsystematic methods of formulating and reporting on research. In monographs, particularly, conclusions, implicit and explicit propositions, and even problem statements may occur anywhere in the body of the text. Page references have been inserted in brackets in the abstracts in order to facilitate the location of such information more exactly within the context in which it occurs in the primary source. Many interesting questions have occurred to an author apparently as outgrowths of his original investigations, and are inserted into the main argument or narrative as speculative asides. An attempt has been made, therefore, to draw these insights out and to place them under an appropriate category in the abstract.

It has obviously been impossible to cite in detail all recorded statements of fact and descriptive materials of any work, and particularly of those over ordinary article length. Mention of virtually every piece of evidence has been attempted, however. Tests of the reliability of abstractors have been made by requesting each of the abstractors to undertake a breakdown of randomly chosen studies. In each instance there was almost com-

---

[2]It should be emphasized that no attempt was made to include either primary sources, like missionary documents and government reports, or popular or semipopular accounts for public consumption, even when they were written by professional anthropologists.

[3]The complete form finally adopted contains the following items:
  Author, Title, Bibliographic Data
  Purpose or Problem (including hypothesis or class of phenomena treated)
  Definitions, Assumptions, and Hypotheses
  Methods and Techniques
  Graphs and Charts (if any)
  Data
  Conclusions (explicit and implicit)

[4]As an example of a study which closely approximates it the reader is referred to E. Spicer, Pascua: A Yaqui Village in Arizona, 1940.

plete agreement on information selected and recorded. Nevertheless, because it was felt that a more extensive context from the sources would be desirable for certain purposes not so concerned with the aims for which these materials were specifically intended, page references are given in brackets.

Problems of Organization. — One of the principal barriers to undertaking the task of codification is the rarity with which the "assemblage" of fact has been geared to any explicit attempt at "systematization," to use Whitehead's terms.[5] The observer very often uses a minimum of organizing concepts to grapple with his data, if indeed he uses or develops any at all. A first step in the analysis of these materials, therefore, has been the organizing of contributions into meaningful theoretical categories — leadership and innovation, factionalism, cultist and nativistic movements — which might further be subsumed under the broad headings of contact conditions, intercultural relations, and effects of contact. A second, really concomitant, step has consisted in isolating and discriminating between studies which are, respectively, theoretically conceived, descriptive and hypothesis eliciting, and ethnographic but largely geared to evidence of change in process.[6] In this way it is hoped, among other things, to introduce some useful degree of comparability to the impressive documentation of empirical evidence on the subject matter, and also to qualify relationships between variables more concretely. Different investigations might vary with respect to degree of conceptual and theoretical formulation, but data from the one might nevertheless be integrated with insights achieved in the other(s); or they might simply be noncomparable in terms of levels of analysis. Indeed, such distinctions have been made according to the degree to which problems were defined and delimited, and data were selected and organized in relation to them.

For purposes of illustrating the degree of comparability and complementarity existing within a given class of problems, I shall consider briefly the results of two contrasting studies of nativistic movements.[7] At this stage no attempt will be made to specify implicit or suggested propositions in such a way as to make them amenable to further testing. It is this goal however, toward which such an analysis is directed.

Mode of Analysis: An Example. — Studies of nativistic adaptations

---

[5] Alfred N. Whitehead, Modes of Thought, p. 2.

[6] Miss Rose Wax, graduate student in Anthropology, undertook a preliminary analysis of this type for a Master's thesis, using the present collection of materials as her primary sources.

[7] The sources used are Cora DuBois, The 1870 Ghost Dance, Univ. of Cal. publs. in Anth. Records, Vol. III, 1939, pp. 1-152; and Philleo Nash, The Place of Religious Revivalism in the Formation of the Intercultural Community of Klamath Reservation, Social Anthropology of North American Tribes (Fred Eggan, ed.), 1937, pp. 377-442.

range from empirical descriptive histories of specific movements to the testing of general hypotheses. DuBois, in her statement of purpose, simply remarks that her study ". . . grew out of a desire to trace the introduction and course of the 1870 Ghost Dance in northern California. No preliminary problem was set beyond the accumulation of data bearing on this subject."

Nash, on the other hand, engaged himself in "A study in the relationship between deprivation and participation in a religious revival on the part of three tribes on one reservation."

If we were to characterize these studies from the point of view of methodology, we should speak of the former as following the method of natural history and the latter as using the method of controlled observation, which in turn is a variant of the controlled experiment. In the natural-history method an attempt is made to trace the development of forms of phenomena in order (1) to understand more fully the particular characteristics of the specific case, by means of documentation and more vivid concreteness; and (2) to establish a range of such cases within a given class in order to facilitate genetic analysis. Thus, DuBois was interested in studying a "series of generically related religious movements" which "not only symbolize but also represent in part the whole struggle between two divergent social systems."

By the completion of the study, the career of these cults has suggested certain conceptual ways of organizing and interpreting the data. Factors operative in the presence or absence of the doctrine complex were given special attention. Absence was construed, moreover, in an active rather than passive way: it involved rejection and not mere indifference. All of the groups in the area investigated had to make some decision. If their members did not feel moved to emotional and psychological reaction in consequence of their contact with whites, they were secondarily affected by intercultural relations with one another. Coping with these forces involved the operation of perceptual and integrative processes. The nature of these processes, at least within the context of her study, is not spelled out by DuBois, but can be inferred from her interpretive statements. I shall respond to the following concluding remarks:

> Once an idea or complex has been introduced to a group there are factors making for its acceptance or rejection. Certain factors which made for the rejection of modern cult elements are . . . (1) insufficient deterioration of a culture as a whole; (2) too great sophistication (because with no grounding in the old culture, an adventist and revivalistic doctrine was meaningless. There was no emotional need for even diluted forms of the old life. The cults to be acceptable had to strike a group at that precise time when the old culture had deteriorated but faith in it had not); (3) skeptics and conservatives both; (4) certain specific doctrinal ideas (e.g., the teaching that half-breeds would

suffer the same fate as the white people; a fear of ghosts and the dead in general). . . . Balanced against the rejective factors were an equal number of factors which must have made the cults acceptable. . . . (1) the hope which the doctrine offered for the rehabilitation of the shattered aboriginal culture and the attendant improvement of economic conditions; (2) a real aesthetic appeal; (3) the direct emotional appeal to recently bereaved persons [136-37].

Once a complex has been accepted it is frequently adapted to local cultural forms. This phenomenon has been observed frequently and has been labeled by anthropologists with the catch phrase "pattern theory". . . . It might be . . . more desirable to give the concept an active connotation by using a word like patterning [137].

The Shasta, Yurok, and Hupa . . . illustrate nicely the relative stability of the three groups involved and may indicate tentatively that patterning is in proportion to stability. That is, the greater the stability of a group, the more pronouncedly it will pattern foreign traits to established institutions. . . . Among these three tribes, who were territorially contiguous, we find three degrees of stability. The Shasta, who enthusiastically embraced the new cults with a minimum of patterning; the Yurok, who accepted the cult provisionally but largely on their own terms, only to reject it subsequently; and the Hupa, who were completely resistive to it. These three grades of receptiveness suggest that social integration and stability are closely allied [138].

The author apparently displays two concerns with her material: (1) the cultural conditions under which nativism, as a mode of adaptation to new environmental situations, strikes a responsive chord and is embraced, and those conditions under which it is actively rejected; and (2) the forms of acceptance when the behavior complex is adopted. Since each of these problems requires special analysis I shall limit myself to a consideration of the former.

Each of the factors making for rejection must be re-examined in terms of operational utility. What, for example, do we mean by "cultural deterioration," and how do we measure it? If it is represented as a continuum, no doubt there would be a very high degree of agreement about a culture in the last stages of deterioration. It is very nearly extinct as a consistent way of life for a distinctive aggregate of individuals; value consensus is at a minimum; choice behavior becomes randomized instead of patterned, etc. At the other pole, however, one might almost define absence of deterioration by frequency of rejection of nativistic cult behavior.

That is to say that a culture whose value system has a positive valence for the majority of its adherents will not seek to recreate itself (metaphorically speaking) by action or symbol. Such behavior is an index of deterioration rather than a correlate of it. At best, one is left with the impression that he must intuit what the author means by the concept. It should be possible to define it operationally, as suggested above, so that one could predict at what point receptivity to nativism becomes maximized.

"Sophistication," "skepticism," and "conservatism" are somewhat easier notions to handle, particularly if we speak of "consistent skepticism" and "consistent conservatism" instead of "tendency toward skepticism" (that is, a polar statement rather than a modal one), etc. Sophistication appears to be equated with degree of "faith" in the forms of the old life or, perhaps more operationally, in the degree of emotional reluctance to change. Of the factors stated as being favorable to acceptance, only one is a direct counterpart of the negative factors. That is, the hope for economic rehabilitation when earlier patterns failed to afford adequate satisfactions to a significant segment of the population. Unfortunately we are not given any clues as to when, theoretically, this point may be expected to occur. Nor are we enlightened about who feel that their culture is "shattered," and what they consider to be an "improvement of economic conditions." In short, one is left with a series of descriptive statements about the conditions under which groups are resistant or responsive to nativistic reactions. These statements, moreover, attempt to answer what happens, rather than why or how it happens.

Finally, the concepts of "stability," "social integration," and "patterning" require some comment. One is again left to intuit from the body of the text just what is meant by these terms. Integration appears to be synonymous with patterning, both of which would consist, then, of mechanisms by which a people assimilate either the forms or meanings — or both — of alien culture elements to their own patterns.[8] Greater or lesser integration might be said to exist, therefore, to the extent that new stimuli are patterned after, or made consistent with, prevailing modes of doing, having, and understanding. This explication perhaps fits more precisely with the concept of cultural, rather than social, integration. There is no general consensus about the latter, but the most widely held conceptions about social integration appear to take one of the two following forms:

(1) An expression of the degree of agreement between normative role playing (statements about what these alignments should be to achieve certain

---

[8]This roughly is what Herskovits speaks of as reinterpretation. The dynamics of this process have been best explicated to date in a paper by Homer Barnett, entitled "Culture Processes," American Anthropologist, Vol. 42, 1940, pp. 21-48.

means) and actual role playing; and (2) an expression of the extent of overlapping personnel in the various groups and associations of a society (kinsmen, friends, and neighbors, for example, also collaborate on productive enterprises, ritual activities, community decisions, etc.). Now it is apparent that, while there is a real difference between the cultural and social dimensions of integration, a significant positive correlation ought nevertheless to exist between them. To the extent that a people perceive new reality objects and events in terms of prevailing tendencies in the sharing of belief and action, we should expect correspondingly a high degree of social integration in either of the respects mentioned above.

<u>Comparison</u> <u>of</u> <u>Method</u> <u>of</u> <u>Correlation</u> with <u>Natural</u> <u>History</u> <u>Method</u>. — From the kind of analysis attempted above it would appear that a natural-history approach lays considerable groundwork for determining the class characteristics of societies and cultures amenable to or resistant to nativistic cult reactions. Important questions still remain concerning <u>why</u> and <u>how</u> changes occur from the latter type of those which favor such reactive tendencies. Hypotheses intended to answer such questions are implicit in the basic data of this study. They will become explicit only in that sort of investigation which states its conclusions in the beginning, as it were, and then sets out to verify or disprove them.

Nash's approach represents such an attempt and is, therefore, useful for comparative purposes. The hypothesis which he proposes is that:

> Nativistic cults arise among deprived groups. They follow a shift in the value pattern, due to suppression and domination, and are movements to restore the original pattern, which they do by the construction of a fantasy situation. The nature of this fantasy, which is basic to the cult, is a function of (1) the original value pattern and (2) the successive changes in the value pattern under white domination.

If the hypothesis is correct, then it is further expected that "those groups which participated most fully in the revival should be those which suffered most deprivation in their contacts with whites."

Deprivation is only generally designated as "feelings of loss or damage" at the very end of the study [442]. Loss, moreover, is to be interpreted not merely in concrete physical terms, but principally in psychological terms. It is loss perceived in relation to expectations about results attendant upon a particular course of action. It is clear from the basic data brought to bear upon the above propositions that the addition of alternative courses of action based upon differing value patterns did not of itself create a sense of damage. Of the three groups compared in southeastern Oregon and northern California, the Klamath suffered least cultural shock. They did not fight the whites, and they remained on their ancestral lands. None of the traditional roles were forcibly deactivated by white contact, but concepts, valuations, and choices associated with them were made amenable to reinterpretation and reorganization by virtue of the intercultural relations established.

Life chances, in short, became subject to re-evaluation on the part of males particularly. Thus, traditionally, highest prestige attached to older chiefs and shamans, lower ranking to younger chiefs, commoners, and of course slaves. In the early contact period none of these positions were displaced, but many individuals with more disvalued statuses could work at various non-Indian jobs on the reservation (jobs at the agency involving the use of English). We learn that the only category which did not take part in the revival were a number of the younger Klamath who did go to work in the agency. These individuals were not the only ones to identify with and accept white skills and values—at least insofar as they were enacted on the reservation—but they were the only ones who had "unequivocally benefited" by same. Deprivation, therefore, is a _relative_ term. Commoners apparently did not feel any great loss by the mere fact of accepting the idea and practice of working on individual farms instead of engaging in community production; some did, many did not. They might have succeeded in materially ameliorating their status had not unforeseen destructive weather conditions undermined their gains, and so caused dissatisfactions with the benefits attached to their roles.

These observations suggest important areas of agreement with certain hypotheses advanced in connection with reference-group theory. Merton and Kitt, for example, in considering the individual who adopts the values of a group to which he aspires but does not belong, have stated the proposition that:

> Within [a relatively closed social system], anticipatory socialization becomes dysfunctional for the individual who becomes the victim of aspirations he cannot achieve and hopes he cannot satisfy. But . . . precisely the same kind of reference group behavior within a relatively open social system is functional for the individual at least to the degree of helping him to achieve the status to which he aspires.[9]

The appearance and continued presence of whites in the area investigated created potentially an open system for those who did not actively oppose them. For the Klamath particularly, new channels were opened up for the achievement of reward. The establishment of permissive intercultural role relations, therefore, made possible the reorganization of choice behavior in the context of an expanded perceptual field. "Anticipatory socialization" for the Klamath meant readiness to learn certain new techniques—

---

[9] "Contributions to the Theory of Reference Group Behavior," in Merton and Lazarsfeld, 1950, p. 88.

individual farming, English, and keeping records on the agency—and to value, for example, the kinds of interpersonal relations and concepts of success associated with them. To the extent that they were successful, these adjustments were certainly functional for the individual. When he failed to achieve the satisfactions anticipated he suffered not only loss relative to expectations, but also the further loss involved in strained if not alienated relations with his in-group.

Group participation in revivalistic cults, or the individual expressions of such behavior, are indices of negative evaluations about means and end values of some outside group, in relation to previous expectations or desires to assimilate to the norms of the latter. But they are also indices of frustrated attempts to maintain prevailing value and normative standards of belief and behavior realistically (involving resorting to open conflict) in the face of alien group pressures. All three groups—the Klamath, Modoc, and Paviotso—shared the common experience of forced adaptation to the same outside group. The channels which they pursued differed, and this fact undoubtedly caused them not only to appraise their respective positions in terms of in-group damage suffered or advantage gained, but also to compare them with respect to each other. About the latter, unfortunately, little is said except by implication or indirection.

In addition to defeat in warfare with the whites, the Modoc are also said to have suffered severe ridicule and loss of self-esteem at the hands of the Klamath and to have been denied access to skills of individual enterprise. The Paviotso, who came to the reservation for protection, simply wanted to avoid all areas of intercultural interaction. Their problem consisted in maintaining traditional orientations without either vigorous self examination or opposition. This was admittedly a most difficult position to maintain over the years.

Anticipated benefits, the perception of opportunities to maximize participation in traditional or new goals, and the degree of initial and later skepticism about white values (as interpreted from agents on the reservation) conceivably were different in each of the groups compared. It is therefore probable that reactive dispositions to the common experience (evaluations of the developing situation) took place with reference to nonmembership groups (whites and other Indian males) as well as to membership groups. In this respect categories of younger and older males within the group also appear to be important frames of reference for developing attitudes and making decisions. Was this equally true in each of the three groups? These status distinctions were obviously important among the Klamath: the younger men could now circumvent earlier modal avenues to the achievement of success. The fact that a number of them did so successfully further accentuated the latent generation cleavages inherent in their social structure. Did the environmental changes so affect the Modoc and Paviotso groups as a whole that no such latent cleavages manifested themselves? Or, to ask the question another way, why did the younger males fail to perceive themselves as being differently affected by the new and challenging experiences than the older, more prestigeful males?

The answer to these and a number of other questions about the contextual structuring of behavioral responses to felt deprivation require some considerations about the nature of comparison and frames of reference used by individuals. Cult behavior in itself is not a homogeneous phenomenon. It may be rather quickly adopted by a large number of individuals (or by a whole group) and intensively pursued over a long period of time;[10] or it may have relatively short-term appeal to a small number of persons. Frequencies, percentages, and value commitments of participating individuals can probably be hypothesized as correlating with systemic characteristics of societies and cultures, as well as with certain personality characteristics. Of the two studies considered here, DuBois' data bear more upon the latter part of this function, Nash's to the former. In order to formulate propositions of the sort suggested, it is first necessary to refine concepts, so that some kind of measurement and greater comparability of evidence and conclusions can be attempted.

Relation Between Studies Compared and a Typology of Nativism. — By way of concluding this partial analysis of cultist behavior I should like to relate certain hypotheses by Linton from a typological analysis of nativistic movements to understandings derived from the papers considered above.[11] Linton suggests the following propositions:

1) Dominant groups which consider themselves superior tend to initiate perpetuative-rational forms of nativism as soon as they achieve power;

2) a dominated group which considers itself superior will normally develop patterns of rational nativism;

3) a dominated group which considers itself inferior may develop nativism of the revivalistic-magical type if subjected to sufficient hardships — including the dominant group's opposition to their assimilation;

4) the threshold of suffering at which movements may develop will vary, and will also be influenced by the patterns of reliance upon the supernatural; a devout society will turn to nativism before a skeptical one will.

5) Nativistic movements are unlikely to arise in situations where both societies are satisfied with their current relationship, or . . . finding themselves at a disadvantage can see that their condition is improving. However, such movements may always be initiated by particular individuals or groups who stand to gain by them.

---

[10] Pubelo societies today are products of this sort of adaptation.

[11] The above citations are taken from a paper entitled, "Nativistic Movements," AA 45, 1943, pp. 230-40.

INTRODUCTION 13

All of these statements imply different frames of reference for comparing one's present and past situations with future expectations. Attitudes, states of mind, and patterns of selective behavior in the face of new alternatives are, to an important degree, functions of (1) identifications with one or more status categories within a community, or (2) identifications with one or more nonmembership groups, or (3) both. To statement (5) we should have to add that satisfaction is not felt simply with reference to nonmembership groups, but also with reference to intragroup relations and sharing of values. In brief, what is needed is a greater refinement of the structuring of crisis situations in intercultural relations.[12] A problem of special interest exists in cases of multiple-reference groups, namely, the regular bases of choice between two or more competing units of identification. Feelings of superiority or inferiority are obviously closely related to the notion of the "crushing impact of European culture" (DuBois) and of "deprivation" (Nash). Because superior or inferior considerations seldom apply to whole cultures, the concept of deprivation or of relative deprivation is perhaps to be preferred.

The "threshold of suffering at which movements may develop" is difficult to translate into operational terms, except with reference to concepts of integration. We may ask: when does the balance between gains and losses within a social system or a value system reach a state in which nativistic reactions appeal to some segment or segments of a population as a rewarding line of response to present crisis? Linton's broader theoretical considerations thus appear to tie in very closely with the more limited descriptive materials and hypotheses generated by the two studies considered above. More comparative work needs to be undertaken, in order to support or qualify these tentative generalizations, and perhaps to add others as well. Several dimensions of cult behavior have deliberately been omitted from our discussion: their esthetic appeal; the shift from doctrinal, ceremonial appeal to individualized, personalized expression; leadership characteristics, to name some of the more important and recurring features. Many particular experiences, however, can be incorporated within broader hypotheses about the role of deprivation, of integration, and of group identification, as in Fauset's statement that:

> . . . one is led to believe that, for many of their members, certain religious cults in northern urban communities assist the transplanted southern worshipper, accustomed to the fixed racial mores and caste requirements of the South, to adjust his psychological and emotional reactions to conditions in the North, where

---

[12]The concept of "crisis" is used here in the sense suggested by W. I. Thomas, Source Book for Social Origins, 1909, p. 18. ". . . crisis, as I am employing the term, is not to be regarded as habitually violent. It is simply a disturbance of habit, and it may be no more than an incident, a stimulation, a suggestion."

all life and living are more fluid and intermingling of the races is inevitable.[13]

Range of Problem Areas.—Revivalistic or nativistic movements comprehend phenomena of very wide occurrence among the societies of the world, including "isolationism" in America, "rising nationalism" (viz., in the Middle East, India, Africa, and Southeast Asia), the creation of new states (Israel), and the continued, long-range, hardened opposition to experimental change by certain ethnic groups within complex populations (viz., the pueblos in Arizona and Mexico). They offer, therefore, an excellent opportunity for testing propositions about the occurrence and characteristics of such patterns of adaptations in a variety of particular intercultural contexts.

Nativism represents one widely recurring process of adaptation to crisis situations inherent in acculturation. Factionalism (perhaps to be included within some wider frame of reference such as *dissociation*) is another equally important pattern to assess. It also assumes several forms, derives from varying rationales, and occurs in many broadly multicultural contexts, including need-fulfilling associations like political parties and labor unions. If, indeed, there is any possibility for a theory of change, it should lead to a better understanding of comparable data from the entire range of problems investigated within social science.

These assembled abstracts do, in fact, demonstrate the wide range of phenomena under observation by the anthropologist— and, as the project continues, by the sociologist and social psychologist—concerned with culture change. They should prove provocative and stimulating to the testing of such tentative theory as has so far been attempted, and provide materials for co-operative exploration by tangential disciplines such as history, philosophy, economics, and political science. The more immediate theoretic contributions will bear upon the nature of equilibria in sociocultural systems, and the conditions under which and processes by which they change. From this point of view they will have greatest implications for sociology and social psychology. In the course of the investigations planned in the co-ordinated program of cultural dynamics at Stanford, it is hoped that a systematic simplification of the enormous welter of empirical evidence will lead ulti-

---

[13]Arthur Huff Fauset, Black Gods of the Metropolis, 1944. Hill's comments on the rejection of the Ghost Dance by the Navaho because of an intense felt fear of the dead in no way disproves or negates the deprivation hypothesis or the role of integration. Nativistic reactions in general are thought to constitute just one of several possible alternative responses to situations which involve feelings of loss. A specific cult form may be avoided or actively rejected (that is, removed from the perceived field of possible choices) when it conflicts with intensely shared values. See W. S. Hill, "The Navaho Indians and the Ghost Dance of 1890," AA 46, pp. 523-27.

mately to the establishment of a series of compendent propositions at the middle level of theory, that is, intermediate between hypotheses geared to specific groups of data and highly generalized theory.

Part Two
MONOGRAPH ABSTRACTS

MONOGRAPH ABSTRACTS*

1. Adair, John J. A STUDY OF CULTURE RESISTANCE: THE VETERANS OF WORLD WAR II AT ZUNI PUEBLO. 1948. Ph.D. dissertation, Univ. of New Mexico.

Purpose or Problem. — 1. How does a pueblo resist the values, ideas, and habits of contemporary Western culture which are pressing in on it from all sides? Specifically, the way in which the Zuni veterans of World War II met with a buffer of resistance when they returned to the pueblo from war service, bringing with them nonpueblo values, ideas, and habits which they had acquired while away from home [1]. We shall examine some of the forces at play which served to perpetuate the ideas and habits of these people, and what cultural techniques were used to combat these forces pressing in from the outside.

2. This resistance to the values of the white world to the culture which surrounds them will be examined from the following points of view, once the contemporary historical background is laid: from the point of view of the force of witch beliefs in Zuni culture; from the point of view of religious pressure; and from the point of view of the other techniques of control that are so important in the pueblo way of life: gossip, rumor, ridicule, and formal action on the part of the pueblo council [6].

Definitions, Assumptions, and Hypotheses. — 1. The pueblos have survived many crises, in part because of their cultural conservatism, possibly the most remarkable of all pueblo characteristics [2].

2. It is reasonable to think that many of the cultural techniques, whereby Zuni is able to reincorporate this great number of men into the traditional life of the village, may indicate a process which remained the same throughout its long history [3].

3. It is my belief that more may eventually be learned of the basic pueblo ethos by studying that point of contact between the white and Indian worlds where values are in sharp conflict, where the resistance is greatest [5].

4. The importance to the present study of witchcraft (defined as "power used improperly") as a motivating force, is that it acts as a control and is one method by which the action of the individual is culturally determined, thus rendering witchcraft immediately relevant to maintaining the status quo of the society and to resisting diffusion [49].

---

*The abstracting procedure has been to retain wherever possible the actual wording of the authors themselves. Thus the bulk of the material consists of direct excerpts; minor editorial revisions or comments have been made only when these were believed to add to the clarity and continuity of the volume. It has therefore not been considered advisable to set off direct quotations from the remainder of the material.

Methods and Techniques. — Zuni was chosen because: it had the largest veteran population (213) of any single pueblo; the author had previous contacts with Zuni; it was the best known single pueblo; a group of Navaho veterans was being studied in the adjacent Ramah area.

Use of previous studies for "depth of focus." Direction of some interviews; not of others. Four oral life histories and two written ones obtained [23-30].

Graphs and Charts. —Appendix I: Clan Census of Zuni (174).

Data. — The pueblo of Zuni went through a period of great tension during the years of World War II because the impact from the outside world was greatly intensified. The nature of this critical period consisted of the following: about 10 percent of the population was removed from the village by the draft; the cash income of the village was greatly augmented by a tremendous increase in the demand for Zuni jewelry for the curio trade, and by government allotment checks, resulting in a rapid change in the material culture of the pueblo. The impeachment of the Zuni governor in 1943 brought about a split in the village; the return of the veterans created a period of uncertainty for the elders, who had lost to a great degree their traditional techniques for dealing with returned warriors. There was also at this period an underlying trend toward disintegration in certain parts of the religious structure of the village. The economic base of Zuni life has been greatly changed in the last twenty years by the tremendous growth of craft work; approximately one-half of the silversmiths and all of the bead workers are women. The ownership of sheep, as well as of cattle and horses, has given the men a certain economic independence of the women which they did not have at an earlier day. While residence is matrilocal, there are many deviations from this pattern, as there were in Kroeber's day, and as there probably always have been. A new development that seems to be gaining favor among the younger generation is the establishment of residence independent of either family. There is also a growing number of Zuni marriages outside the pueblo. Civil authority has become divorced from religious authority to a much greater degree than was formerly the case, making it easier for the United States government to deal with native authority. The governor and his assistants are much more important in village affairs than they used to be, but they still do not have the prestige which goes with high religious office.

A number of changes were evident since Adair's stay at Zuni in 1938: there were many more houses along the Black Rock road, nonpueblo in style; automobiles were everywhere, and relatively few men were seen on horseback; in the houses there was much more furniture; there was also definite indication that Zuni had changed in its attitude towards whites. The architecture today presents a totally different appearance, but this physical appearance is misleading: only the façade is modern. The greatly increased cash income immediately affected other phases of village life. A great many automobiles were bought, and this allowed more and more of the young people to get to town and to the saloon just outside the reservation line. The number of divorces grew, creating hostilities between families and increasing the total friction within the community. Agriculture declined, because silversmithing brought a greater return for time spent. In 1943, there was a change of village officers—and a political split affecting the whole pueblo. Thus when the veterans returned home they found the pueblo in a state of unrest, and this confusion was increased by their unpueblo behavior.

A description of witchcraft as it operates in Zuni society follows. The Zuni is careful not to arouse the enmity of others, but it is equally important not to have anyone suspect him of witchery. To avoid acquiring the taint of suspicion it is necessary to conform as strictly as possible to the Zuni ideals of behavior. Thus the institution of witchcraft serves to help maintain the status quo: individual action is blocked; no one wants to be an innovator and run the risk of arousing jealousy which may lead to being bewitched or being charged with witchcraft. There is good evidence of the fact that the Zuni are more preoccupied with witchery now than they have been at some periods in the past. With the increase in anxiety due to uncertainties in the minds of the villagers and conflicting values in the minds of the men returning home, there was an accompanying increase in witch beliefs, and this in its turn acted as one of the controls which served to subjugate the individual to the will of the community. Thus, many of the veterans have not utilized the knowledge, or followed the ideas and habits picked up while they were in the service.

Religion and its expression in ritual is the single most outstanding aspect of pueblo culture, the point of greatest cultural elaboration. Many veterans while in the service observed both Zuni and Christian religious practices. There did not seem to be any great stress or confusion as a result; it seemed quite possible for the Zuni to believe in both germs and witches, with the following of one set of beliefs not excluding othe other. While the men were away from the villages, religion was an individual matter; as soon as they returned, they were forced to conform with traditional ritual practices enforced by the public opinion of the pueblo. There was a very definite "bid" for the men on the part of the curing societies, but it is not known whether this whole process is a carry-over from the old war practices of the past, or a new development based on a conscious desire of the leaders of the various curing societies to recruit new members. There is a slackening of activity in the katchina cult on the part of the young men, but this probably represents a general trend rather than a function of acculturation among veterans. Lack of faith in the katchina cult and in the ritual procedure of the rain priests is in striking contrast to the firm belief of these men in the efficacy of treatment offered the sick by the curers. Lack of belief in the weather control has been undermined by the changing economy; since there is an alternate way of obtaining food, that is, working for wages, the motivation for dancing to obtain rain for the crops has shifted from one of necessity to one of social conformance. Medical treatment offered by the government has not become an alternate method of curing in the sense that wage earning has become an alternate means of obtaining food, because of the necessity of dealing with witches as long as anxieties are expressed in that way.

The following techniques of enforcing public opinion are discussed: gossip, rumor, ridicule, and formal action taken by the pueblo council. Ridicule, rumor, and gossip— because of the strong sense of shame— are especially effective devices. These three (other than formal action) form a kind of superstructure which rests on the underlying sense of shame, and they are as important as witchcraft in determining "social timidities" (Parsons) and shaping the Apollonian (Benedict); as a result of the sense of shame, a Zuni feels uncomfortable whenever he is made to feel conspicuous. All aspects of behavior which deviate from the norm become the subject of village gossip; two "subjects" of gossip are presented: (1) the feeling of the Zuni towards those of their fellows who aspire to "act like whites," and (2) gossip leveled against those who deviate from the religious patterns. It is quite possible that gossip of the first sort proved to be a greater block to these men, as carriers of new traits and ideas brought back from the outside, than any other cultural technique. It forced many of these men to change their ways shortly after their return: if they persisted in their ways they were made to feel uncomfortable. This gossip is so powerful that the veterans have not been effective as culture carriers.

Conclusions.— 1. The cultural continuum which we find in the pueblos is most noteworthy. The socioreligious structure remains basically unaltered. So too the Zuni language is a vital part of their cultural heritage, and is not only the language of the elders but that of the young children. In contrast to this resistance of foreign socioreligious values, we find today that the Zuni accept elements of our material culture which may be conveniently fitted into their way of life. This differential has often been commented upon, i.e., the way in which change in the ethos of a people "lags" behind the change in their technology [3-5].

2. I thought that the veterans would be important agents of diffusion of new ideas and habits which could be observed and described. But this was not the case, and I began to think in terms of resistance to diffusion, in terms of a reaction within the pueblo whereby a tightening took place that made the diffusion of new ideas not only ineffectual but even impossible. The study was reoriented from one of culture change to one of cultural stability, of cultural conservatism [23].

3. In much of the literature on acculturation the conflicting sets of values of the dominating culture (economically speaking) juxtaposed with the native values is supposed to lead to frustration and social maladjustment. Here we certainly find an exception. The rationalization of the Zuni allows him to hold both sets of values with a minimum of conflict [69-70].

4. Because of the period of stress created by the war the anxieties of the people have increased. Witchcraft is, at Zuni, a traditional method of displacing these anxieties, that is, attributing one's personal difficulties not to individual failure, but to a conceptualized scapegoat: the witch [74].

5. The 213 Zuni men who served in the armed forces learned new habits, ideas, and techniques, and acquired new attitudes and values while they were away from their pueblo. Native belief in witchcraft and religious activities have acted as controlling forces and have drawn the men back into their native way of life. Public opinion in the pueblo as it is expressed in the form of gossip, rumor, and ridicule has been a most effective technique in the enforcing of the traditional way of life and has acted as a deterrent to these men. As a result of these barriers no nonpueblo traits of significance had been introduced by these men into the pueblo at the time of the research [161].

6. There is a narrow margin between the years of plenty and the years of want, and this margin was overcome only by close co-operation in ritual. The controls are unconscious techniques of making the people conform. [162].

7. There is an indication that the women have a stronger economic position in the pueblo than they had twenty or thirty years ago because of the store credit they are able to maintain as a result of their crafts. This is emphasized here because of the fact that it is not the women who are the agents of contact with the outside world: it is the men; and it is the men who have taken on more of the attitudes, ideas, and habits from Western culture primarily because they are the ones who have been exposed to them [163-64].

8. An equally significant point is the "drifting-out" process that is a most important dynamic in modern pueblo culture, and has been of great importance in the retention of the old ways. There is a steady drift from the pueblo of those who are not willing to conform to the traditional ways of the Zuni. The result of this is that those who might be cultural innovators are lost from the stream of Zuni life. A selective process is at play: it is the nonconformist who leaves the village [164-65].

9. Zuni is a much less friendly pueblo, insofar as its relations with whites are concerned, than it was thirty years ago. It is probable that this attitude towards whites has diffused from the Rio Grande pueblos, which have been hostile to whites for a long time. Growing hostility toward whites is certainly in part a result of the encroachment of the white world on what was until quite recently an isolated pueblo. The Zuni are acutely aware of the fact that certain aspects of their ritual are being lost. It is basic to Zuni belief that to share a religious secret is to destroy its efficacy. By the same token, becoming more secretive may increase the power which has gotten out of hand. Is it a successful technique of handling the same situation (as at the Keresan and Tanoan pueblos) — secrecy and hostility toward whites? This recent antagonism toward whites is another reason the white ways carried back to the pueblo by the veterans have not taken root [165-67].

10. Accompanying this hostility toward whites is a certain "nativism" that may be seen in the revival of ceremonies at least three of which have been given for the first time in many years. It looks as if, in the face of certain aspects of disintegration of the total religious structure, other parts are flourishing, at least for the moment [167].

2. Barnouw, Victor. ACCULTURATION AND PERSONALITY AMONG THE WISCONSIN CHIPPEWA. 1950. AAAM, No. 72.

Purpose or Problem. — To contrast the acculturation of the Wisconsin Chippewa with that of neighboring tribes, such as the Dakota and Cheyenne, and show how some of the Chippewa reactions to white domination reveal culture and personality patterns which were characteristic of the Chippewa but not of the Dakota and Cheyenne [7]. To analyze behavior and also the characteristic group responses of the Wisconsin Chippewa to a series of historical events stemming from the impact of western culture [8]. To find out whether "group personality" traits had any bearing on the historical events, and how these traits may have been displayed [29].

Definitions, Assumptions, and Hypotheses. —1. Patterns in acculturation have varied greatly from one tribe to another, even when similar problems and conditions were met [11].

2. Such differential reactions may be ascribed to: the great diversity of geographical, sociological, and economic conditions in the different culture areas of aboriginal North America, and to a complex of cultural, sociological, and psychological factors. Differential reactions of the second type often tell us something about the constitution of these Indian societies, the personality characteristics of their members, and the central values and preconceptions embedded in the native cultures [11-12].

Methods and Techniques. —An application of the culture and personality approach to the domain of history [8].

Several summers' field work (1944 to 1947); most of the work with four individuals. (See Appendix for their life history materials.) Drawings, TAT, and Rorschach records collected.

Data. — The Chippewa seem to have accppted white domination very readily. They quickly arrived at a modus vivendi with the fur trader and became very dependent upon him. There has been a discernible continuity of social patterns among the Chippewa. The social structure was atomistic in the past, and so it remains today, and the personality structure associated with the former way of life persists to a considerable extent, contrasting markedly with the situation on the Plains, where a tradition of co-operative activity seems to have persisted even on the reservations. Among the Chippewa the social atomism was reinforced by cultural-psychological factors which served to imbue the individual with a sense of isolation. Culturally induced fears, and particularly the fear of sorcery, led to mutual suspicions which inhibited the development of co-operative activities.

Various possible explanations are presented to account for the Chippewa ready acceptance of white domination, in contrast to many of the surrounding groups. (a) The Chippewa were more fortunate in the types of white men they had to deal with. This is shown to have been partly true; however, the attitude of the Chippewa toward the successive white conquerors did not vary very much. (b) Familiarity with the white man's strength; while this did much to dissuade Indian groups from rebellion, it was not always enough to serve as a deterrent to warfare. (c) The individualism of the Chippewa and their inability to co-operate successfully in large group ventures. While important, this does not explain the remarkable rarity of isolated outbursts against the white man, despite the many reasons for resentment and the fact that out-groups were generally regarded with mistrust and dislike by the Chippewa.

Early contact was mainly through the trader, whose power lay in his possession of vital supplies, the access to which depended upon his willingness to extend credit. The relationship was a symbiotic one, he needing their furs, and the Indians dependent on his trading goods. In many cases he was really the crucial authority in the band, of greater functional importance than the "chiefs." This relationship between the Indians and the trader is an important one because it apparently formed the prototype for later attitudes toward the American government and its representative, the Indian agent. In both cases, the white man represents "the father," the source of goods and rations, the promiser of gifts, the organizer and initiator of new schemes of social action. This identification of the white man with the father is related to the characteristic father-child relationship in the society which is characterized by unsatisfied needs for affection and dependence. This is shown, too, in the submissive approach to supernatural power through the appeal to pity.

The Plains tribes were generally not willing to enter into the kind of dependent relationship which the Woodland tribes soon developed with the white man (as exemplified by the Chippewa, Menomini, Cree, etc.). This is seen to be related to the kinship structure and child-training patterns, which in the Plains tribes did not foster an inflation of the father image or tend to the development of submissive attitudes toward authority. Because of their long and stubbornly preserved autonomy, the Plains Indians were crushed into submission, not gradually absorbed as the Woodland peoples were; this catastrophic change resulted in an alteration of the character structure of many Plains tribes. However, among the Chippewa there does not appear to have been any marked shift in personality patterns from one generation to the next. This is ascribed to the fact that Chippewa acculturation resulted in no disorganization of social structure, no change in the nature of interpersonal relationships. The long apprenticeship with the trader served to induct the Chippewa gradually into their present place in the western world. Differences in tempo between the Woodland and Plains acculturation are evident, as well as differences in the nature of the acculturation.

Woodland expression of anti-white hostility and resignation to white domination also set in sooner. An early nativistic movement, the Shawano cult, developed among the Woodland tribes in the early nineteenth century. This was based on revelations received by an Indian prophet from the Great Spirit and was characterized by certain anti-white features, including the expectation of eventual deliverance from the white man. In many ways it was more realistic than the later Ghost Dance, which was too violent in its expression of anti-white aggression to appeal to the Chippewa, and therefore was not accepted by them, although they did accept the Drum Dance from the Dakota, which was organized to promote peace and harmony and did not run counter to Chippewa values.

Conclusions. — 1. Although some friction and irritation were unavoidable during the contact period, the Chippewa adjusted without any real protest to the new state of affairs, because the white man brought many gratifications which they valued highly. The atomism of their society favored a gradual and piecemeal type of acculturation. The Chippewa did not have to undergo the traumatic organization experienced by the Plains tribes, for in their case there was no marked change in the social order attendant on the white man's assumption of power over them. Patterns of interpersonal relationships did not significantly alter, and consequently there seems to have been no change in the personality structure of the Chippewa [76].

2. No analysis of historical causation can afford to leave personality variables out of the reckoning. Those differences in Chippewa and Dakota acculturation were not only the results of contrasting socioeconomic conditions; they reflected as well emotional responses and attitudes characteristic of personality structures which had been moulded by different cultural environments [76].

3. Caudill, William. JAPANESE AMERICAN PERSONALITY AND ACCULTURATION. 1952. Genetic Psych. Monographs, Vol. 45, 3-102.

Purpose or Problem. — To investigate the personality and societal dynamics of the conflict situation faced by the Nisei [18].

Definitions, Assumptions, and Hypotheses. — There seems to be a significant compatibility (but by no means identity) between the value systems found in the culture of Japan and the value systems found in American middle-class culture. This compatibility of values gives rise to a similarity in the psychological adaptive mechanisms which are most commonly used by individuals in the two societies as they go about the business of living [9].

2. A value system, following Parsons, may be defined as a limited

set of interrelated principles governing conduct—a set of normative ideas, rules and symbols, shared by members of a society and coloring the actions of individuals in every sphere of their life. Adaptive mechanisms, as discussed by French, may be defined as general techniques used by the ego to meet many different situations arising in everyday life. The psychological adaptive mechanisms most commonly used by individuals interacting with each other in a society may be called the socially approved mechanisms of that society [9].

3. Japanese and middle-class American societies, and the personalities that are developed in these societies, seem to share several parts— the value systems and the adaptive mechanisms—that appear to be similar, but these parts are differentially combined with others to produce dissimilar social structures and personalities in the two groups. Because they are not identical, there are many points of conflict as well as agreement for the Nisei individual attempting to adjust to American middle-class life. [10].

4. Theoretical constructs used as general framework [11]: The common psychological adaptive mechanisms of a group of individuals can be thought of as integrated with various degrees of success into a wide range of personality adjustments. The society in which these individuals live will favor certain types of these personality adjustments so that modes can be found in the total range of adjustment and these modes will vary in different societies. However, all individuals in the total range will share a complex of basic personality characteristics which allow them to utilize their social personalities as they act out their roles within the social structure of a society which is conditioned by a set of symbols and a value system [11]. A society is seen as composed of a group of individuals who mutually interact in terms of values and symbols within the framework of an interlocking network of social structures. A social structure is defined as a system of formal and informal groupings by which the social behavior of individuals is regulated [12]. Operating within the social structures of a society are its status systems composed of a series of status positions which individuals can occupy [12]. Each status position calls for the playing of a different role by an individual, and the composite of his social role behavior may be called his social personality.

5. Psychological adaptive mechanisms are considered to be a less complex construct than "basic personality," etc. (cf. Alexander). These ideas stem mainly from a theory stated by French of the goal strivings of individuals which give rise to adaptive mechanisms by which individuals seek to reach their goals. The integrative capacity of an individual may be defined as the amount of tension he is able to withstand in striving after a goal without showing signs of disintegration [15]. Some adaptive mechanisms may be considered as defenses erected by the ego against inner conflicts arising in the personality.

6. Individuals in a society share certain basic personality character-

istics because, especially as children, they experienced similar culturally patterned pressures to complete their early and crucial developmental tasks within a society having a particular social structure and value system. More than this, the individuals share a common set of adaptive mechanisms which are, however, capable of a wide range of types of integration resulting in many variations in personality structure. The types of integration of the adaptive mechanisms which occur with greatest frequency in the total range of personality structures are probably the result of social influence [16].

7. Immigrant individuals identify with, not just imitate, that class or group in the host society with which they feel most familiar (cf. Ruesch) [17].

Methods and Techniques. — Analysis of 70 TAT records (30 Issei, 40 Nisei), compared with an analysis of 40 white lower-middle-class and 20 white upper-lower-class records in terms of values and psychological adaptive mechanisms. (There is an attempt to include individuals representative of all types of adjustment.)

Part of a collaborative research.

Graphs and Charts. — Table 1: Percentage Distribution of Issei and Nisei ISC Placement, 26; Table 2: Percentage Distribution of Nisei ISC and ILA Placement, 26; Table 3: Values and Themes on Selected TAT Pictures, 39-40; Table 4: Values and Themes on Selected TAT Pictures, 48-49; Table 5: Values and Themes on Selected TAT Pictures, 58-59; Figures 1-4: Types of Adjustment from analysis of 15 TAT Records, 74-77.

Data. — The Nisei as a group tend to be solidly oriented toward the "common man" level, and to lack any upper- or lower-class orientation. From the high level of education and training of the Nisei, from the jobs they have and the evaluations of their employers, and from their socio-economic placement, it can be seen that the social personalities which they exhibit, as the sum of their social roles, are very close to those found in the lower middle class. Where Japanese-American values differ in emphasis by comparison with middle-class values, these differences are not of such a nature as to draw unfavorable comment from the middle class. But despite the compatibility of values and adaptive mechanisms between the two groups, when these cultural and psychological characteristics are drawn together for each group, two recognizably different basic personality patterns emerge.

The most distinctive feature of the social organization of the rural Japan from which most of the Issei came was the consanguineous family system, usually composed of members from three generations; with its rigid code of obligations subordinating individual interests to those of family units, submission is demanded in the name of the supreme value of a common loyalty to the family. The main teaching and disciplinary techniques are teasing and ridicule, mainly by the mother. Thus, the approval of the outside world becomes exceedingly important, with the best defense in a precise knowledge of exactly what is expected. Moral conflict is a matter of being caught between conflicting external obligations and not of conflict between principle and the pressure of social custom, as it is most often with Americans. The Japanese individual receives much support and security from his family, but also in all his dealings with the outer world he must carry the heavy burden of being the representative of the entire family group rather than operating as a single individual. In Japan, an outlet for this heavy load of tension is provided in sensual, physical pleasure; the Nisei however are barred from a release of tension in physical indulgence because middle-class values learned in school and among white peer groups place a negative sanction on such behavior. The Nisei thus felt the full effect of the tension and anxiety aroused by trying to live up to Japanese obligations in the widened competitiveness of an American middle-class world, but were denied most of the traditional Japanese techniques for releasing such tension.

The Issei place a high value on the attainment of such long-range goals as higher education, professional success, and the building of a spotless reputation in the community. These goals they willingly help the Nisei to attain because it is their unquestioned expectation that they will in turn fulfill their obligations to their parents. It is this "unquestioned expectation" that is the source of greatest conflict for the Nisei who feel deeply their obligations to their parents, but who also are striving for integration into American middle-class life. Both Nisei and Americans of the middle class have an ego structure that is very sensitive and vulnerable to stimuli coming from the outer world, and a superego structure that depends greatly upon external sanction. However, this is much more true of the Nisei, where parents must uphold society's values and act as censor regardless of their more personal feelings, without providing protection against the outer world.

Conclusions. — 1. An analysis of the data presented here seems to bear out the initial hypothesis of the study that there is a significant compatibility (but by no means identity) between the value systems found in the culture of Japan and the value systems found in American middle-class culture, and that this gives rise to a similarity in the psychological adaptive mechanisms which are most commonly used by individuals in the two societies [94].

2. The situation seems to bear out Ruesch's hypothesis that in the acculturation process from ethnic to American the individual strives for substitution of cues of essentially similar value. This phenomenon points to the further hypothesis suggested by this research, that immigrant individuals identify with, not just imitate, that class or group in the host society with which they feel most familiar, and that their mobility strivings are centered on the problem of obtaining membership in this more familiar class or group. Thus, it would seem that the Japanese Americans strove with considerable success to be like the American middle class because middle-class values were those that were most like Japanese values [93-94]. Substitution of cues of essentially similar value cannot always be achieved successfully.

3. The harshness of Japanese child rearing is consistently mitigated

by the indulgent affection of the paternal grandmother. The Nisei never knew their grandparents, and this source of gratification was closed to them. By extension, this is equally true for the second generation of any immigrant group, and this important fact has been too little stressed in the literature on the personality dynamics of various ethnic groups [32].

4. It is now possible to restate the hypothesis in general terms so that it may serve as a guide to future research. If the value systems of two societies can be shown to be compatible in many areas of life, this compatibility, often in the face of surface dissimilarities, will give rise to a similarity in the psychological adaptive mechanisms found in the personalities of individuals in the two societies [94-95].

5. Since the same adaptive mechanisms may be integrated with various degrees of success by a number of individuals into their personalities, it is possible to examine in a systematic fashion the range of personality adjustments in a society, and also to begin to determine the modal adjustments in this range [95].

4. Chêng, David Tê-ch'ao. ACCULTURATION OF THE CHINESE IN THE UNITED STATES. 1948. Fukien Christian University Press, Foochow, China.

Purpose or Problem. — Not a problematical approach, but an attempt to penetrate into a confined area of human behavior by analyzing and scrutinizing its forms, its processes, and its principles as experienced and manifested by this particular group of Chinese in Philadelphia [4]. Before a more clear picture can be drawn and the concept generalized it is highly necessary that the data of acculturation of different groups should be made available for comparison [4].

Definitions, Assumptions, and Hypotheses. — Discussion of concepts of "human nature," "acculturation," etc. [6-16].

Methods and Techniques. — Participant-observation; personal interview; use of documents and historical records; re-evaluation of historical analyses and reconstructions [17-18]. The author was missionary of the Chinese Christian Center (1940 to 1944) and teacher of the Chinese Public School for children and Sunday School in Philadelphia's Chinatown.

Graphs and Charts. — Twenty-eight tables: Density of Population; Occupations; etc.

Data. — The Chinese immigrants in Philadelphia are practically all Cantonese, and from a specific area along the southern coast of the province of Kwangtung. This area has always been looked upon as a cultural frontier, and has served as the last foothold of national defence against northern aggressors. Due to its long contact with the outside world, and widespread emigration, the people are looked upon as liberal and progressive.

Canton has been one of the most important hinges upon which the culture of West and East came to meet. The main causes of emigration—which was common—are economic pressure and previous migration or relatives; the peak of migration to this country being 1880 to 1890. Discovering their high visibility, they adapted themselves to this new situation (1) by geographical dispersion, and (2) occupational adaptation, in noncompetitive areas.

In tracing the history of development of the Race Street Chinatown in Philadelphia there are two factors to bear in mind: (1) the tribal relationship, and (2) the geographical provincialism, both of which are deep-rooted Chinese cultural traits. The first stage was characterized by the individual establishment of laundry shops evenly scattered through the whole city, with some central figure gradually emerging as leader. The second stage was marked by the beginning of organization of recreational activities, such as opium smoking, Chinese tea, and card games. The third phase was characterized by the mushroom growth of vicious practices, e.g., gambling, with feuds between clans starting—the tong wars. The fourth stage was that in which the store became the leading center in all affairs among the Chinese people, affording a milieu where the Chinese could feel comfortable and safe. Chinatown thus provides for the Chinese aliens a neighborhood of primary relations.

The occupational variety of the Chinese in Philadelphia, as in the rest of America, is very limited. Laundry operatives outnumber all others; a fair second are the restaurants. There are a few grocery stores and curio shops, and a very few professional people. During the war period there has been much labor mobility, with the number of unemployed being reduced, many going into industrial work, and a gradual increase of professional and semiprofessional workers. The majority of the Chinese in America were peasants and most of the occupational activities in this country are new to them. Laundrying, as a specialized vocation, is a Western trait; in the old days, the laundry work was done by the women. Its adoption is entirely motivated by pecuniary gain. The Chinese restaurant men are more inclined to approximate the American standard of living. They are comparatively better educated, expecially in English, and are relatively well-to-do. Most are second generation or came rather early in life; their families usually reside in the white men's residential zones, with a higher standard of living; this group is accorded not only economic advantages but also social prestige. Changes in the menu to suit the American taste have been a tendency during the last score of years. The modernization of the kitchen is also significant. In trying to meet increasing demands, the store has become the community center, post office, family bank, tribal house, and cultural center, besides serving in the orthodox function as supplier of Chinese goods. The lonely life of most of the immigrants increases the desire for some form of social life; in addition, the storekeeper (or bookkeeper) is usually a literate person, commanding high respect and honor, and with business connections in China enabling them to handle the financial affairs of the immigrant, especially supporting the big family left behind in China. The Chinese storekeepers (1) are the most conservative group; (2) have a much better Chinese education than others; (3) usually have their families here and live in Chinatown; (4) deal almost exclusively with the Chinese, and are the least able to speak English; (5) are the loyalists to China; (6) have an antagonistic attitude toward white people. All the professional Chinese, except the Christian ministers, are second generation; the number in this group is exceedingly small. The largest group is that of the engineers; these are the most Americanized, and most of them intend to go back to China after the war. That most of the ministers are from China indicates that there exists a religious incompatibility between the first and second generations. There is only one Chinese M.D., with few patients among the Chinese, since they usually resist medical advice, other than traditional herbs. Government officials are looked upon as symbols of power and authority; the conception of government as a personal relationship makes workers in the government office popular (in this case, an interpreter). The one practicing barber has eliminated the Chinese specialties (e.g., eye cleaning), but still provides a social experience rather than the impersonal one of a non-Chinese speaking barber.

There are various kinds of social organizations: (1) Tribal organizations, composed of a small group of immigrants who have the same surname and are more or less related to each other. Membership is by popular election so that homogeneity can be maintained. This was the earliest form of organization here. (2) Regional organizations which have had a very powerful influence in Chinese society in America; all people who come from the same district are included. The function is (a) to provide mutual aid for the sick and impoverished; (b) mutual protection; and (c) a respectable funeral. They are also active in providing special relief in their own particular district in China. (3) Economic organizations, e.g., guilds—only recently formed in the large cities. An over-all Chinese Public Association handles all the big affairs which concern all Chinese. There are also tongs—Chinese secret societies "gone wild." Since their inception, the tongs have been connected with all the organized vice in Chinatown; wars between them are frequently only a pretext for the traditional enmity existing between groups and involve all the Chinatowns, in view of their strong organization. These are apparently dying out in importance although they may possibly transform themselves into civilian benefit organizations.

Chinese family life in the United States has undergone many changes. Since emigration is a means for a better family life in China in the future, there was in the earlier period no desire on the part of the Chinese to bring their wives. Four different types of families are described: (1) "mutilated"—with wives in China; (2) "divided"—with the rest of the extended family in China still looking after the emigrant's; (3) "grafted"—marriage to an American (culturally); (4) "emancipated"—Chinese born in the United States, and their families, ranging from least to most acculturated. The only traces of Chinese culture in the latter group are to be found on their dining table, with Chinese food served some of the time, and the casual observance of Chinese festivals; they have little relationship with relatives in Canton. Marriage is as important an event as ever; now, however, the intricate ceremonies are replaced by the elaborate Christian church ceremony, although the marriage partners are not necessarily Christian by faith; divorce is still extremely rare, and the traditional concept of marriage has not been altered. Changes in parent-child relationships are occurring in China, with the younger generation becoming more independent and assertive. This process is being accelerated in America, although the bond between parents and children still seems to be closer in a Chinese-American family than among average white Americans, despite the conflict between generations to be found in American groups. Husband-wife relationships are undergoing change, despite cultural resistance in that (a) the personality of the wife is gradually being recognized both because of the law and because of appreciation of her economic value; (b) the relationship is becoming more American, i.e., more democratic, as in control of the family purse.

Education in China is regarded as one of the supreme social values; it is instrumental rather than ethical; to become a government official, by succeeding in the civil service examinations, is the highest honor one can bring one's family, as a life-long guarantee of comfortable living. Western influence in China has swung the emphasis from classical to utilitarian; the major subjects of Chinese students in this country are overwhelmingly in practical scientific training rather than theoretical philosophical studies. The percentage of children in school in the United States is much higher than in the homeland; in nearly every Chinatown a Chinese public school is also established in which Chinese culture can be taught.

A discussion of the festivals, and of the ceremonials and celebrations in the life cycle follows. The custom of marriage, it is pointed out, has been rapidly changing in China itself. The old belief that marriage is predestined is giving way to the new doctrine that marriage is a civil contract. The ceremony is becoming simpler, with the financial obligation greatly reduced. Conflict with respect to parental consent is common in this country. The many Chinese customs relating to death, because of their religious significance, stubbornly resist change. Reasons given for the slowness of the Chinese to take on Christianity are (1) China for many centuries had never known or met any culture and civilization equal to her own; she had always been a giver and teacher. (2) The inconsistency between Western religion and practices has weakened its appeal. The Sunday School is attended (a) primarily for utilitarian purposes, mainly to learn English; other reasons are (b) to seek personal help; (c) to gain social status among the white group; (d) to avoid troubles during tong conflicts; and (e) the fear of deportation. The Chinese attitude toward religion is tolerant, and they discern one common purpose in all religions, to persuade all men to do good.

In the area of recreation, the process of acculturation is going on pretty rapidly: teahouse going and feasting is retained, as is amateur music; the Chinese theater is almost absent, although the influence of American movies is growing; public holidays and festivals no longer are as important. Recreation for the second-generation Chinese is entirely different from the immigrants' except for mah-jongg; theirs are similar to Americans' generally— e.g., movies, funnies, baseball, and social parties; increasing recognition of the vacation idea is noted.

Conclusions. 1. In nearly all cases, the dates of celebrations have been changed to the nearest Sundays to suit the convenience of people living under the new culture pattern. There are many customs which have adopted new forms but have preserved the spirit and the implications of such practices (e.g., Kite Day—representing height or aspiration). In several cases, both the spirit and the form of the custom have disappeared; what may be left is only an occasion for feasting. There are also customs whose traditional forms have been maintained but their spirit is lost. Last is the kind of custom whose form and content have both been changed, as evidenced in the customs surrounding births, weddings, and funerals [186].

2. The emotional and psychological life which the Chinese immigrants acquired during their childhood in China has by no means been transformed, but rather temporarily submerged into a dormant state by the new cultural pressure, although there are some outworn superstitious practices that have utterly failed to survive in the new cultural climate. Many old taboos, however are still preserved and new ones have been created in order to safeguard their good luck in earning a fortune for which they have come to this country [203].

3. We find three different aspects of the process of acculturation, with respect to recreation: (a) The aspect in which the recreation satisfies a certain desire, involves little effort of learning and requires no direct personal association with white Americans, e.g., in a movie theater. (b) The aspect in which the American trait is similar to the Chinese trait and can be easily made to fit into the Chinese trait, e.g., adoption of violin and guitar. (c) The aspect in which an entirely new want is created, e.g., in the adoption of vacations for employees [210].

4. The acculturation of the Chinese immigrants in America, as affected by the situations and American reactions, may be differentiated into the following four stages: (a) The first stage, infiltration, was characterized by mutual toleration and cultural curiosity. The relation was pecuniary, pure and simple. (b) A stage of conflict, characterized by racial antagonism and persecution, as soon as the economic justification for the presence of the Chinese did not exist. (c) Cultural diffusion, which began when the storm of conflict was over. Only after the conflict situation had been removed, and the duration of their sojourn had been prolonged, and their desire to go back to China had been gradually diluted, did they begin

to adopt the cultural traits of the white people. The most conspicuous changes were in the more tangible things. In turn, they offered to the American people chop-suey and art goods. (d) The fourth and present stage is assimilation. With the growing up of the second-generation Chinese, the process of Americanization has been greatly accelerated. If there were no special disturbing factor (i e., racial difference) the children of Chinese could be assimiliated as well as those of English, German, etc. [222-24].

5. In the contact of cultures, the borrowing of material traits invariably comes before the borrowing of nonmaterial traits; women adopt the Western clothing much more thoroughly than do the men; food habits are the most persistent and will probably never be exterminated. Under nonmaterial traits, the Old World traits in business, social organization, and religion are still very dominant, while in education and customs they are greatly weakened by the adopted traits. Both in family and customs we find that there are many traits which have been mixed and changed. In language and recreation, both the old and the adopted traits are about the same. All in all, it is quite clear that so far as the Philadelphia Chinese are concerned, the culture traits which they have adopted from the American culture are definitely more than the culture traits which they have transplanted from the Old World and retained [238].

6. There will always be a Chinatown composed of some Chinese stores and restaurants and inhabited by some Chinese immigrants. But it will remain only as a "cultural cushion" for a remnant group because the majority group— the American-born Chinese— is definitely moving out, once the pressure from the outside is removed [258].

5. Codere, Helen. FIGHTING WITH PROPERTY: A STUDY OF KWAKIUTL POTLATCHING AND WARFARE. 1950. AESM, No. 18.

Purpose or problem. — To utilize both the historical and the cultural materials in order to achieve understanding of the processes at work in Kwakiutl life under the conditions of contact, from 1792 to 1930 [v]. To trace the various tendencies in Kwakiutl life as they were furthered or inhibited by the pressures of the contact culture and to determine both the binding force and the dynamics of this historical process [118].

Definitions, Assumptions, and Hypotheses. — 1. Within this period Kwakiutl culture was in intensive contact with the new European culture and changes occurred which were at once the development of tendencies already present in Kwakiutl life and the result of pressures put upon it by the powerful surrounding culture [v].

2. Analysis reveals a major shift to have taken place. This change was the great increase in the vigor of the potlatch and the coexistent decrease and final extinction of warfare and physical violence [v].

Methods and Techniques. — Analysis of the historical and ethnographic material available on the Kwakiutl, oriented toward an understanding of the Kwakiutl as they were revealed by their history. Particular prominence was given to the economic developments.

Graphs and Charts. — Twenty tables scattered throughout the monograph, mainly related to Kwakiutl economic activities, population, and potlatches. Tribal and linquistic map of Vancouver Island and adjacent territory.

Data. — The Kwakiutl plane of living was one of the highest of any North American Indian group. Their wealth was closely related to the great natural wealth of the region in which they lived, but was actually produced by their magnificient technical and artistic virtuosity and by their unusual energy. They are remarkable for the degree of their preoccupation with social rank and the manner in which every aspect of their culture seems to focus upon this preoccupation. The rapid decline in population from at least 1837 to 1924 brought about a higher proportion of potlatch positions in relation to population, making that access to a position easier than it had been, with more people active in support of the potlatch.

The Kwakiutl were a people of marked economic ability who adjusted successfully to the new and expanding economy created by the Europeans in the area, and who used the proceeds of this success for potlatching. Certain attitudes and practices of Kwakiutl economic life from the time of the earliest records facilitated this adjustment. They were extremely able and industrious. Their own industrial procedures and food-getting techniques were varied, specialized, and concerned with production far in excess of mere need. These were assets in meeting the new economic conditions and in taking advantage of their expanded opportunities. The habituation to standardized and pluralized manufactured objects was carried over; they had a potential demand for European goods in excess of any practical utility the goods might have possessed. The relatively cheap and impressive abundance encouraged the potlatch. Since they required only a limited amount of manufactured goods for consumption needs and since they did not hoard, any surplus was used in potlatching. Already familiar with the natural resources of their land and trained in their exploitation, they were able to take an indispensable place in the commercialized fishing and lumbering industries of British Columbia; this was aided too by their flexible and migratory occupational habits.

Kwakiutl warfare was suppressed as a result of historical developments and was eradicated within twenty years after the period of intensive contact with the new culture. The character and tendencies of Kwakiutl warfare itself helped to bring about its extinction. No particular advantages were to be gained from it that were not available in other areas, nor was it a special area for the development and exhibition of "war-like" qualities highly valued by the society. Rather, it was bent to the services of a vast and intricate system of rivalry for purposes of social prestige and this rivalry had always been more fully expressed and dramatized in the potlatch. While the use of force had some effect in eliminating physical violence in Kwakiutl culture, forces were involved in this historical development that were far more pervasive and positive in effecting a cultural change than the occasional use of military force.

Conclusions. — 1. The binding force in Kwakiutl history was their limitless pursuit of a kind of social prestige which required continual proving to be established or maintained against rivals [118].

2. The main shift in Kwakiutl history was from a time when success in warfare and head hunting was significant to the time when nothing counted but successful potlatching [118]. The new economic situation stimulated the peaceful warfare of the potlatch and furthered the tendency already present in Kwakiutl life to eliminate violence against persons [129].

6. Dollard, John. CASTE AND CLASS IN A SOUTHERN TOWN. 1937. Institute of Human Relations, Yale Univ. Press.

Purpose or Problem. — An attempt to see the social situation as a means of patterning the affects of white and Negro people as a mold for emotional forces. The aim of the study is to grasp and describe the emotional structure which runs parallel to the formal social structure in the community [17]. To understand the white-Negro adjustment in the community with specific reference to emotional factors.

Definitions, Assumptions, and Hypotheses. — 1. The adult man will tend to develop the feelings appropriate to his reality situation, and all men in the same situation will tend to develop essentially the same feelings; if adult personalities do not possess the expected uniform responses, explanation must first be sought in the life history of the individual for variant circumstances which might produce unique attitudes [18].

2. The lives of white and Negro people are so dynamically interdependent and integrated in one system that neither can be understood without the other.

Methods and Techniques. — Basically participant observation. In general two kinds of observations were made, first as to what people said, and second as to what they did and seemed to feel. Practically none of the material was gained by direct interrogation and none of it by set questions [19-20]. Life histories were collected over a five-month period. The author was aware of observer biases such as sectional, personal, sociological, and psychological forms of perception, and has attempted to discount for them in collection and analysis of the material.

Data. — The southern plantation economy and the northern industrialized economy are primarily products of a geographical selectivity and a historical continuation of two currents of European mores: the slave-feudal organization and the free, competitive, individualistic tradition. This produced two competing modes of life in which the conflicting mores were reified in rival states, political philosophies, and finally civil war. Previous to the Civil War, slavery was a method of subordinating Negroes that, once established, required no active accommodative adjustments to arise between the races. After the Civil War, the caste system arose as an adaptive method of replacing slavery. The increased racial hostility following the Civil War may be explained in terms of the insecurity in subordinating the Negro and therefore the requirement of active aggression against them. Also, it may be explained in terms of a deflected expression of hostility against the North turned toward the Negroes. Even today it is only when the differing views on the Negro and his status are focused upon that the old attitudes of hostility toward the North are reinstated. There is a conflict between the dominant American mores and the regional mores of the South which have had to deal with the Negroes. Two different and contradictory conceptions of human worth are operating in one social field [61].

Any description of social life must inevitably include caste and class. Caste and class distinctions are ways of dividing people according to the behavior expected of them in the society [62]. Essentially caste seems to be a barrier to legitimate descent. It does not completely exclude social contact; the distinctive features are marriage and sexual prohibitions. Within the caste system there is also a class system which may be divided into lower, middle, and upper. Class status is defined in terms of cultural factors and is focused on economic position and advantage, whereas caste conflict is focused around social contact. In Southerntown there is essentially a white middle-class group and a Negro lower-class group, with a small percentage of the other caste-class groups.

There are differential advantages and disadvantages of membership in any particular caste or class. From the standpoint of the individual the white middle class may claim three "gains": economic, sexual, and prestige. The white middle class is so placed that it makes all of these gains from the Negroes and some of them from the lower-class whites.

1. Economic: The lower-class people do the laborious and monotonous work but receive a smaller share of the purchasing power in the community. It is this lower-class labor supply that supports the white middle class in its position and is therefore a vulnerable point. Negro tenant farmers show a propensity toward migratory habits, much to the annoyance of the planters. The possibility and fact of geographical mobility may be seen in psychological terms as a manifestation of insecurity and/or one of the few aggressive responses the Negro can make toward the whites.

2. Sexual: We mean by sexual gain the fact that white men, by virtue of their caste position, have access to two classes of women, those of the white and Negro castes [135]. This is not so for Negro women because they are objects of gain rather than the chosen. Negro men and white women

are strictly limited to choices within their own castes. The following points may be noted: (1) There is still a tendency toward the idealization of white women in the South [137]. (2) Access to Negro women is a continued reaffirmation of caste superiority and white dominance. (3) The taking of other people's women is in general held an aggressive act in one society and Negro response along expected lines is not absent but suppressed [154]. (4) The mores among the white caste seem to be becoming stronger and exerting more pressure against cross-racial sexual contact. (5) The sexual issue exemplifies the whole caste problem, and is one of the most acute issues requiring the utmost in defense and aggression on the part of the white caste. (6) Any move toward social equality may be seen on its deepest level as really a move toward sexual equality [170]. (7) In attempting to describe how a person may act as a result of his social position, it must be realized that not all individuals with caste privileges actually make use of them.

3. Prestige: In the South a man has prestige solely because he is white. Thus membership in the white caste automatically includes the right to demand from Negroes forms of behavior which serve to increase his own self-esteem. From the standpoint of the Negro, there are two possible motives in his submissive behavior. (1) The repressed antagonism is often replaced and concealed by a servile behavior. (2) Identification with the socially powerful white person, accompanied by idealization, pride in the white man, permissiveness, and a wish to serve him [174]. This may give rise to a desire to be like the white man.

Southern society is not desirous of educating the Negro to full participation in the culture, but rather for slave or caste participation; however the educational process is set in motion, it is very difficult to control. The caste principle functions in education in the South by stressing craft and vocational training for the Negro which prepares him for, but not beyond, the opportunities of his lower-class status. Voting is similarly treated.

The church has had a profound influence in inducting the Negroes into American society. The church today serves a number of functions: (1) The Negro is individuated in the church and can play a significant role [247]. (2) It offers an opportunity for intensive impulsive expression. (3) It acts as a social control by focusing attention on a future life while negating the value of this one. (4) It is a form of collective activity which gives pleasure and is a center of social solidarity for the Negroes [248].

The Negro people are caught in a conflict between total American and southern regional definitions of their role. The Negro faces a situation of chronic frustration to which he may respond in five possible courses of action: (1) Become overtly aggressive against the white caste. (2) Suppress aggression and supplant it with passive accommodative attitudes. (3) Turn aggression from the white caste to individuals within his own group. (4) Give up the competition for white caste values and accept forms of gratification other than those secured by the whites. (5) Compete for the values of white society, raising his class position within the Negro caste and managing aggression partly by expressing dominance within his own group and partly by suppression of individual impulses. The aggressive manifestations permitted to the white caste, in defense of Negro aggressions, are much more overt and decisive, as in mob violence and lynchings, and in their control of formal force such as the police, judges, juries, etc. Other forms of aggression permitted are moral intimidation or personal derogation of the Negro, as exemplified in caste etiquette and social isolation. White people fear Negroes with a special context, that is, when the Negro attempts to claim white prerogatives. Because the white southerner is caught between his regional mores and our national democratic mores, there are certain defense beliefs in the South to reconcile this discrepancy, such as that Negroes are culturally inferior, and expect aggression and mastery from the white man.

The position of the Negro from the standpoint of American cultural values is one of disadvantage. On the other hand, the gains of the Negro caste may be defined in reference to the pleasure orientation of an organism. In this sense, the lower-class Negro may be seen to have three gains: (1) greater ability to enjoy sexual freedom possible in his own group; (2) greater freedom of aggression and resentment within his own group; (3) the luxury of his dependence relationship to the white caste. The Negro enjoys an impulse expression less burdened by guilt and less threatened by his immediate social group to a degree not customary in the white middle class. It seems that direct and instinctual gratification is offered to lower-class Negroes in exchange for the money and mastery which are the chief cultural values of the whites.

Conclusions. — 1. The greater freedom of aggressive expression among Negroes seems to be related to the value of Negro disunity from the standpoint of the master class. This differential of freedom is likely to exist as long as the caste pattern of relationships itself, since it seems to be functionally related to white superiority and Negro subordination. The possibilities of socially effective aggression for the Negro caste in Southerntown do not seem to be increasing. Aggression as a force tending to alter social relations has had very little effect.

2. The Negro is perfectly capable and willing to accept his position in our society on an equal basis with the whites but is unable to do so because of the caste situation as it exists today. The outlook for any distinct change in this situation in the near future is not very good. The dominant aim of our society seems to be to "middle-class-ify" all of its members. Negroes, including lower-class Negroes, are no exceptions. Eventually they must all enter the competition for higher status which is so basic and compulsive an element in our way of life. This will mean giving up their "gains" and approximating more nearly the ideal of restraint, independence, and personal maturity, which is implicitly attached to our demands for individual competition and mobility [432].

3. Race prejudice may be summarized as follows: Cultural restrictions in childhood and the limitations of daily life in adulthood provide numerous frustrations for every individual; hostility is aroused in response to these frustrations. If expressed, this hostility would tend to break up in-group solidarity; so it is systematically discouraged and suppressed. Though repressed, it is not extirpated but utilizes such permissive social formations as race-prejudice traditions to vent itself safely on an object.

7. Du Bois, Cora. THE 1870 GHOST DANCE. Univ. of California Pubs. in Anth. Records, Vol. III, 1939, 1-152.

Purpose or Problem. — This paper deals with only one minor phase of a recurrent series of messianic or revivalistic movements which have arisen among the weaker peoples throughout the world as reactionary waves to the crushing impact of European culture. The subject under consideration has a double significance. On the one hand, it is allied with a cultural category of universal if sporadic distribution. On the other hand, it is bound up in its specific aspects with the struggle of northern California and Oregon Indians to integrate their cultural life to the unavoidable demands of European invasion [v].

The following study grew out of a desire to trace the introduction and course of the 1870 Ghost Dance in northern California. No preliminary problem was set beyond the accumulation of data bearing on this subject. It became increasingly evident that all approaches were inherent in an adequate description and interpretation [v].

Definitions, Assumptions, and Hypotheses. — 1. The modern cults on the Pacific Coast are more than a religious problem. They not only symbolize but also represent in part the whole struggle between two divergent social systems. Under their native leaders the Indians have sought sanction to reject or adopt the new concepts being forced upon them and have endeavored to preserve some modicum of their native values [v].

2. In the title, Ghost Dance has been used as a general term to cover a series of generically related religious developments, but in the body of the paper the term will be applied only to the first phase of the whole growth, consisting largely of doctrinal stress on the return of the dead and the end of the world, which in some vague supernatural manner would entail the elimination of the white people.

3. In the strict accuracy of the word, acculturation might be used whenever a diffused trait or complex is accepted by a culture upon which it impinges. That is, patterning and acculturation might be practically synonymous. However, acculturation seems to have been given special meaning. It is used most frequently to describe minimal cases of patterning; that is, cases in which dislocations accompanying the absorption of foreign features exceed integrations. More specifically, it seems to have been used to de-

scribe the manner in which a shattered aboriginal culture makes the best of a bad bargain. It may be legitimate to distinguish between external contacts which can be integrated to the dominant social values without destructive dislocations and those which cannot. The difference between patterning (which represents integration) and acculturation (which represents at best only a partial integration) is not always obvious in cultural phenomena [137]. Once a complex has been accepted it is frequently adapted to local cultural forms. This might be called patterning. Whereas diffusion represents the process of expansion in history, patterning represents the process of absorption [137].

Methods and Techniques. — Material collected intermittently from 1932 to 1934; preliminary historical data considered essential. Data obtained largely in biographical form. Obstacles listed in gathering material: (1) the reticence in speaking autobiographically; (2) temporal: limiting the firsthand informants available; (3) the contempt in which earlier cult frenzy and credulity is sometimes held; (4) due to the topical approach, requiring an unsatisfactorily superficial contact with each local group. As much as possible of the detailed raw material is presented in the form of direct statements by informants, since the formulation of modern religious developments in northern California is preliminary and tentative [v].

Graphs and Charts. — Map of Modern Cults in Northern California [facing 1]. Various figures and plates showing diffusion of modern cults in different territories, costumes, etc.

Data. — The religious developments covered in this paper occurred during a period of sixty years, beginning in 1871. It was a time of marked intra- and intertribal flux, during which Indian life underwent progressive disintegration. As a result, the early reactions which were resistive to white encroachments were gradually transformed into an acceptance of European habits and attitudes. Strictly speaking, the Ghost Dance and Earth Lodge cults cannot be called messianic movements since the appearance of no great saviour was anticipated. More properly they might be called adventist or revivalistic cults. No single leader can be considered mainly responsible for these religious phenomena; they were the creation of many religious-minded individuals of varying cultural backgrounds.

The early movement was characterized chiefly by the psychological excitation engendered by the doctrine of an imminent return of the dead. To hasten the dead on their way, faith and continual dancing were essential. The immediacy of the expected advent fostered the rapid diffusion of the doctrine. Skeptics were threatened with transformation, usually into rocks or animals. Anti-white ideas were present but they were minimized by informants. In no instance do there seem to have been plans for overt aggression. The whites were to be exterminated at the time of the advent and there was no need to hasten matters by armed efforts. Half-breeds were threatened with the same fate as the whites, at least among some groups. Each group learned the doctrine from a proselytizer who spoke simply as a messenger for a dreamer. At first, under the influence of mass excitement, dreaming was generalized. Sometimes communications from the dead were secured during sleep or in trances induced by dancing. After a year or two, the general excitement quieted down and dreaming was concentrated in the hands of those few who were most able in composing new songs, directing dancing, and in haranguing the group. Besides these doctrinal and psychological aspects of the Ghost Dance there were certain ritual observations, e.g., the outdoor round dance, immersion, wealth emphasis among the Yurok, Karok, etc.

The necessity for distinguishing between the Ghost Dance and Earth Lodge cult lies in the idea of the Earth Lodge itself. This is obviously a central California innovation and is diagnostic of the new and reversed spread of the cult in the northern part of the state. The Bole-Maru had its most elaborate development in north central California, where ceremonialism was most elaborate in pre-white times. One of the three main dances, the Ball dance, seems to have been a Patwin contribution whose cultural antecedents are undoubtedly European. It cannot be stressed too strongly that dancing was the pre-eminent form of religious expression to these Indians.

<u>Conclusions</u>.— 1. Characteristic of all these movements was the appearance of local dreamers or prophets whenever an external impulse set a new religious form in motion. These local dreamers and interpreters represent a constant recrudescence of local authoritarianism, but always beneath this local authority can be discovered an external stimulus. It is as though taproots were always being sent down into the intense localism of the California tribelets. In most tribes, for short periods, dreaming was epidemic. It soon subsided and concentrated in the hands of particular dreamers or "preachers." The influence of these leaders was everywhere different and individualized, yet on the whole they seem to have been instrumental in reshaping shamanism and breaking ground for further Christianization [3].

2. The movements' influence has made possible the introduction and acceptance of the many marginal Christian sects which now flourish among the Indians of this region. The revivalistic psychology of the Pentecostals, for instance, has made it peculiarly a well-fitted vehicle for the Christianization of those Indians who had had previous experience with the Ghost Dance and its proliferations. At the moment it represents one of the terminal points in a progressively Christianized ideology for which the Ghost Dance and its subsequent cults were transitional factors [2].

3. On the whole, it may be said that the Ghost Dance in northernmost California and Oregon was largely doctrinal and psychological, with a minimum of ritualism, and even that minimum contained few elements new to any of the participating tribes [131].

4. It is significant that the most complicated of the modern cults (the

Bole-Maru in north central California) arose in the area where ceremonialism was most elaborate in pre-white times [133].

5. Diffusion has been obviously one of the major processes which functioned in the history of the modern cult movements under consideration. Some of the factors influencing the diffusion of modern cults in northern California and Oregon were intertribal marriage, language, reservation systems (bringing tribes into contact with each other and splitting tribal groups into two areas of residence), transportation, and employment of Indian labor [137].

6. There were two types of diffusion which were evident. One might be called linear and the other centrifugal. In linear diffusion each tribelet learned the cult in its own territory. The essential point is that one tribe at a time learns a new complex by having it imported to its own territory and into its own cultural sphere. In some, however, a heterogeneous gathering representing many different tribal groups gathered together for joint ceremonies. The guest groups then carried back the new ideas to their own territories. This type of dissemination might be called centrifugal diffusion [136].

7. Once an idea or complex has been introduced to a group there are factors making for its acceptance or rejection. Certain factors which made for the rejection of modern cult elements are: (1) insufficient deterioration of a culture as a whole; (2) too great sophistication (because with no grounding in the old culture, an adventist and revivalistic doctrine was meaningless. There was no emotional need for even diluted forms of the old life. The cults to be acceptable had to strike a group at that precise time when the old culture had deteriorated but faith in it had not); (3) skeptics and conservatives both; (4) certain specific doctrinal ideas (e.g., the teaching that half-breeds would suffer the same fate as the white people, a fear of ghosts and the dead in general). Balanced against the rejective factors were an equal number of factors which must have made the cults acceptable: (1) the hope which the doctrine offered for the rehabilitation of the shattered aboriginal culture and the attendant improvement of economic conditions; (2) a real esthetic appeal; (3) the direct emotional appeal to recently bereaved persons [136-37].

8. Once a complex has been accepted it is frequently adapted to local cultural forms. This phenomenon has been observed frequently and has been labeled by anthropologists with the catch phrase "pattern theory." It might be more desirable to give the concept an active connotation by using a word like "patterning" [137].

9. The Shasta, Yurok, and Hupa illustrate nicely the relative stability of the three groups involved and may indicate tentatively that patterning is in proportion to stability. That is, the greater the stability of a group, the more pronouncedly it will pattern foreign traits to established institutions. Among these three tribes, who were territorially contiguous, we find three

degrees of stability. The Shasta, who enthusiastically embraced the new cults with a minimum of patterning; the Yurok, who accepted the cult provisionally but largely on their own terms, only to reject it subsequently; and the Hupa, who were completely resistive to it. These three grades of receptiveness suggest that social integration and stability are closely allied [138].

8. Elkin, Henry. THE NORTHERN ARAPAHO OF WYOMING. 1940. In Linton, 207-58; see Sec. 25.

Purpose or Problem. — See Linton.

Definitions, Assumptions, and Hypotheses. — See Linton.

Methods and Techniques. — Field work; otherwise not indicated.

Data. — Before contact with white civilization, Arapaho life can be said to have followed a fairly harmonious course. The society had achieved a fairly high degree of balance and stability both in its adjustment to external conditions, and in its inner organization. At the beginning of the historic record, they had lost all direct traces of settled agricultural life. The possession of the horse was the basis of their way of life. Intertribal trade was small and relatively unimportant, their own resources supplying practically all their needs, although they did exchange for horses. Warfare was one of the major activities closely related to the age-graded system. The vision quest had a more limited role among the Arapaho than among most Plains tribes. It supplemented the society structure as a means of conferring supernatural power, and primarily served as a preparation for membership in the two oldest groups. Government was more complex than is general in societies of equally simple social differentiation. The conditions of Plains life subjected the Arapaho to quick changes in the availability of food supply and to sudden and unexpected attacks from enemy raiding parties, thus forcing them to plan tribal movements and activities and to enforce regulations. The qualities of behavior most prized were bravery, good judgment, kindness, and generosity. Accumulation of property for the exclusive aim of personal possession beyond that required for sustenance was relatively nonexistent. The spoils of a successful raid were equally divided among all participants, though those who acted most effectively received first choice. The principal means of attaining high status was through outstanding activity in warfare, government, and religion. It is of fundamental significance that in the tribal life of the Arapaho the individual engaged in these various activities at different times in his life; thus the individual's sphere of achievement was limited at all points of his life. In this society, where intense pursuit of glory and distinction might have led to a condition of thoroughgoing and uncontrollable rivalry, the age-society structure cast it into a formalized mold which directed it along conventional and socially desirable lines. Men with high standing were required to demonstrate great modesty and reserve in all except the conventionalized pattern of reciting their record of military prowess.

In comparison with many of the other Indian tribes the Arapaho have not been badly treated by the whites. Their warfare with the conquerors was less bitter and prolonged than that of many of the other Plains Indians. The part which the semilegendary Friday played in this affords an example of the influence which particular personalities may exert in crucial situations. The Arapaho also had the advantage of being placed on a reservation within their aboriginal range. The destruction of the buffalo by whites eliminated the most important aboriginal resource of the territory, while the region was poorly suited to the agriculture which the whites offered them as an economic substitute for hunting. They were reduced at once to a condition of economic dependence on the whites and could not have survived without government rations and the small income derived from unskilled labor. Farming was completely discordant with their ingrained attitudes and habitual patterns of behavior — they were accustomed to constant mobility, cooperative endeavor, and quick changes in speed of activity; their prestige values centered about warfare and the giving away of goods.

In its material aspect, reservation life shows an extreme diversity accounted for by a heterogeneous pattern of values derived from an elaboration of their older norms to fit the new conditions of life. That they have never bodily accepted the standards of American civilization is apparent throughout. Whatever they have taken over has either conformed to their aboriginal set of values, or its function has been appreciably transformed. Despite the fact that there is no longer a material need for their old pattern of mobility, the Arapaho have retained it to a surprising degree. This pattern has made the Arapaho take over the automobile more enthusiastically than any other white trait. The automobile has given the Arapaho his most thorough sense of value and prestige since warfare and the buffalo hunt. White styles in clothing and personal adornment have generally been adopted. Aboriginal food habits have scarcely changed; all forms of men's handiwork have long since passed away, although a number of old techniques practiced by women remain.

In view of the fundamental changes in the conditions of Arapaho life, the extent to which the traditional social forms have continued to function is striking. The tribal community has remained as coherent and well-knit as in the old days; the kinship organization has changed little, while the age societies have passed out of existence as organized bodies. The band structure went through a marked transformation and survived in the form of neighborhood groupings. Of all religious phenomena, the attitudes and practices associated with the Sacred Pipe and Sun Dance have remained most intact. These had a distinct tribal character and serve, now as then, as symbols of the communal solidarity. The disappearance of the society lodge dance has confined the younger men to a meager role in the traditional ceremonial life. This has facilitated the spread of the Peyote cult, which also serves as a bond between the Arapaho and the Shoshoni members of the two groups on the reservation. The Arapaho seemed to take to the missions more easily than to any other phase of white culture. The widespread conversion to Christianity, with a preference for the more highly ritualized forms, has been a simple addition to the culture, accomplished without the elimination of the older beliefs. The adjustment to reservation life has affected diversely the life patterns of different strata within the society. Women lead lives little different from those of the older women; the pattern of men's lives was more complex and its equilibrium has been shattered by reservation life. The young and middle-aged men fare the worst since they cannot occupy themselves with religion and practice as do the old men, who thus gain deference and respect from the whole community. White personality patterns are in direct conflict with the deep-seated aboriginal patterns of generosity and recognition of kinship obligations, and in this conflict the aboriginal patterns seem to have won.

Conclusions.— 1. The adaptation which the Arapaho have achieved so far is of a superficial sort, leaving most of the aboriginal values intact. There has been a considerable loss of culture content. Acceptance of white institutions has taken place mainly in two fields, technology and religion.

2. Tribal solidarity seems to have been, if anything, exaggerated by the conditions of white contact, and the social pressure exerted upon individuals who behave in ways differing from the cultural stereotypes is a serious bar to successful individual adaptation. This is the more remarkable in view of the apparent loss of faith in the aboriginal culture.

9. Embree, John F. ACCULTURATION AMONG THE JAPANESE OF KONA HAWAII. 1941. AAAM, No. 59.

Purpose or Problem.— The study is concerned with changes in the social organization, the network of social relations, which have taken place in rural Japanese society when transplanted from Southern Japan to the island of Hawaii. An investigation of changes brought about when a number of people from many regions, but with a common cultural background, formed a new social group in a new and alien environment. A study of readjustments made by a group of individuals to a new geographical and social environment [5].

Definitions, Assumptions, and Hypotheses.— 1. The new social environment differs in that (a) there are several different racial groups in Hawaii as against a single group in rural Japan; (b) of the Japanese in the new region practically all were strangers to each other on arrival [5].

2. The common cultural background of the group will show itself in many ways, gaining strength by contrast with the alien social environment, but being greatly modified by it and by the new geographical background.

It is these modifications in social structure and their causes which form the primary problems of this study [5].

Methods and Techniques. — Field work, August 1937 to February 1938, with less intensive research carried on among the Japanese on Oahu. 1935 to 1936: an intensive social study of Kumamoto, Japan, from where 40 percent of the coffee farmers at Kona have come.

Kona was chosen as the primary field for study because (1) it has a somewhat uniform origin in Japan; (2) it is a one-crop region (coffee); (3) coffee growers are more independent than plantation workers, so that Kona is comparable to a Japanese village where local affairs are administered autonomously; (4) the Japanese form a majority of the population of Kona; thus they are able to form their own integrated social life better than if they were merely a minority.

Graphs and Charts. — 1. Prefectural Origin of Japanese in Kona [6]. 2. Kona Population by Racial Groups [25]. 3. Tabular Comparison of the Local Group in Kona and Japan [37].

Data. — Indications of amicable racial relations are apparent in the interchange of culture traits, e.g., in parties and language borrowing, food, etc. The direction of cultural interchange is preponderantly from white to Japanese and Hawaiian, possibly because of the dominant economic and political position of the former. The size of the average household in Kona is smaller than in Japan— because of the lack of permanent household servants, more children away at school or employed elsewhere, the lack of a grandparental generation until recently, and the decrease in adoption. Banquets are much less common and much simpler; because of the lack of trays, much of the polite formality of a Japanese feast is lost, along with the careful frugality which it entailed. Many other material objects had to be left behind in Japan; an attempt was made, however, to retain many of the old social customs. Three things have been preserved with remarkable tenacity; the Japanese style of bath, food, and kitchen, these being the habits acquired in early childhood and those most deeply ingrained. This too is the sphere of women, who here tend to be culturally more conservative. An exception to this is the encouragement the mother gives her children to learn the American mode of life, while the father attempts to mold them in the old Japanese tradition.

The most important social groups of Kona are the kumi, groups of neighborhood homes which co-operate on the occasion of emergencies. It is here a utilitarian organization founded by the first-generation immigrants, functioning chiefly as a burial society, which has taken the place of the Japanese buraku— a local group united by a common religious structure and a tradition of many generations. Houses are scattered rather than forming a close neighborhood group as they do in Japan; this affects the relative social solidarity of the two groups in many ways — in general, the friendly, neighborly spirit of the Japanese local group is lost in Kona. Another hindrance to co-operation is the fact that the inhabitants did not know each other as children, that they hail from different regions of Japan with slightly different customs and so never quite trust one another. Relative mobility, too, is greater, so that the rotating forms of co-operation by which a man receives aid one year and is expected to return it the next are weakened. Emphasis on climbing by individual effort is one of the major causes of the decline in co-operation.

Marriage has not lost its importance in the community (as have the naming ceremonies and the ceremony of presenting the child to the village gods a month after birth), but it has changed considerably and many American customs have entered into the picture. Arrangement is still made with the aid of go-betweens, but the opening steps are frequently begun by the individuals immediately concerned, emphasis all along being on the individuals concerned rather than on family arrangements. The formal etiquette of a wedding has been undermined by the American influence in types of food, clothes, etc. The role of the ancestral spirits in family life is weaker, and an important corollary of this is the fact that adoption of sons is less frequent; very few of the old household gods are found in Kona. Much Christian influence is found in the religion— adopting the word "church" for a Buddhist temple, sitting in pews instead of on the floor, and singing Buddhist hymns at intervals instead of leaving the service up to the priest. The observance of the old holidays and fiestas in honor of the old pantheon of deities has largely disappeared, largely because they have no seasonal significance in Kona. The old routine of taking each day and season as it comes, celebrating festivals together, having rest days, has been replaced by a capitalistic ideology of making money. The festivals which have persisted have done so in a commercialized form. Religious gatherings have come to serve as integrators of social class groups, not of local geographical groups. Japanese Christians rate a little higher with the white community than Buddhists, a fact sometimes entering into conversions. Those who become Christian may do so as a way of "reforming," as an aspect of Americanization. Christianity has not affected the older generation appreciably, but the fact that children may become Christian may affect family solidarity. The custom of young people exchanging gifts with contemporaries at Christmas but not with their own siblings may be a characteristic acculturation phenomenon in America for other immigrant groups as well.

The society termed peasant as it exists in rural Japan is fundamentally a co-operative one, while that of Kona, made up of men from this same co-operative peasant society of Japan, is fundamentally a competitive one. In rural Japan there is a clearly defined pattern, a well-knit social structure of co-operative forms based on common territory and kinship. Everyone has his place, and there is no struggle for status. In Kona, on the other hand, this set structure is largely lacking. There is no local religious center belonging to a local group, and the traditional forms of funeral co-operation, exchange labor, etc., while operating to some extent, are not the automatic functions of the local group in Kona that they are in Japan. Another aspect of the accepted framework of life in Japan is the calendar, the seasonal round of nature, which is missing in Kona. Throughout the social organization in Kona we find the effects of this changed emphasis from group cooperation to individual initiative, from Japanese peasant ways to those of the American pioneer and business tradition, from an emphasis on the sacred to the secular. Much of the process of change in Kona is of this nature, due in part to acculturation through continuous firsthand contact with modern American culture, in part to pioneer conditions, and settling in a new environment which lacks the associations and traditions of an old Japanese village. Evidence of the lack of unity is the comparative slowness of the spread of news, and the greater number of suicides. There is less security, either economic or social, for the member of Kona society.

While one important cause of these changes is the fact that the social organization in Kona is a newly formed one based on old patterns by an immigrant group, another important factor is the influence of the American culture pattern of individualism and the strongly capitalistic emphasis of the American economic system. The greater emphasis on money may also be due in part to the fact that the people of Kona are a selected group— selected because they left Japan and so were in some way dissatisfied at home, selected further because they left the sugar plantations in the Territory and set themselves up as independent farmers. American individualism is also partly the cause for the lessened family unity, as is the fact that the children born in Hawaii go through a different educational system, often leading to family disputes. Some evidences of this weakening of family ties are: fewer adopted sons; more marriages primarily arranged by the individuals concerned; abandonment of farming by many young people and a yearning for city ways. Correlated with this is the lack of relatives in Kona, so that each family must get along without kin and the strong sanction of the approval or disapproval of behavior by the extended family is lacking.

Groups based on common occupation, especially in the second generation, are also coming to replace those based on kinship or common territory. New social groupings thus arise, sometimes replacing old ones; corresponding with this type of change there is a loss of clear-cut function in some of the older types of groups. There is a lack of formalized behavior in the face of changed conditions which also contributes to the breakdown of old patterns. An interesting thing about some of the institutions whose functions have changed or weakened is the way in which people become self-conscious about them, as in discussing the pros and cons of the kumi system, etc. In the cooperative society of rural Japan such aspects of the social organization are traditional and taken for granted. Most of these observations hold in the field of religion as well as of social and economic organization. Periodic gathering of local groups is less frequent, actually creating a social solidarity by age lines rather than by common territory. The recreational aspect of seasonal festivals and recurring banquets tends to be replaced by movies and baseball games, with the concomitant decrease in participation. There is an attempt on the part of the older people to maintain contact with the nation of Japan—through letters, visits, and war contributions, and through language schools, whereby they attempt to impart some of their cultural values to the second generation.

Japanese society in Hawaii, then, shows an attempt to recreate the old social forms in a new environment. The local group organization has been recreated but its functions are somewhat different and less clear-cut, kin groups have been replaced by local groups, occupational groups, and especially tokoro groups (people from the same locality in Japan). Social solidarity in Kona is weaker than in Japan due to weaker local group organization, conflicts between first and second generations, and to the American influences of individualism and a capitalistic economy. The old religious values are seriously modified and the seasonal festivals mostly lacking. The direction of culture change is predominantly from American to Japanese society—from emphasis on kin and local solidarity to occupational solidarity, from a rice economy and gift exchange to a money economy with an emphasis on specialization of occupation and a selling rather than exchanging of services and goods, from a co-operative culture to one of competition.

Conclusions.— The direction of most of the acculturation process has been from American (as donor) to Japanese, probably due to the former's dominant political and economic position [146].

2. When a cultural item is losing its function, sentiment comes in as a rationale to the defense of the weakening custom—and people take up attitudes for and against it [50].

3. There is no evidence of a revivalist cult among the Japanese of Kona, such as is sometimes found among "deprived" groups. One possible reason for this is that while economically suppressed, they are members of an ethnic group whose native land is a great world power, so that they regard their own hardships as being personal and in no way a reflection on the ability and virtues of Japanese as a whole. They do not feel deprived in the sense of having their whole governmental system made subservient to some foreign power [130].

10. Fauset, Arthur Huff. BLACK GODS OF THE METROPOLIS: NEGRO RELIGIOUS CULTS OF THE URBAN NORTH. 1944. Pub. of the Philadelphia Anthropological Society. Vol. III.

Purpose or Problem.— 1. We shall be interested in only one phase of the religious life, namely, the influence of the so-called religious cult in the lives of some Negroes who inhabit certain sections of our large northern cities [1]. We shall subject to scrutiny five of these special groups, or "cults," selected because for the metropolitan areas referred to these are among the most important and best-known cults of their respective types, and hence among the most representative [8, 10].

2. We shall be interested in the question which Herskovits has revived: "Does contemporary religious practice among Negroes in the United States disclose definite African survivals?" Do the cults under observation indicate "Negro" form and "Negro" content in the practices now prevalent among them, rather than "American" or "European" form and content, as students like Frazier and Wilson are inclined to believe [10]?

3. We shall scrutinize the evidence for indications of functional expressions (as against "pure" African survivals) destined to transform certain social needs of the American Negro folk into cultural necessities and imperatives which are derived from their cultural milieu [11]. (Cf. Frazier, Wilson, etc.)

4. Borrowing a suggestion from Reid, we shall observe some of the avenues into which these practices have been directed [11].

Definitions, Assumptions, and Hypotheses. — 1. The influence of that overwhelming African heritage still must persist within the cultural nimbus which surrounds the religious beliefs and practices of the descendants of these African slaves [2].

2. Underlying the life of the American Negro is a deep religious bent that is but the manifestation here of a similar drive that, everywhere in Negro societies, makes the supernatural a major focus of interest [4]. (Testing Herskovits' hypothesis.)

3. Thus the American Negro church represents the one institution among Negroes in the United States where we are privileged to observe the seeds of revolt, so inherent in the institution of slavery, taking root and sprouting [6-7] (because of separatist habits of worshiping apart from the whites, conflict over slavery, etc.).

4. The chief reasons for these separatist tendencies were the reluctance of white Christians to accept Negroes in the already established churches on a plane of equality and the desire of Negroes to worship in churches where they could feel free to express themselves along the lines which the general condition of their lives prompted [8].

5. Undoubtedly the cults are able to shed light on some of the questions concerning the Negro and his religious attitudes [10].

6. The cults have the great significance which their rapid and increasing spread in urban communities would seem to indicate [11].

Methods and Techniques. — The method of approach has been to visit a place of worship frequently enough to become accepted as a friendly spectator and participant in the rites. From this point it has been possible to establish cordial relations with members and leaders, who usually are only too willing to spend time with a stranger in order to impress upon him the virtues of their particular form of worship. Notes taken afterward, except in case histories [11-12].

Graphs and Charts. — I. Organization of Cults. II. Functional Developments of Cults. III. Factors Which Attract Communicants to the Cult. IV. Negro Church Denominations in Philadelphia.

Data. — The effect of separatist tendencies (in the nineteenth century) was to establish a Negro church, which became an instrument of, by, and for Negroes. About the beginning of the twentieth century, new types of Negro churches made their appearance, more nearly representing doctrinal splits within the older established models. Later and further developments in the tendency to form splits show pronounced "nationalistic" characteristics, that is, churches which tend to emphasize the racial qualities of the communicants. Although the tendency of Negro religious cults to spread in the large northern centers has been marked during the past two decades, still the aggregate number of cult members in these centers does not represent a sufficiently large proportion of the total Negro population to warrant more than tentative generalizations; nevertheless, the number of cult worshippers is substantial and appears to be increasing.

Details of five different cults are then presented, touching upon their origins in America, including in some instances the character and life history of their founders, their organizational form, practices, rituals, and attempts to achieve their objectives. The five cults are: (1) Mt. Sinai Holy Church of America, Inc.; (2) United House of Prayer for All People (Bishop Grace); (3) Church of God (Black Jews); (4) Moorish Science Temple of America; (5) Father Divine Peace Mission Movement.

There is little substantial difference in fundamental belief between the first two cults and the more orthodox evangelical Christian denominations. A comparative study of this and other factors shows considerably more difference in the other three cults, although various taboos, etc., are found to be common to all.

Conclusions. — 1. These four compulsions, then — the supernatural being, the personality of the leader, relief from physical and mental illness, and race consciousness — appear to be most prominent factors in the respective attractions which these cults have for their members [76].

2. The striking increase of cult groups in the large northern centers is to be related in part to the psychological factors which are implied, first, in a change from rural to urban life, and, second, in the adjustment of mental attitudes to new mores. Hence one is led to believe that, for many of their members, certain religious cults in northern urban communities assist the transplanted southern worshipper, accustomed to the fixed racial mores and caste requirements of the South, to adjust his psychological and emotional reactions to conditions in the North, where all life and living are more fluid and intermingling of the races is inevitable [80-81].

3. Other factors of importance in the cults' attraction are: personal reassurance, music, a sense of the esoteric within the group [83-86].

4. They are characterized by a diversity of activities, notably in the

economic, political, and educational spheres, which tend to compensate for the paucity of analogous activities in the life outside the cult. In the Father Divine Peace Mission Movement the function of the cult to transform social needs by means of secular enterprises is most clearly demonstrated. Essentially a religious organization, it becomes, in effect, the mechanism by which various social urges, particularly those of its leaders and more socially dynamic members, may find outlets of expression. By making it possible for agencies to be established to fulfill these needs, it tends to transform these urges into the imperatives of American culture [88, 91, 95].

5. The development of the Negro's church came as a result of the Negro's need in America for a place to express himself in various ways; it did not result from some inexorable law peculiar to his nature; neither did such a law, or as Herskovits expresses it, a "drive," constrain the Negro then or later "to turn to religion rather than to political action or other outlets for his frustration" [98].

6. There is an indication that as American Negro cults become more intent upon social, economic, and political problems, the literal adherence to the Bible diminishes. Those cults with original economic, social, and political programs tend to develop their own set of rules [108].

7. Singing, dancing, etc., while generally characteristic of American Negro cult worship, are not essential features. The Moors definitely contradict such an assumption [108].

8. The theory that Negroes in the United States demonstrate survival characteristics of African influence in the form, ritual, and spirit of their religious worship must be received with considerable caution. That there is a modicum of such influence undoubtedly is true, but this is overwhelmingly outweighed by American cultural influences [108].

11. French, David H.   FACTIONALISM IN ISLETA PUEBLO. 1948.
    AESM, No. XIV.

Purpose or Problem. — To demonstrate that factionalism is caused by the inability of men of prestige and authority in the pueblo—the men who make the decisions—to achieve the unanimity that is necessary there for the proper functioning of government. In addition, the weakening effect of the acculturation process on the political motivations that lead to unanimity has been underlined [v].

Definitions, Assumptions, and Hypotheses. — 1. In a community which was once well integrated and which believes strongly in co-operation, this series of factional disputes may be considered examples of political pathology.

2. Factional disputes may have occurred regularly in the prehistoric pueblos. The multiplicity of villages at times in the past may have been caused in part by frequent divisions following disputes [vi].

3. Considering the frequency of factional disputes in the pueblos, the

question arises as to whether or not there is something in the nature of Pueblo culture that produces factionalism [vi].

Methods and Techniques. — (1) An introductory sketch of the pueblo as it was in 1870; (2) a description of the political organization of Isleta at that time; (3) a history of the last seventy-odd years in which factionalism is stressed; and (4) a discussion of causal relationships in Isleta factionalism.

Data. — Isleta is first described as it was in 1870 as, while factionalism may have existed in earlier times, the only information available concerns the breakdown of the relatively stable political patterns of the nineteenth century. Quotations follow from an account of the elections of 1870 of the governor and officers, and of an attempt to reform the principale system from 1890 on; since governors were able to choose which of the principales they would consult, there was always the possibility that governors would choose only the men whom they could control. Also at this time the acting cacique began to make arbitrary use of his power in respect to nominations. The pueblo was split into two factions which came to be known as the "Progressives" and the "Conservatives." The picture of factionalism from 1919 to 1922 is one of "reactionaries" in the majority, most of them simply interested in retarding Americanization; but being used by men who wished to hold office and thus to have access to community money. In 1941, two factions developed on issues involving the governor who, with a minority, wished to serve as president himself, select all the councilmen, etc. The split widened, with friendships, kinship ties, and ceremonial organizations disrupted. Each Faction began to seek the support of the United Pueblos Agency. A third party also made its appearnnce. Recent information indicates that the pueblo has still found no satisfactory solution to its political problems.

An examination of the part that acculturation has played in shaping the recent disputes follows, referring primarily to Spanish and American influences. The Isletas believe that their town organization is an integral part of an elaborate and supernaturally controlled universe, and the priests are respected because they preserve the welfare of the village. The government is thus theocratic in nature. The Isleta factions have more often been split over political matters than they have over questions of religion. By contrast, the issues in other pueblos have usually been more purely religious in nature. Many of the secular offices in the pueblo are filled by appointment, but this does not carry the same idea of responsibility for the appointee as is usual in American government. There is a lack of clear definition in regard to questions of authority; in times of crisis, such unsettled authority questions become crucial, and, in Isleta, they are the core of factional disputes. If unanimity is impossible, the government of the pueblo is seriously hampered; even after years of contact with white Americans, questions are not settled in terms of majority rule. When men of high prestige disagree, the ordinary members of the pueblo tend to divide and distribute their support among the leaders; thus, factions or political parties are formed. There are no formal mechanisms for settling a factional dispute after it has started. In the past, strong social pressure could be exercised to deal with individual dissenters. But today there is no way to get men of authority or their followers to agree, once a split occurs. Differences tend to increase with time, and the breach remains open until the issue disappears, or one group abandons its position, or a settlement is effected by an outside agency like the Indian Service.

In Isleta, wealth and descent are stressed much less than the contribution that an individual makes to the communal welfare. However, there have been a number of leaders during recent years who have displayed individualism and self-assertion. Men who are ambitious can often achieve their aims with little opposition. To avoid trouble, the rest of the hierarchy may fail to oppose their activities. Influences from outsiders, especially in recent years, have led to changes in the attitudes of the people and, to a lesser extent, in the form and functions of the government. One reason that changes are not easily effected in the Isleta government is that it has no recognized system for initiating them. They are aware of the fact that the Spanish made additions to their governmental organization by introducing offices; these offices have been incorporated into the theocracy, but in their minds are probably more open to modification than those which are considered aboriginal. It may be easier to set up new offices and political functions than to eliminate or modify existing ones.

Important factors in recent acculturation have been education, work for wages, and the automobile. White influences have not penetrated quickly, but they have gradually changed the life of the individual and finally the life of the village as a whole. Thus many general changes cannot be ascribed to any particular cause but to the total impact of the whites. Important changes have taken place in values. There has been a secularization of life, and a loss in the strength of the religious sanctions underlying the theocracy, as well as a growing lack of active participation in ceremonies. Dependence on the village has decreased. Opportunities for employment outside the pueblo have opened avenues of support other than the traditional occupation of farming. No longer is there a threat of Navaho and Apache raids, thus encouraging isolated dwellings. The community is losing its cohesiveness. There has also been a decrease in identification with the village and in loyalty to it, as reflected in a growing tendency to dissociate oneself from politics. The big change in values has occurred in the sphere of individual demand, in the economic sense, resulting in a greater need for money. In the factional strifes, however, it is the community monies that have been significant. For many men, personal gain has come to predominate over an interest in the community welfare; the Isletas still do not express the hope that they will be elected to the annual offices, but from the behavior of many individuals one must conclude that such a desire is present. Changes in the pueblo have caused the appearance of a new type of political organization, such as the Isleta Union and the third party (organized in 1942). These are essentially pressure groups. Their appearance undoubtedly indicates a growing realization that their traditional theocracy and political techniques are not well adapted to modern conditions. The disruption caused by factionalism seems to be sufficiently great to outweigh the conservatism of the Isletas in regard to changing the nature of their government.

Conclusions.— 1. The key to an understanding of the causes of factionalism in Isleta is the unanimity which must be reached if problems are to be settled in the traditional way [46].

2. The desire for unity was strong enough to cause one of the potential factions to abandon its position (during the nineteenth century).

3. The influence of white culture has been such as to decrease the identification with, and dependence on, the village, and to increase self-interest. The principle of unanimous decisions has not changed, but the motives which make such decisions possible have changed [46].

4. The Isletas' conservative attitude toward their culture may have been strengthened by the early attempts of the Spanish invaders to deculturate the Pueblo. The attack on the native religion may have caused the Pueblos to defend their religion by surrounding it with great secrecy and by attaching symbolic values to it, thus enabling them to better keep their culture intact.

12. Goldfrank, Esther S. CHANGING CONFIGURATIONS IN THE SOCIAL ORGANIZATION OF A BLACKFOOT TRIBE DURING THE RESERVE PERIOD. 1945. AESM, No. VIII.

Purpose or Problem.— An analysis of Blackfoot adaptation to a reserve situation, focused on changes in social organization and the effect of new patterns on the individual and the group [1].

Definitions, Assumptions, and Hypotheses.— 1. Blackfoot society is competitive, although in the prereserve period hunting the buffalo demanded a high degree of co-operation; goals have remained competitive, behavior individualistic, hostility overt [3].

2. The Blood offer an exceptional opportunity for analytic examination: within a short sixty years of reserve life, economic change has been surprisingly frequent. Its influence on the structure of Blood society and the status of the individual in it has been marked.

Methods and Techniques.— Part of a collaborative study—the Columbia Laboratory—in the summer of 1939; nine weeks spent on the reserve (ten days at the Sun Dance). Interviews; extensive personal histories from two men in their fifties. Use of historical documents.

Data. — The Blackfoot were buffalo hunters and horse raiders. They traveled in bands, loose organizations whose members were frequently close relatives and whose essential purposes were economic and political. Equally significant were the men's societies. Their early possession of the horse and the gun, and their comparative freedom from white pressure gave ample opportunity for effective hunting and substantial profit from the expanding fur trade. This profit was measured in horses. The chief road to social recognition was through organizing or directing a war party which could be done only by the man with wealth, although there was considerable opportunity for vertical mobility. Co-operative mechanisms, emphasizing interpersonal responsibilities, counteracted to some degree the competitive trends, but these trends continued nevertheless to dominate Blackfoot life.

The reserve period — the abandonment of hunting and raiding, and the acceptance of a sedentary existence within a restricted area, was the greatest change in the life of the Blood. The Canadian government was primarily interested in making its wards self-supporting; it did not enquire into the effects of its policies on those patterns of tribal life that did not immediately affect the success of its programs. Increase in horses became the sole important source of accumulated wealth, while initiative that had found expression in the old manner of life was blocked by poor rewards and legal prohibitions. In the past, skill, daring, and ambition were more apt to have brought success than earnest hard labor. The one activity that assured them a place in their society — horse stealing — was now forbidden them. That such a radical change was accomplished without resistance was due to the fact that there were no more buffalo on the plains. Rations offered by a friendly government alone made life possible. Much of the traditional living was destroyed, but the economic mechanisms developed in the buffalo period survived. Social stratification became more marked in these early years of the reserve period, with only those who had horses before 1877 able to participate in ostentatious displays. With the increased opportunities for making a living, social differences became less conspicuous, but the dominance of the large owners of horses and cattle was never threatened. As the economy expanded, the rich spent more lavishly, and those who shared in the new wealth imitated as successfully as they could the behavior of the wealthy tribesmen. The new herding economy functioned comfortably within the framework of prereserve values. From 1910 to 1920, income spread was greatest and Blood prosperity at its peak.

With few exceptions, the new farming program received its strongest support from those individuals who had the smallest stake in their society. Quick rewards soon set them on a par with the successful herders, but lacking a surplus of horses they did not validate their position in the customary manner. For the first time in the history of the Blood, a money economy, entirely divorced from the traditional horse economy, flourished successfully. After a decade of prosperity, an accident of climate created a social upheaval among the Blood, reducing the successful herder to penury, at least in terms of a money economy. But he still possessed sufficient horse wealth to validate his prestige as he had always done. His waning security, however, led to a compulsive buying of privilege. The farmers suffered, but only temporarily. Discouraged as a result of the drought and depression of the early thirties, they have ceased to cultivate their crops. Today, the better land is being concentrated in the hands of the few. Wealth has become the determining factor in status, increasingly divorced from the old horse economy.

Program and accident frequently effected radical changes in Blood economy and social stratification, as well as in such institutions as the bands, men's societies, women's society, and the bundle transfers. These can be understood only in terms of historical events. Band leadership has been considerably modified both by political and economic change. In the nomadic past, a leader's power depended upon strong support from family and band. For this he paid in "generous giving." Today, it is the Canadian government that distributes the rations, so that the need to support native leadership is reduced. Moreover, the early emphasis on individualistic behavior has survived; when chiefly authority fails to win co-operation, the Administration can still hope for success by appealing directly to interested members of the tribe. In the past, women enjoyed a comparatively strong position; this has been maintained in reserve life and the white man's law, which protects their property and person. Some few women on the reserve are called "manly-hearted," usually coming from families rich in horses. In this society, jealousy has become obsessional, with men exhibiting the greatest sexual insecurity. While the Blackfoot are very fond of their children, where families are easily broken, where abandonment is not unusual, and where a child on his own initiative frequently seeks a parent substitute, the parent-child relationship necessarily lacks the intensity that distinguishes it in our culture. Adoption is frequent—as an old-age insurance. Patterns of escape established in childhood are repeated in adult life. The basic competitiveness of the society is frequently expressed in the sibling relationships, as for instance, the institutionalization of the favorite. The age grade is an important mechanism for solidarity, but alternate grades of the men's societies call each other "fighters." This institutionalization of hostility, however, only reinforces behavior patterns implicit in the basic structure of the society. But when economic advantage demands co-operation, hostility may be repressed, if only temporarily.

Conclusions.— 1. Blood society, in the buffalo days, was basically competitive, but required considerable co-operation in order to function. The substitution of an impersonal government agency for a freely chosen band leader offered a more certain security on the material level, but reduced the need for mutual help and joint responsibility among the members of the tribe [70].

2. The quick divorce of a money economy from a horse economy by

those who began to farm in 1910 must be laid to the fact that they had the smallest stake in the benefits offered by their society [71].

3. The paternalistic programs of the Canadian government have not succeeded in resolving the social conflicts in the Blood community. Competitive and rivalrous trends, which functioned destructively in the buffalo past, find ample expression in the more recent present [71].

13. Goldman, Irving. THE ALKATCHO CARRIER OF BRITISH COLUMBIA. 1940. In Linton, 333-89; see Sec. 25.

Purpose or Problem. — See Linton.

Definitions, Assumptions, and Hypotheses. — See Linton.

Methods and Techniques. — Field work; otherwise not indicated.

Data. — Two phases of Carrier acculturation can be viewed as representing a continuum, from the period of integration of the potlatch-rank system of the Northwest Coast to the present period of disintegration of this system. Contact between the Carrier and the Bella Coola of the Coast was continuous and direct, and there is a general resemblance between the formal structure of the potlatch-rank complex in both cultures. It is assumed that, prior to this contact, loose social structure, lack of chieftainship, seminomadism, absence of ceremonialism, were characteristic of the Alkatcho Carrier, as of the simple Athabascans. It is probable that not until white trade became important, with the Coast Indians performing the function of middlemen between the Europeans and the natives of the interior, did Coast culture make its strong imprint upon the Alkatcho Carrier. The process of trade, intermarriage, and acculturation was characteristic of coast-interior relationships. With patrilocal residence recognized by both groups the women of the Coast were brought to Alkatcho, where they must have inevitably become foci of acculturation.

The potlatch complex of the coast developed under conditions of economic abundance and was not very common prior to the coming of the white fur traders and the subsequent enrichment of the Coast peoples. With the Carrier operating on a subsistence economy, either the potlatch-rank system had to be markedly altered or the social and economic base, or both. Carrier trade with the Coast resulted in increased economic productivity, and they were quite conscious of the differing effects in potlatches between themselves and their Coast neighbors. Symbolic destruction of property rather than actual destruction) among the Carrier was not only significant of their particular attachment to material goods but represented a way out of the continually mounting property exhanges. As elsewhere on the Northwest Coast, Carrier potlatching was never an individual enterprise; under the conditions of potlatching and the drive for building social prestige, the extended family became a more cohesive unit and leadership was strengthened.

The Carrier accepted none of the Bella Coola religious ideology; their own religious practices and beliefs remained unchanged. In material culture, a crude counterpart of the Coast plank house was introduced. Social stratification was based, in theory at least, upon genealogical distinction as on the coast; attitudes toward the few slaves they had were modeled precisely upon these prevailing at Bella Coola. All dominance relations and rivalries found formal expression in the potlatch-rank system; social distinctions that tended to lapse during potlatch interims suddenly leaped into prominence as soon as a potlatch approached. However, nothing resembling the fierce rivalries and the great destruction of property that take place on the coast appeared at Alkatcho. Rather striking personality differences among women seemed to have been correlated with social status. Property here too was given a high valuation; its possession gave the individual tremendous prestige. The emphasis was upon useful work—everyone had to participate to the full extent of his capabilities in the household economy. For the upper class at least all interest centered around the potlatch-rank complex.

With the early fur traders contact was brief and intermittent since none of the early traders settled closer than seventy miles from Alkatcho. The independent trading activities of the Carrier have brought them in touch with some of the larger white settlements, mainly at Bella Coola. None of the white traders was consciously concerned with changing the native forms of life beyond attempting to develop in them a taste for the trade commodities in which they dealt, and the Indians have become increasingly dependent on them in food, clothing, and implements, as well as items such as victrolas which they have been induced to purchase. Relations with the Church are highly tenuous. The Canadian government attempted to outlaw the potlatch, but because of the isolated position of the village, its enforcement depended on the willingness of the Indians to forsake these forms. The life of the neighboring white settlers differs little in outward respects from that of the Indians; poverty has reduced them to much the same level of material comforts. On the whole, the population has tended to remain relatively stable. Economic life has remained fundamentally unchanged, but a tendency can be observed for the gradual acceptance of cattle herding as a sideline to trapping.

Rank distinctions based on the potlatch-rank system are no longer acknowledged; a more significant economic stratification is developing as a consequence of the introduction of the horse and the steel trap, creating changes in economic relations which are certain to affect the culture markedly. Reasons for the elimination of rivalrous potlatching and social-rank distinctions are: (1) the contact with the whites and the gradual acceptance of Western evaluations upon property have tended to make the Indians rather reluctant to give up property; (2) the changes in trap-line ownership and their effects upon the structure of the extended family, the co-operative potlatch unit, removed the essential props from the body of the potlatch-rank system. These operated together with direct external pressure. Today the basic social group is the individual family, which is economically and politically independent. The new attitude toward wealth, adopted from the whites, has not yet achieved universal acceptance, and successful men are regarded scornfully by many as misers. The most socially acceptable use of wealth today is its expenditure on luxuries. The weakening of rank distinctions that in the period of first contact with the missionaries became associated with church offices, must be considered as a contributing factor to the loss of interest both in Catholicism and in aboriginal religious beliefs and practices.

Conclusions. — 1. The changes which have taken place have been voluntary and not dictated by necessity, even the individual ownership and registration of trap lines, which was perhaps the most revolutionary change.
2. The first series of culture changes, which resulted from contact with the Bella Coola, seem to have been motivated primarily by considerations of prestige illustrating the importance of the factor of prestige in certain cases of acculturation.
3. Lack of integration of the borrowed patterns is indicated by the ease with which the Carrier abandoned them when they came under white influence.
4. The first results of white contact were profound changes in the native technology, trade goods replacing most of the native manufactories. On the social side, white contact resulted in a sloughing off of the crest and potlatch patterns and a reversion to the older and simpler forms of organization; these forms were enough like those of the whites to be compatible with the new contact situation.

14. Hanks, Lucien M. and Jane. TRIBE UNDER TRUST, A STUDY OF THE BLACKFOOT RESERVE OF ALBERTA. 1950. Univ. of Toronto Press.

Purpose or Problem. — 1. The problem of the direct effect of social security [xv].
2. The interrelations of agency policy and practices to the Indian inhabitants [xv]. The agency applied the official policy of promoting self-sufficiency among the Blackfoot. How did the Blackfoot react to these measures? What conditioned this reaction, and what measures did the agency adopt in response to this?

Definitions, Assumptions, and Hypotheses. — 1. This is a community with basic social security; but we had drifted into the assumption of a priority of economic factors over others. Reserve residents could be protected against the dangers of starvation, but could not be provided with the kind of inner psychological security that would encourage them to make their own way in the world [xiii-xiv].

2. The expected placidity of a secure people was not present [xiv].

3. An Indian reserve presents some of the same administrative problems encountered all over the world. Possibly there is also light that may be shed on the problem of the relation of security in social life to initiative [xvi].

Methods and Techniques. — Field work: 1938, summers of 1939, 1941, by two psychologists and one anthropologists. Data from interviews — Blackfoot informants paid; data from official documents; and the two classes of data compared with each other and with certain memoirs and local histories.

Graphs and Charts. — Ten: Summary of the Annual Round; Reserve Income; Distribution of Cash Income from Cattle; Incomes of Selected Reserves; etc.

Data. — In 1870 the great era of the fur trade ended. To transform the land from wilderness to civilization required two immediate steps: the bringing about of "order," which was entrusted to the Northwest Mounted Police, and abrogation of the claim of the Indian inhabitants to the land and the formal establishment of white sovereignty. Reasons for the Blackfoot signing the treaty are given: Crowfoot, chief of one of the bands, tended to favor the whites in all his dealings (especially Father Lacombe). While a crucial figure for the first treaty, the Blackfoot never considered Crowfoot a leader authorized to make decisions on their behalf and responsible for tribal conduct. Disposal of land was completely foreign to the Blackfoot; it was not property. They thought that they would be permitted to continue hunting on the land indefinitely; that life would continue in much the same way, with the added benefits of sums of money every year. The people seem to have been influenced by immediate considerations rather than the remoter consequences of signing the treaty.

In order to gain the new possessions brought by the whites (such as iron blades, guns, woolen blankets, colored beads), the Blackfoot began to kill buffalo at a greater rate; to their subsistence needs was added the exchange motive. Yet despite an increasing number of white settlers, Indian life persisted in its old forms, and not until the coming of herders and agriculturists were the beginnings of social upheaval clearly felt. However, the buffalo gave out almost immediately after the treaty was signed, and the government program had to be developed overnight. The Agency planned on turning the Indians into gardeners; in the meantime the first step was to give out food rations until the gardens were well grown. So was begun the ration system, a system which in the future was to have exceedingly important consequences for these people. Overcoming their initial distaste, the people, gradually seeing tangible rewards for their efforts, went ahead with gardening, with many changes in the social structure following. There was a conflict between Indian ways and white ways, in relation to gardening, where following the Indian way served as a slogan to rally the disaffected.

Much of the failure of the Indians to co-operate with the government occurred because the whites failed to deal with the key men in the tribe; instead they made their own key men, who lacked the necessary authority to ensure co-operation. They also created distinctions between head chiefs and minor chiefs such as were unknown among the Blackfoot. Many young men, taunted by their elders, tried the warpath as a means for showing their worth; those who did not, turned to a new kind of competition. With food issued weekly, and the old activities of hunting unnecessary or impossible, the Indians found themselves with time on their hands. In former days these were the occasions for dancing and celebration. Consequently, a veritable epidemic of society dances and ceremonials sprang up, providing those who knew the songs and rituals a new opportunity to be known and to espouse the Indian way of life, even without war deeds to their credit. Officialdom looked askance upon these activities, for it took time away from gardening and prolonged the process of making the Blackfoot self-sufficient. Further attempts to increase Indian self-sufficiency were made, especially by the introduction of cattle (which met with considerable opposition), and working for wages, such as harvesting of hay. The old bands had subdivided into smaller groups that were of a more suitable size for carrying on gardening activities. The new ways of earning a living broke these units down still more. The original band organization was a suitable social structure for a collective nomadic life but not one likely to flourish under sedentary conditions where individual accumulation is rewarded. The early pattern was to hand over all earnings to the chief, who was responsible for the welfare of the whole band. Gradually the idea of the individual's right to his earnings began to filter in. The old obligation of the more successful Blackfoot to help his relatives contrasted with the individual rewards of the white culture.

In order to reduce the cost of maintenance of the Indians, the Department specifically recognized the policy of selling land for their support. Today, through management of the Indians' cash accounts, the Agency partly determines the amount of cash that an Indian may have; yet the manner of spending lies to a great extent beyond the agent's control. Thus, only in part is this an Agency-controlled system. In general the trust fund has provided a steady and fairly reliable source of income for the Indians from cattle (although no one considers them to be intrinsically valuable in contrast to the highly cherished horse). Wages are earned through (1) work off the reserve; (2) permanent jobs on the reserve; (3) wages from temporary jobs on the reserve. The present distributing mechanisms on the reserve may be divided into two groups: (1) those introduced by the Agency associated chiefly with production on the reserve; (2) those which are retained, though perhaps in a modified form, from the social fabric of prereserve days. Fundamental to the Blackfoot distributing system is one central concept which appears in some form in many institutions; it is the Plains concept of the virtue of generosity; one must be sagacious and resourceful in handling affairs so that one can give away much but still have enough to continue the show. Indian entrepeneurs who make comfortable livings mainly through the sale of horses, may be considered the lingering exemplifications of the old band system, providing a source of income for thier bands. In general, the function of the band as a distributive system has been assumed by the family. It assumes a characteristic pattern when the head of a prosperous family has his circle of dependent relatives who furnish him a market for generosity in return for homage. In addition to providing for indigents, the family contains a system of relationships to its own members that makes for distribution. Near extinction is the institution of the favored child, which centers about the family. Outside the family an important system of distribution is gambling. Visiting, both on and off the reserve, constitutes another form of distribution, as do religious ceremonies. In general, possession of wealth is an index of class.

The trust funds, under Agency management, made possible the introduction of white technology to the Blackfoot. It was initially conceived as a device for assisting individual Indians to become independent workers. Because the Agency saw a gradually increasing need for supervision, it assumed a greater managerial role. Except for the Agency's primary obligation for the welfare of the Indians and its lack of special interest in showing a profit, its role is similar to that of a business enterprise. The Indians themselves urged many a paternalistic feature, in the interest of retaining and extending this basic guarantee of subsistence. Specialists, aside from the medicine man, have disappeared. Recreational groups are made up of people who by chance happen to be in a given locality at a particular time. A reduced kinship group alone preserves most of its functions with its obligations of cooperation and sharing. In many respects the reserve residents are thus more unified than ever before, but in earning and sharing they are more divided. Today the size of the kinship group is partially limited by the geographical distribution of houses, but a more important factor is the generally increased and better distributed wealth. Today too there is greater stability and, as a by-product, the diminished possibility of status mobility, a key incentive in the old system of individual competition. There lies no broad avenue for the ambitious: as compared with buffalo days, the capital investment necessary to become productive is much larger today. Certain basic attitudes of a market economy have crept in. The virtue of exhibitionistic generosity has decreased in value, and the virtue, formerly soft-pedaled, of sagacity with property has gained. Yet there remain significant differences between white and Indian consumers. Of low status in terms of skills which they can contribute, the Indians' returns are less and their share proportionately smaller. As participants in the white world they would be living without opportunity for social advance on the bottom rung. On the reserve there is little freedom or encouragement of enterprise; the emphasis has been on collective advancement rather than on using the trust funds to capitalize individual enterprise. Today the reserve distribution and security system is balanced between two opposing forces. To the extent that the trust funds can provide them, this security will be a rallying point for many who seek even greater benefits. To the extent that these are provided, the trust funds will stabilize the present system. The other side of the picture reveals the inroads of white economic ideology, dissolving important distributive channels and isolating groups that formerly stood together. This has fertilized the ground for a competitive market system, so that when valued skills have been obtained, disintegration of the social body may continue. But at present these Indians are unable through poverty and unwilling through taste to forego security for potential benefits, though most make every effort to have white produce and their own basic security too.

It can be inferred that despite the presence of means satisfying their needs, these needs are not fully satisfied. Improving the standard of living is not purely a matter of increasing the annual income, since there is the practice of letting the future take care of itself, while responsibility for upkeep and improvement of the reserve houses has been shunted into the Agency's hands. Two types of Indians are distinguished on the basis of needs: (1) those whose needs concern mainly the demands of food, clothing, etc., and (2) those who, despite having these needs fairly well satisfied, still strive for things over and above these. The first group is, to a large extent, cared for amply by the trust fund; the second is not and consists, generally, of the younger, more energetic Blackfoot who desire to have some of the features of existence found in white homes. The trust fund has thus made the comforts of white existence more available to Indians but at the same time has raised their aspirations.

There are on the reserve two systems of headmen, the one surviving from the old band organization, the other growing from the system of elected officials. The old pattern, hinging on the chief's ability to provide for his followers, has been modified into a role of good neighbor, counselor, and planner for the welfare of the reserve as a whole, with the elected chiefs exerting the main influence, for Agency recognition is necessary to be effective. To become chief, a man must show energy and persistence enough to bring some sort of tangible return. This has striking parallels with the old war pattern and the related validation of supernatural powers, for both paths require persistence, and both are publicly recognized only in terms of tangible results. Education is becoming an important requisite, in that information about conditions beyond the reserve is becoming necessary to solve the problems on the reserve. As a group the council of chiefs forms a two-way communication device between Agent and Indians; a serious consequence of Agency policy is the destruction of the morale of the council of chiefs, due to the lack of policy for Indian participation in reserve management. The most sanguine aspect of the political situation is the current Blackfoot demand for chiefs with education and familiarity with techniques of white culture.

The vast majority of Indians remains voluntarily segregated on the reserve. Lack of employment opportunities in normal times have further contributed to this end. Maximum security is found on the reserve with people of their own kind. When they must leave, they go mainly in groups to places known for being receptive to them. Such attitudes do not extend to the Blackfoot alone; thereby solidarity among Indians living on different reserves has been fostered. The band having disappeared, there remains as the present nucleus for living the individual family, variously expanded by the addition of siblings, in-laws, the aged, and children. In these groups considerable mutual help exists. There is comparatively little group stability, with change of residence frequent, due to season, the character of employment, sociability, etc., often with any kinship affiliation serving as a liaison. Solidarity within the extended family is gained by such events of common interest as a marriage. There has been an increased fragility of marriage bonds due to the many changes such as increased proportion of males to females after the cessation of wars. The status of women has also been enhanced through the application of white law. Today, households that are economically successful tend to become independent; white law and administration have further weakened the extended family system by the assumption that the conjugal biological family is the social unit to be preserved. There exists, nevertheless, a strong feeling on the reserve that the extended family is the proper social unit for living.

Today at the age of seven all Blackfoot children leave home to attend one of the two missionary boarding schools on the reserve, from August to June. Association with children of one's own age fits nicely into the Blackfoot pattern of age grading. There is evidence of the continuation of informal interage grade rivalry and joking, but little of solidarity between alternate age grades. With many concepts established by their years of school life, the twenty and thirty-year-olds try to lead a life as much like whites as possible. But reserve income is scarcely geared to the speedy attainment of their ends; the old epitomize the exact opposite of this way of life, and with each poor year the young men come closer to the circumstances of the "reserve Indians," whom they consider to be lacking in interest in the worthwhile things of life. While a few change to Indian ways shortly after leaving school, the majority change in about the fortieth year of life. Women, too, make the transition, but at an earlier age; since they have received the submissive role in the culture, they are less free to maintain the outward manifestations of white ways. White dress for Indian girls is negative in the extreme as far as reserve attitudes are concerned. In addition, many of the techniques for living which she learns in school are inapplicable to her; also with obligations centered in the household, she is not free to prolong her contacts with the white world. Such a transition does not necessarily mean giving up one's mode of earning a living, etc. It is mainly a reorganization of values so that the same behavior occurs, though directed toward different ends. From abnegation of the past one becomes a devotee. This is the present position of much ceremonial life, and people participate eagerly. There are only two immutable requisites for acceptable Indian conduct: first, the obligations of a social role within the extended family must be observed; second, there should be no active sabotage of Indian ways. Thus, attendance at the Anglican church is thoroughly permissible. Though all other aspects of life may have changed, the ceremonial details continue, reaffirming solidarity with the past.

Conclusions.—1. In general, we see a white system of production welded onto a system of distribution in itself a modification of the original indigenous system [55].

2. Effects of the trust funds are; (a) the Indian has been reduced to the status of worker in an Agency-managed enterprise; (b) the Blackfoot system of distribution within the tribe has been displaced or transformed; (c) the population has been forced to turn to the white economy for satisfaction of certain basic needs [103].

3. Despite greater social contact than formerly between various sectors of the reserve, the general picture is one of biological families looking to the Agency for income and distributing it within a reduced circle of kinsmen. Life within these units has become more stabilized, and old incentives have decreased in effectiveness [107].

4. The Indians lie midway in social structure between two types of economy. The one is the indigenous system where goods and services flow on a basis of reciprocal obligations between members of a common group of kinsmen. The white system places even subsistence on a fee basis and dissolves the community of obligations within most groups beyond the family [109].

5. Differences in the reception of the benefits of the trust fund are due to three main factors; (1) the trust fund does satisfy the needs of the older generation brought up to expect little more than subsistence; (2) there has been an increase in expectations among many due to the decade of prosperity after the surrender of land; (3) a new generation has grown up which is unfamiliar with the difficulties of its fathers, and has taken for granted the advantages accruing from the trust fund, and which has gained new standards from closer association with whites [120].

6. Despite the fact that these people have basic economic security and one of the largest incomes of any Indian reserve in Canada, as a whole their needs have not been satisfied but augmented. By satisfying their wants it has made others more acute and brought about the emergence of new ones [122-23].

7. There are several factors involved in accelerating or decelerating the transition back to Indian ways — successive years of hard times, differences in personal industriousness, with the more easily discouraged joining the Indian ways earlier; membership in an extended family that is dominated by an espouser of Indian style of living; the sheer pressure of conformity [169].

8. The assumption of economic and political management and the fail-

ure of reserve enterprises to produce a return commensurate with Indian expectations have produced frustration of the needs for political and economic self-expression [177].

9. The Blackfoot would receive their benefits gladly if they could be brought to see the undertaking as their own endeavour and not one being done for the benefit of an alien group [179].

15. Harris, Jack S. THE WHITE KNIFE SHOSHONI OF NEVADA. 1940. In Linton, 39-118; see Sec. 25.

Purpose or Problem. — See Linton.

Definitions, Assumptions, and Hypotheses. — See Linton.

Methods and Techniques. — Field work; otherwise not indicated.

Data. — The focal point of the pre-white culture of the White Knife Shoshoni is the bare subsistence level and the activities of the Shoshoni to maintain it. Circumstances of food supply and poor transportation facilities prevented the occurrence of large or frequent group gatherings over an extended period of time, and true band organization was impossible. The camp group was therefore fundamentally independent, a fact that is extremely important in understanding the informal, amorphous character of the culture. The acculturation process falls into four clearly defined time periods of contact. (1) The first fifteen years of contact (1825 to 1840) brought a few trappers into the area and resulted in the beginnings of ecological disturbances and a few clashes, but no significant changes. (2) 1840 to 1850 saw a number of emigrant trains passing through Nevada on their way to the coast. There were some pilfering raids and the horse was acquired, but only to be eaten. (3) Following on the heels of the gold rush and the discovery of silver and gold in Nevada itself, the stream of emigrants, miners, and settlers now reached major proportions, and were being raided by the White Knives, who had acquired the horse and gun. An incipient band organization arose, and these Shoshoni experienced their greatest degree of consolidation. (4) 1860 to 1877 saw the disintegration of the weak band, but, because of the severe drain on the aboriginal food supply and settlement by the whites, a return to the former mode of life was impossible. This new phase resulted in a period of breakdown and partial adjustment.

Many natives still remain in this fourth phase, living outside of the reservation and attempting to adapt themselves to white culture. But the majority of the White Knives moved to the Western Shoshoni Reservation where they entered the fifth phase of the acculturation process. The transition from a food-gathering economy to agriculture, and later to herding, was accomplished with relatively little difficulty— the food quest needed no incentive other than the actual desire for food. Lack of outside income from leases or land sales has made the White Knives solely reliant on their own efforts. The material culture has been considerably changed and enriched. Political organization has become somewhat more formalized under white contact. Two factions have arisen—one insisting that it looks after the interests of the Indians, while the other caters to the white officials. The prime motivating factor in this split is a deep-seated resentment against the whites, and particularly the Agency officials.

Supernaturalism had a wealth of traditional customs, beliefs, and practices on which to draw, and curing ceremonies are still very important. Missionary activity on the reservation has not been very significant; the three families who are leaders of the "progressive" group attend fundamentalist services. Only those few who have been most affected by the church's teachings now feel it necessary to make some compromise with the aboriginal religious beliefs. Nativistic movements have never been important. The only formal perpetuation of the old ceremonies is the annual Fourth of July "fandango" held on the reservation-- a development from the Gwini ceremony.

Within the past few years, the acculturation process has been accelerated by a new road through the reservation; automobiles are becoming a prestige factor; there are visits to the larger cities. Movies are being shown, making the Shoshoni more keenly aware of the customs and habits of the whites. Resentment against the whites coexists with the aboriginal attitude of resignation; the resentment militates against wholehearted adoption of white standards.

The first attempts at directed culture change came with the agency period, in the form of additions to the culture, with little if any attempt to interfere with aboriginal practices. The abandonment of many of these seems to have been gradual and almost unconscious, with no resulting derangement to the individual. The population is increasing; the present culture is a well-integrated mixture of aboriginal and European elements, with the latter on the increase. There seem to be no internal factors which would prevent their complete Europeanization.

Conclusions.— 1. The acculturation process has been comparatively free of maladjustments. Perhaps the most important factor is that the aboriginal society was both meager in content and simple in structure and the impact of a strange civilization, therefore, could not result in such sharp conflict of values. Furthermore, the White Knives were spared the removal to strange territory or the close association with whites which have operated as disintegrative factors in other cases of Indian acculturation [113].

2. The shift from a hunting-gathering to an agriculture-herding economy was easily effected, primarily because the incentive to work was independent of those cultural institutions which usually break down under white contact. Once the economy had risen above the bare subsistence level, the strict limitations which it had imposed on the aboriginal culture were lifted and the White Knives enjoyed a period of cultural efflorescence formerly

denied them. The expanding economy, moreover, is developing toward the white pattern of prestige gain and ego gratification through property possession and display.

3. The pattern of White Knives culture which existed before white contact corresponded at crucial points to that which the whites brought with them. There was the same general type of family structure and the same preoccupation with economic factors [113].

4. Religion was the aspect of Shoshonean culture least dependent on the economic organization and, consequently, the one least affected by its changing phases.

16. Honigmann, John J. ETHNOGRAPHY AND ACCULTURATION OF THE FORT NELSON SLAVE. 1941. Yale Univ. Pub. in Anth., No. 33.

Purpose or Problem. — The primary aim of the present study is to demonstrate the configuration of aboriginal Fort Nelson Slave culture, and the changes occurring in that configuration following contact with Europeans [11].

Definitions, Assumptions, and Hypotheses. — 1. In accordance with the principles of organismic logic, any additive or aggregative notion of culture has been rejected. A particular culture is regarded as a unified whole, a configuration or Gestalt. The full meaning of any aspect of culture therefore cannot be conveyed without considering the interactive operation of the total culture. Every culture possesses a distinctive "life style" which colors and gives meaning to all its activities. This style reflects the goals, ultimate values, and orientation of the culture [13].

2. We assume that cultures are dynamic organizations, with an inherent order and direction that is knowable [14]. The adoption of new elements into a culture may sometimes alter the orientation of the culture as a whole by introducing new values and goals [15].

Methods and Techniques. — 1. Description.
2. Interpretation of integration of the descriptive data according to a theory of the dynamics of culture [11].

The descriptive data were based on communicated information and observed behavior. Because it was assumed that any pattern of culture perceived and rationalized by one person may differ from that perceived by another, the empirical data were presented independently of any interpretation. Brief notes on the informants used are included [15].

Graphs and Charts. — (1) Fort Nelson Population. (2) Calendar of the Fort Nelson Slave. (3) Calendar of the Providence Slave. (4) Slave Kinship Structure. (5) Fort Nelson Food Prices (1943). (6) A Month's Basic Fall and Winter Rations. (7) Ecology of Contemporary Fort Nelson. (8) Acculturation as Reflected in the Configuration of Fort Nelson Culture.

Data. — The geographical setting, demography, and social history of the Fort Nelson area are presented, and a description of the general background material follows.

Honigmann then discusses the Contemporary Fort Nelson Slave Culture

1. Technical Culture. Trapping: The principal product obtained from exploitation of the natural environment is fur. Fur is exchanged for money or credit and this in turn is the medium of exchange by which the people obtain most of the necessities of existence. The direct relationship between subsistence and the animal resources of aboriginal times has been modified and integrated into a money economy and, therefore, subsistence is only indirectly dependent upon the exploitation of the natural resources. There seems to have been little of the catastrophic disorganization which followed the acculturation process elsewhere in this shift of economic patterns. This may be explained by the fact that the basic economic patterns of the culture were maintained. Meat obtained by hunting still forms an important part of the Slave diet, along with European foods purchased from the traders. Collecting is practiced and gardening is of growing importance, but fishing is so rare as to be almost nonexistent. Water transportation is mainly by plank boats with outboard motors; toboggans and snowshoes are still used; dogs were introduced about fifty years ago and are used as pack animals; horses were introduced about thirty years ago and their use appears to be increasing. Included in the discussion of technology were the following categories: cutting, tanning, lines, sewing, dyes and paints, weapons, containers, bead weaving. In general, only those elements of the aboriginal culture have been retained for which the new white culture offered no adequate substitutes. The development of mechanical aptitude, it is noted, represents an entirely new cultural pattern.

Dress and Adornment: The greater part of the clothing worn today is purchased ready-made.

2. Integration of the Contemporary Technical Culture. The adaptive goals of the Fort Nelson Slave culture have veered from a direct dependence on the forest environment to an indirect dependence on resources. In the main, however, the Slave have become overwhelmingly dependent upon the dominant white culture of the area for subsistence and for physical well-being [123]. In some aspects the contemporary culture is failing to serve adequately the goal of adaptation as reflected in the tendency toward a decline in population. Although mobility is still of value, a new orientation towards sederunty has developed. (Sederunty is the tendency of the society to abandon unlimited mobility in favor of settled or permanent patterns of residence [125].) This represents the symbiotic dependency of the Indian culture on the manufactured resources of the white culture and has reduced the necessity of the aboriginal type of mobility. Because of the shift in the economic patterns of the culture, money has become of prime importance in the culture. Game and fire still retain much of their aboriginal value. Individualism is still of value in the technical culture of today.

3. Nontechnical Culture. The general tendency is toward the collapse of the aboriginal band organizations in favor of village groups: where the former were based on relationship, the latter are not. The Slave do not appear to have developed verbal patterns for distinguishing sharply between themselves and other ethnic groups in the area. Few elements of the native religion have remained functional in the culture today. The people's relationship with the supernatural is largely patterned along the lines of Roman Catholicism. The Indians are still not firmly integrated into these patterns, however, and their adjustment is largely passive.

4. Integration of the Contemporary Nontechnical Culture. In general, white values and white sanctions find only slight reception in Slave culture, where they are unrelated to survival goals [147]. The new value of sederunty finds little reflection in the nontechnical culture. As a value, money pervades the entire culture. Game is only of secondary importance now for subsistence, but it still retains a strong emotional value. Despite the patterns of community living, individualism is still one of the basic goals of the culture. This self-maintaining goal may be termed cultural exclusiveness when considering its ramifications in Slave relationships with other ethnic groups and especially the dominant white culture.

Conclusions. — One orientation, that directed toward maintaining individualism, we found to persist from the aboriginal to the contemporary horizon. Acculturation did not change this basic outlook of the culture and, in some nontechnical aspects, acculturation has been delayed by this value. In other instances we found values to alter in importance through time and, in at least two instances, new values to enter the configuration. As a whole we can characterize the configuration as having moved from a position of strong independence or self-sufficiency to one of symbiotic dependence on white culture in which self-sufficiency was abandoned [150].

17. Joffe, Natalie F. THE FOX OF IOWA. 1940. In Linton, 259-332; see Sec. 25.

Purpose or Problem. — See Linton.

Definitions, Assumptions, and Hypotheses. — See Linton.

Methods and Techniques. — Field work, otherwise not indicated.

Data. — The dominant leitmotif in the acculturation of the Fox tribe with the white man is that of vigorous and planned counteropposition to pressure. Coupled with hostility was considerable political skill and foresight, which enabled them through military and pacific means to withstand the impact of white culture that came to them through the channels of exploiting colonial governments and the general westward migration of the nineteenth century. Their acquisition of land by purchase is unparalleled in the history of the American Indian, giving them status as tax-paying residents of the State of Iowa. Even the horse did not prove to be as disruptive to Fox life.

The acceptance of new cultural elements has proceeded along the lines of gradual substitution of new traits rather than sudden and complete elimination of old ones. It is in the field of law and politics that the major social changes have occurred. With the signing of the treaty of 1804, the Fox began to abandon the native scheme of internal control; the disappearance of warfare weakened the power of the chief, whose principal function had been of an intertribal nature. As police service rendered by the braves was no longer needed, and there was no field open in which to gain war honors, this group soon died out. In the acceptance of white culture there have been sexual, lineal, and factional differences. For the women to adapt themselves to new ways, a less drastic readjustment was involved than for men: their role remained essentially unimpaired, while it was much more difficult for the men to adapt themselves to a new technology and to agriculture. Schism into progressive and conservative factions began with the first white contact, on the basis of pro- and anti-white groups, resulting in a bitter feud.

The Fox as a tribe have never embraced Christianity. Peyote and the Drum Society are two religious cults that have been imported from other Indian groups. Aboriginal culture is valued, but the Fox are not blind to certain obvious benefits to be found in white ways, such as technology and medicine. Today money is well understood and appreciated. Personal evaluation has not changed. The mental activities of the Fox have been utilized for reaching a working adjustment to each situation rather than preserving the outward formal shell of life when the inner meaning had gone. As each element of their culture lost its use, it was rapidly discarded and not retained.

The two crucial incidents that serve to demarcate changes in the mode of Fox life are the purchase of land in 1854 and the severe smallpox epidemic in 1902, when the village was burned at the order of white authorities, and the Fox dispersed and took up residence in various parts of the tribally owned land. Because the Fox geared themselves to a money economy early in their history, and depend on trade goods for many necessities, conditions in 1933 to 1937 were crucial. The soil is extremely fertile, and irrigation is unnecessary. Half of the families owned automobiles. To the white man the Fox does not display any feeling of inferiority. He feels that the Agency is supported by his funds; persons who have developed servile attitudes of accommodation are looked down upon. Fox life is so full for the average Indian that he does not need to go outside of his own group to achieve satisfaction and prestige. The working adjustment that Fox culture has reached by acculturation is vigorous, with the great in-group feeling buttressed.

Conclusions. — 1. The most complete shift has been in the economy of the Fox. The present economic basis of the Fox existence is farming, and their technology is that of the white man.

2. That the Fox have been able to adjust themselves to a completely new method of making a living is in a large measure owing to the lack of conflict between the old institutions which made for personal prestige, and the prestige standards of Western culture.

3. While present-day Fox life is based on the white man's technology, the other major cultural foci are Indian.

4. Common possession of the Algonquin syllabary may have introduced the conflict which often arises between a literate and illiterate group.

5. The survival of the Fox can be attributed to four major factors, all of which may be understood in terms of a strong in-group feeling and tribal solidarity.

6. The Fox were fortunate in having a long period of not too close contact with Europeans before the intensive contact which began with the arrival of white settlers in numbers. Adjustment was also facilitated by their continued residence within the same ecological area. They were given time to make a transition from one set of economic techniques to another and it is in this sector of their culture that they have borrowed most extensively and willingly from the whites.

7. They seem to show little if any resistance to the acceptance of new mechanical appliances, but show a very high resistance to changes in language, religion, or social organization. The integrity of their culture has been maintained by the attachment of symbolic values to those elements of the previous culture which were still able to function under the new conditions.

18. Joseph, A., Spicer, R. B., and Chesky, J. THE DESERT PEOPLE: A STUDY OF THE PAPAGO INDIANS OF ARIZONA. 1949. Univ. of Chicago Press.

Purpose or Problem. — 1. The immediate objectives of the Indian Education Research Project were to investigate, analyze, and compare the development of personality in five American Indian tribes in the context of the total environment setting for implications in regard to Indian administration.

2. The ultimate aim of the long-range plan of research is to attempt a systematic evaluation of the whole Indian administrative program with special reference to the effect of the new Indian Service policy on the Indians as individuals, to indicate the direction toward which these policies are leading, and to suggest how the effectiveness of Indian administration may be increased [vii].

Definitions, Assumptions, and Hypotheses. — Regional differences in the degree of white contact and local variations in culture required that children from two areas, one representing a more acculturated, the other a less acculturated, group be selected. These areas belong to different dialect groups to which different personality traits were attributed by the Papago [viii-ix].

Methods and Techniques. — Research since 1941: co-operative efforts of a large staff drawn from several disciplines. Personalities and life histories of a representative sample of children—projective and performance tests, interviews with parents, teachers, etc., medical examinations. Participant-observer technique, for the anthropological background study from October 1942 to July 1943 (by Rosamond B. Spicer).

Graphs and Charts. — Eighteen; five maps. Appendix: Personality Sketches of Eight Papago Children (A. Joseph).

Data. — The Papago live on the land, as they have for centuries, by farming small fields and raising livestock, but in recent years they have depended increasingly on wage work on near-by ranches and farms and in mines as well as on employment by the government. The area is one of the hottest and driest in the country, offering little in the way of surplus — they were thus not pushed off their land.

In the early 1870's the Papago were placed under the jurisdiction of the Indian Agent on the Pima Reservation. They were then living almost as they had before they ever saw white men; at the end of this period (about 1933), many individuals had made an adjustment to white culture, and they foresaw that the tribe as a whole would also have to make a similar adaptation. Education, especially for persons from the southern and eastern districts of the reservation, was made possible away from the reservation. This area is now progressive in American ways and supplies many of the leaders of the tribe who have some understanding of Western culture. The majority of these students came home and made a satisfactory adjustment, reintegrating themselves with the old culture, but also bringing back with them certain new values which are obvious today. Other effects were the digging of wells, building of the hospital, establishing of the Indian court. This period also saw a renewal of Catholic missionary work, which had lapsed during the nineteenth century.

The period since 1933 is one of more intense contact with white culture, of the beginning of public works and wage work in the Civilian Conservation Corps, of the acceptance of the Indian Reorganization Act, and of a quickened cultural change. Conflict arose because of the new independence of the young who could now earn money and need not be tied down to the fields nor depend on their fathers for the knowledge and direction which it took to earn a living. With the advent of war, Papago were drafted, and both men and women began to leave the reservation in large numbers to work in the cotton fields, ranches, mines, railroads, and airplane factories. However, the old culture is still strong, although it seems on the surface to have changed a great deal. There is no rigidity in the Papago adherence to their old ways. From their first contact with white men, they began to take from white culture what appealed to them. The white men came as allies, not as conquerors, and there was no catastrophic conflict. The Papago were always fairly secure in the ownership of their land, and no overwhelming force was exerted on them to change their ways; in addition, adaptability seems to be a fundamental part of Papago character. Thus, the Papago were able, without deep emotional conflicts, to add to their own culture many of the values and traits of a foreign way of life.

Up to the eighteenth century, the Papago were semisedentary farmers, who supplemented agriculture with hunting and the gathering of wild plants; this was a way of life in which everyone had to work in order to eat. Horses and cattle, oxen, and wooden plows were introduced in 1700, bringing with them the concept of individual ownership. Well into the twentieth century, their ways of making a living remained fundamentally unchanged. With the establishment of the reservation in 1917, and particularly with the change in the Indian Service policy in 1933, the economy shifted to one of agriculture, livestock, and wage labor. The old Papago house has not been used in most parts of the reservation for fifty years; modern houses are of the Mexican type: wattle-and-daub, adobe, or stone construction. The type of house is something of an index to the occupant's economic status. In the more prosperous eastern districts, adobe construction has been so widely accepted that a wattle house is a fairly sure sign that the occupants have a below-average income. In the western districts, however, a wattle house is far more often a sign of resistance to white culture. The type of house roof is also an index to prosperity or acculturation or both, as are the house furnishings. No longer does the desert furnish all the food; decreasing use of wild products has followed the introduction of stores on the reservation, and Papago food is now rather like lower-class Mexican or Yaqui food.

The family is the most important unit in the Papago social structure; family solidarity is strong. Nowadays the trend is toward greater independence of young families; they frequently go for long or short periods to places where there is employment, but the husband's father's house is always home. Increasingly women are working outside the home and so are becoming financially more independent of men. It is possible that the pattern is changing and that women will come to have more status in spheres now dominated by men. Where parental or political authority has broken down among the Papago, it is often because an attempt has been made to force upon them new patterns which do not fit in with the old. Village and dialect groups have a deeper and more personal meaning to a Papago than membership in the tribe; now that communities are more stabilized, the place has also become important. It is likely that at least the difference between dialect groups which result from differing outside influences will remain for some time.

The Papago will brook no American interference in the one thing they have left which is their very own — their religious life — a fear of interference based to some extent on the government's attempt to stop the summer rain ceremonies because they involved wine and intoxication. Illicit liquor is easily acquired when one has money, and with the prevalence of wage work almost every Papago man has cash. Possibly the speed of acculturation has brought with it conflicts and maladjustment for which compensation is sought in drinking. The disappearance of the old village games and races, which used up much surplus energy and sometimes required arduous training, may also have brought about recourse to other forms of stimulation and excitement. Despite the loss of the group ceremonies and the coming of Christianity, medicine men still receive their power and practice their cures, and the Desert People go on believing in and performing many of the rites they have followed for centuries. Sonora Catholicism antedates other Christian faiths on the reservation today, for their belief and practice are remnants of the teachings of the early Spanish missionaries. All the Sonora Catholics adhere to aboriginal beliefs; the old and the new exist side by side or are inextricably blended. Many individuals have also accepted Presbyterianism, which urges the Papago to live according to the moral code that prevailed in many American towns a generation ago. The change to Presbyterianism was not always made by whole families, and group solidarity was badly shaken. Since in itself it was a condemnation of many of the old ways— the ceremonies, marriage customs, drinking, and dancing—a schism spread to all aspects of life, dying down only in the past decade. Though the number of Presbyterians is relatively small, there is a high proportion of leaders among them. Reasons suggested for this are that the Presbyterians learn English better through the church hymns; that they are more aware of the benefits of education; that the Agency gives them unconscious preference in hiring employees; that the southeastern part of the reservation where they live has had longest contacts with whites and thus is more acculturated; and the probability that it was the more aggressive individuals, dissatisfied with the old ways, who adopted the new.

Contact with non-Papagos is mainly with Mexicans—with the liquor trade the chief link and little real social intercourse between them; with traders—a main channel of white culture; with the Indian Agency; with teachers, who are often among the few white people with whom the Indians have much contact. In the government schools, the immediate focus is upon teaching the children how to make a living, to understand and make use of white culture. Most of the village chiefs and the rising leaders are men who have learned to speak English in school, and the majority come from districts where schools are well established. There is also evident among the Papago who have been to school a tendency to mingle more freely with people other than relatives. School friendships are helping to break down the old barriers between kin and non-kin and thus are helping to make the Papago more one people.

The main areas in which the Papago people have been caught by the re-evaluation of their concepts of life are: (1) Competition and personal achievement are stimulated and encouraged much more than co-operation. (2) The value of personal property is being brought home to them, where before prestige and power came from the wisdom of age and experience or from grace given by the supernatural. (3) New symbols and representatives of authority have appeared, where before authority lay chiefly in the family. While rivaling the family, they are nevertheless not models whose authoritative position may be achieved by any appreciable number of the Papago, thus strengthening the impression that they are clearly superimposed from outside. (4) The relation of young adults to their elders is being changed by what they have learned in school and by their position as wage earners. Education in schools is also breaking the continuity of experience and common sharing between adults and children. (5) Against the belief in supernatural influences is now placed the Western concept of cause and effect. (6) A moral law based on complete adjustment to the society that has developed it is being confronted with a morality of personal goodness and badness which does not necessarily coincide with such adjustment and may demand from the individual attitudes and reactions opposed to it. With this goes a far-reaching reevaluation of the very meaning of goodness and badness in the religious sphere and in that of interpersonal relations. Christianity has become the most important new source of security. Indoctrination of such concepts as the evil of stealing is characterized by the introduction of new principles through a vanguard of restrictive rules which have no organic basis in the minority group's experience and are only slowly assimilated with opportunities for such experiences and for development of corresponding positive values.

Conclusions. — 1. The people who carry the extremely complex white culture to the Papago country are recruited from different classes, with greatly divergent backgrounds, reactions, attitudes, and aims [235]. The Papago, accustomed to the relative simplicity and consistency of his own patterns of life, soon discovers that accepting the concepts of modern American civilization at face value throws him into conflict not only with his own culture but even with many practical demands and aspects of white civilization [235]. What to believe and whom to trust are much more crucial difficulties to the Papago than to white people, who are conditioned to accept the intricacies and inconsistencies of their culture as normal and to make a distinction between those persons whom they believe to be represenative models of their culture and those whom they consider atypical [235-36].

2. Where values similar to those already existing in Papago society have been introduced from outside with comparatively little coercion, there is a certain equilibrium between the development of positive behavior standards and those of restrictive, negative significance. Where, under pressure from a differently oriented society new principles are encroaching upon the Papago, this equilibrium seems to be lacking; and the constructive, positive standards are outweighed by the negative [214].

19. Keesing, F. M. THE MENOMINI INDIANS OF WISCONSIN: A STUDY OF THREE CENTURIES OF CULTURAL CHANGE. 1939. Amer. Philos. Society.

Purpose or Problem. — 1. The study represents primarily an experiment in methods of studying the all too little known and documented processes of culture change, or as now often called, "acculturation" [4].

2. To test out how far ethnologists working in recent decades can reconstruct with any certainty the pre-Columbian life of such a tribe [ix].

Definitions, Assumptions, and Hypotheses. — The Menomini were chosen as being more or less in their original habitat and still retaining their identity while yet having changed vastly under new influences [2].

Methods and Techniques. — Historical survey of all the available records. Museum collections of artifacts. A four-month stay on the reservation.

Graphs and Charts. — Maps of tribal territory, etc. [12, 77, 132, 151, 223].

Data. — This monograph contains the main body of ethnological and historical data from about 1634 to 1929. The Menomini are one of the Central Algonquian tribes belonging to the "Woodland" culture area; their nearest neighbors were a Siouan tribe, the Winnebagoes, who dominated the region. Their sheltered geographical position gave them complete isolation from direct Iroquois attack; however, many refugee tribes fled westward in the early seventeenth century, and almost exterminated them. As a result, when the first whites came, they were a decimated and disorganized group, thus rendering them particularly susceptible to change. These great population movements seem to have favored a leveling down of aboriginal cultures, and an exact picture of pre-white and early tribal distributions and relationships in the area can apparently never be painted [6-17].

The Menomini of pre-white days were apparently a fairly sedentary people, with their economic life centered around fishing, gathering wild rice, and hunting. (Maple sugar is also believed by them to be an ancient food; the author, however, traces its use to post-Columbian times only.) While few clothes were worn, this seems to have been an area of rapid change as a result of white influences and little is actually known of the original dress. Their house styles, on the other hand, being a close and apparently ancient adjustment to the special conditions of the physical environment, changed little until very recent times. This is true also of their travel and transport adjustments which, because of their usefulness, were taken over by the early whites. Weapons and tools were supplanted rapidly by the metal implements of the whites. Intertribal trade was greatly increased; it is difficult to know how much of this was carried on in pre-white days. There apparently was a moiety system, the details of which have passed out of use, the general framework of the system persisting. The aspect of culture in which the totemic system has persisted most tenaciously is in the supernatural connection of the "pagan" folk with spirit powers and ancestors. A band system developed during the fur trade era, brought out by the same forces which broke down the older system. In turn, the band units became obsolete as soon as a more or less sedentary reservation life was adopted. Ancient patterns of individual and family living, however, have persisted to modern times. The fear elements in Menomini belief, too, have tended to remain tenaciously. Individual dreams were important, giving a marked personal character to religion and ritual, excluding the possibility of developing highly institutionalized religious forms, and also giving a potential of variation that was to be significant in the course of modern change. It is suggested that the Grand Medicine Lodge may represent the first of a number of religious and mystical movements among the Indian peoples that were reactions to mission and other white encroachment rather than being "pre-white" [18-52].

The Menomini region became in turn the political possession of France, Britain, and the United States. To the Indian, the fur trader, regardless of nationality, became a satisfier of new wants. This quickly prepared them for penetration and commerce. Especially important were the magic of the gun and of liquor. Continued mixture with whites, especially the French, has been a continuous feature of the Menomini. There were three main types of white influence: the traders, missionaries, and soldiers, each affecting different areas of life. In Menomini thinking the essential test of the opposing systems was how they worked. Behind the one lay all Indian experience, but the other was clearly potent in view of the superior material equipment and political dominance of the strangers. Such change as took place proceeded as a voluntary reorganization from within rather than as a superimposition from outside [53-83].

In the nineteenth century, with the land treaties and movements to reservations, a thorough segregation of Indian tribes again took place. In the meantime, the Menomini had become less self-sufficient, with many Indian manufactures discouraged in the face of white artifacts available. The division of labor between the sexes remained much the same. The economic equilibrium produced in the first two centuries, based on mutual exploitation, appears to have been satisfactory. The agents of trade fitted with apparently no great strain into the tribal organization. A new functional integration seems to have been reached fairly quickly and lasted right up to the end of the fur trading era. Change in the material aspects of life seem to have been determined by usefulness and convenience immediately provable; such artifacts were more or less made over in accordance with their new context, accumulating meanings and uses they did not have before, and losing more or less the functional significance they had in white culture. An elaborate development of art took place, apparently stimulated by white influence. Considerable modification came about in the tribal leadership;

new standards of worth were introduced as regards leadership—the mercenary or orator type, for example. The emergence of Chippewa as a lingua franca was a significant adjustment at the time; however its importance waned when the segregation policy was adopted [84-124].

No attempt was made to refashion the Indian before the advent of the Americans; the French and British were interested in using him, and a stable equilibrium was developed. The years between 1830 and 1850 were crucial; in this period the Menomini lands passed to the whites and the people were removed to a reservation. All that has happened since to them was only a further development of the situation then created. Here pressure was brought to bear to wean them from their old economy, and their contact with whites from now on was to be specialized and selective. White officials, whose activities were directed from Washington, were now constantly in their midst. Attempts were made to turn them into agriculturists; schools were started, having a profound influence on the younger generation in breaking down traditional ways of thought and behavior, even though the results in terms of formal learning were not great. The new relation was a dependent one. Complications ensued because of the lumber interests who wanted control of the Menomini pineries. About 1880, the Dream Dance cult made its appearance among the Menomini, incorporating elements obviously adapted from white religion, while its theology and elaborate ceremonial of dancing and chanting followed patterns essentially old. As a result, the tribe was split far more definitely on the basis of religion than before (that is, between the Christians and the Mitawin—pagans). Menomini economic effort became increasingly stabilized in lumbering rather than farming; it was particularly congenial to them, and more like the fur hunting of earlier days. By 1905 the tribe was one of the wealthiest in the country. At the same time, there was a willing acceptance of the school as a necessary institution. White medicine too began to be accepted more readily. An attempt began, in which policy was aimed toward education and assimilation instead of merely segregation and protection. At the same time, the traditional leadership was undermined, and in their place the government built up a system of direct and paternalistic relationships between itself and the individual Menomini [125-93].

A study of museum and ethnological data indicated that dress shows interesting characteristics of both change and conservatism, with utility the main guiding force as regards everyday wear, and the older and more decorative forms tending to be preserved for religious and ceremonial occasions. The older art specimens appear to be secular and purely decorative. Yet the tendency in all objects seems to be for old forms and meanings of objects to persist even where materials, techniques, and designs are changing. After a period of decay, commercialism is now giving a new stimulus to the Indian artist. The religious and ceremonial life, tenacious as it had proved over the centuries, was now becoming modified; the old beliefs were giving way before Christianity, though magical and fear elements remained especially vital. English words adopted in Menomini fall into three general categories: in terms of use, descriptive terms, and terms bearing resemblance to some known object in Menomini culture. Least touched by such changes was undoubtedly the ancient sacred mythology [194-219].

In recent times (1923), the reservation was linked into the state road system by the building of two main highways across it. Racially, the modern trend is toward stabilization of a mixed type markedly Indian. Concentration schools seem to be more successful in uprooting the Menomini youth from their traditional setting and values than in providing any new integration of personality. The tribe, however, shows no signs of breaking up, although social and racial bonds have slackened.

Conclusions.— 1. Seemingly the form, the material, the technique of manufacture, and the use and meaning of any object are capable of being modified more or less independently, and show different degrees of tenacity or responsiveness to innovation. On the whole, materials and techniques show a greater mobility or modifiability in this sense than have forms, meanings and uses. A complex set of factors, connected with ideas of utility, with tastes and values, and with beliefs and interpretations, were seen to be back of such change and resistance to change [220].

2. Those aspects least affected seem to have been the foods and food-getting techniques, certain other elements of material culture mainly associated with religion, the primary group relationships, the meanings and interpretations of life behind changing religious forms, and the traditional language. These appear closely connected wither with the immediate environment or with deep-seated mental and emotional patterns. Certain other elements, notably the old forms of housing and transportation, and the political organization of the tribe, showed great tenacity, but passed with the vast changes of reservation life. On the other hand, rapid changes took place from the first in such aspects of culture as dress, weapons, tools, art, the larger social institutions, and relationships with other groups.

20. Kluckhohn, C., and Leighton, D. C.   THE NAVAHO. 1946. Harvard Univ. Press.

Purpose or Problem.— (A part of the Indian Education Research Project.) The immediate objective of the project was to investigate, analyze, and compare the development of personality in five Indian tribes in the context of their total environment— sociocultural, geographical, and historical— for implications in regard to Indian Service Administration. The ultimate aim is to evaluate the whole Indian administrative program with special reference to the effect of present policy on Indians as individuals, to indicate the direction toward which this policy is leading, and to suggest how the effectiveness of Indian administration may be increased [vii].

The volume attempts to suggest partial answers to some questions which are vital in dealing with any minority group. How can technical changes best be reconciled with human habits and human emotional needs? How can recommendations made by technicians who have carefully studied a given external situation be most effectively explained to the people whom these recommendations are designed to benefit? What dangers are to be foreseen if facts are to be so communicated to a people of a different tradition that they will be understood? How can knowledge of a people's history, of its unspoken assumptions about the nature of human life and experience, give a responsible administrator some idea of what to expect from a particular policy and how to present the policy in ways which will evoke co-operation [xx]?

Definitions, Assumptions, and Hypotheses. — The central hypothesis of this book is that the incomplete success of the program has been due in an important degree to lack of understanding of certain human factors [xvii]. The writers believe that the Navaho service has been too exclusively concerned with material things, with externals.

Methods and Techniques. — Sources in published literature about the Navahos and in the field work, still largely unpublished, carried on by the writers and others for some years before the Indian Education Research Project began. To these have been added the field work of the project and many conferences with professional students, administrators, and teachers who have had firsthand dealings with the Navahos. The task has been to synthesize the writers' own materials with those in the literature and those supplied in oral conference.

Graphs and Charts. — 1. School Enrollment of Navaho Children, 6 to 18 years (1942 to 1943). 2. Navaho Adult Use of School Facilities (daily average, 1942 to 1943). Twelve figures (four economic; eight linguistic).

Data. — In prehistoric times, the Navaho intruded from the north into what is now New Mexico and perhaps Arizona; their comparatively simple culture thus became enriched by contact with other tribes, especially the Pueblo Indians, and there was a whole series of gradual adaptations to their new physical environment. Major alterations in the Navaho way of living occurred between 1626 and 1846, partly due to returning slaves during the Spanish-Mexican period, and partly due to intensified contacts with the Pueblo Indians. The latter taught them weaving and the making of painted pottery, and also acted as intermediaries in the transmission of various European technologies. The greatest revolution in Navaho economy was that consequent upon the introduction of domestic animals and the associated trait complex of saddles, bridles, branding, shearing, etc. Horses enormously increased the mobility of the Navahos for tribal expansion in warfare and in trade, enlarging the range and frequency of their contacts with many other peoples The character of social relationships within the tribe was also altered, the horse making it possible to supply hogans and outlying sheep camps with food and water from considerable distances. The shiftings were generally confined to well-defined areas rather than constituting "nomadism." Sheep and goats, introduced by the Spaniards, provided a larger and more dependable food supply, a fundamental condition of Navaho population increase. They also supplied a steady source of salable or exchangeable wealth, permitting the acquisition of metal tools and other manufactured articles. A whole new series of demands for goods from the European world was thus gradually created. Livestock, also, formed the basis for a transition to a capitalistic economy, with new goals for individuals and for family groups, a new system of social stratification and prestige hierarchy, an altered set of values.

The American period was characterized by pillaging, destruction of Navaho property, and the shock of a proud people forced to become dependent on strangers, with such incidents as the captivity at Fort Sumner. There followed a period of relative prosperity and rapid growth of population, followed by the building of the railroad in the 1880's: the Navaho were forced to surrender much of their best land. It also brought intoxicants, diseases, and other disrupting forces of white society. The gradual increase in white population in surrounding areas has come to mean economic exploitation and a sense of mounting general pressure. From 1868 to the present, the persistent theme in Navaho history has been the struggle with the whites for land. The problem today is that of making self-support possible in an overpopulated region upon comparatively unproductive, deteriorated lands.

The relationships of Navahos with other Indians are conditioned by geography. Contacts with the various Apache groups tend to be more intimate because of the similarities in language and the sense of a common ancestry and background. With all, there are more or less systematic exchanges of goods; exchanges of ideas and information occur in all contacts—ceremonial, social, and economic. In recent years contact has also increased because of the off-reservation boarding schools. There has been the growth of some sense of solidarity with all other Indians, in spite of historical particularism and animosities. In their relationships with the whites, they have a picture of groupings in white society which differs from the one usually given by the white resident. They differentiate between Americans and "Mexicans," recognizing the fact that the latter too are "depressed groups." Frequently, too, they refer to Mormons and Texans by separate words. Strong feeling is attached to these various terms in their own language, coloring their reactions to the white individuals who play various occupational roles in the Navaho country. The place of traders in the Navaho economy is a highly important one, but perhaps even more significant is their role as white individuals who have spread white ideas and practices among The People. Today, with less isolation from the larger white world, they are no longer so important; however, in many ways they continue to act as a buffer against white society, helping the Navahos market their goods, encouraging native handicrafts, etc. There are many Mission stations on the reservation which serve as centers for religious activities; in addition, the missionaries operate schools and hospitals and various other social services. The number of nominal Christians among the Navahos is fairly large, but most of them continue their adherence to native beliefs and practices. Apart from these activities, the influence of the missionaries would seem to be restricted to rather small clique groups. In general, the effect of any given missionary is chiefly dependent upon his personal qualities; on the whole, their attitude is more tolerant and understanding than was the case in the past.

Education is one of the important functions of the Navaho Service; the present attempt is to provide the pupil with the necessary educational tools to enable him to take his place in either the white or the Navaho world. The principal conscious educational goal expressed by Navahos today seems to be the ability to use English; the greatest single problem faced by the government has been that of communication. Navaho Service Schools also have an important function as community centers where various types of visual education for adults as well are carried out. The system is enlightened and progressive, although at first there was too much haste and unfettered experimentation. The sympathies of many Navahos were alienated because, through lack of proper interpretation, they got the impression that this was a back-to-the-blanket movement. A large and important branch of the Navaho Service is that which deals with health, and in it lies one of the best means of establishing better collaboration.

There is a Navaho Council, whose greatest importance is as a channel for the expression of Navaho opinion regarding the acts and policies of the government. Navahos understand responsibilities to relatives and even to a local group, but are only commencing to grasp the need for thinking in tribal terms. Further, they have no notion of representative government. They are accustomed to deciding all issues by face-to-face meetings of all individuals involved— including the women. Their way of deciding an issue is to discuss it until there is unanimity of opinion or until the opposition feels it no longer worthwhile to urge its point of view.

It is the impression that many Navahos who seek wage work with whites in nonwar years tend to be those who do not get along in their own society. Different sets of Navahos (depending partly upon age, schooling, location of residence with respect to intensity of non-Navaho contacts, and other factors) have shown different major responses to the insecurities, deprivations, and frustrations of the immediate past and especially to the "between two worlds" problem. The Navaho are conscious of the need to develop some compromise with white civilization, but doubt as to the best form of compromise makes them angry and anxious. Thus suspicion and hostility are becoming a major emotional tone of their relationships with whites. In some areas there has been rapid change in their culture in the past generation, yet this very rapidity of change makes for uneasiness. The fact that white American culture has itself been changing rapidly has added enormously to their difficulties. The Indians are exposed to not one but a variety of white groups, too, thus further complicating the matter.

Conclusions. — 1. The Navaho must make tremendous adjustments before any considerable number can take their places as permanent members of the white economic system. The linguistic difficulty will be decisive for a time, but more important is the fact that Navahos simply do not understand the rules for competing in the white world [112].

2. Most of The People today who have not left the Navaho country permanently live in a world which is neither white nor Navaho in the traditional sense, a world where values are shifting and where rules of conduct are in a state of flux. It is the English-speaking generation which must make relentless choices [112-13].

3. Most age, age-sex, areal, and other groups tend eventually to settle down to one or more preferred reaction patterns [113].

4. Adaptation is made more difficult because of the limited degree of homogeneity and consistency of the surrounding society [116].

21. La Violette, Forrest E. AMERICANS OF JAPANESE ANCESTRY: A STUDY OF ASSIMILATION IN THE AMERICAN COMMUNITY. 1946. Toronto. Canadian Institute of International Affairs.

Purpose or Problem. — The purpose of the present study is to describe the social context of the term *nisei* as it has developed between the cessation of immigration in 1924 and Pearl Harbor in 1941, with the chief emphasis placed upon Japanese family and community life [9].

Definitions, Assumptions, and Hypotheses. — 1. **Issei**: those born in Japan; **Nisei**: the offspring of the immigrant group, who are American-born and American-reared; **Sansei**: children of the *nisei*; **Kibei**: American-born but Japan-reared offspring.

2. Though there are variations within the group, the *nisei* are, in general, those American-born Japanese whose behavior and attitudes are most different from the immigrant generation and who have been least affected by their Japanese social heritage [7]. There are profound cultural differences between the groups.

Methods and Techniques. — Ph.D. dissertation. Residence in the Pacific states, and several trips to Japan.

Graphs and Charts. — I. Japanese Population of United States by Division and in Pacific States, 1890-1940 [3]. II. Percentage of Total State Japanese Population for Rural and Urban [40]. III. Occupations by Nativity in California and Washington, 1940 [73]. IV. Training and Occupation of Nisei [74]. V. Major Subjects of College Students [86].

Data. — The United States census of 1930 showed the existence of two main age groups in the Japanese population: an older one consisting of the foreign-born Japanese, and a younger one made up of native-born children of the original immigrants. Between the two principal age groups was a very small third one, representing the immigrants who came from Japan at a very early age. This pattern of age groups is indicative of the profound cultural differences within Japanese communities and families in America. Childhood experiences of neglect, economic privation, and social inferiority were part of the heritage of the American-born children; these had a subtle but potent influence on the personality development of the nisei. In their effort to establish themselves in America, the Japanese immigrants sought to reconstruct here the community and family life of Japan of that time, with many resulting problems: exploitation of the picture-bride system; abuse by the young wives of their new-found freedom and unaccustomed advantages; disproportion of men to women; imitation of the American custom of divorce; absence of primary family control; and the general conditions of immigrant life. Although some features of Japanese family life have undergone change in America, the least affected is the unusual degree of dominance and control of the parents over children. Nothing more clearly discloses to a Japanese family the profound difference between the two modes of life than the return of a Japan-reared child. So great are the frictions arising from the return of kibei that the problem has come to be regarded as a community one; in many ways they seem to be repeating the history of the first generation.

A conspicuous characteristic of Japanese life in America is that it has been lived in well-defined, segregated communities. This was due both to economic pressures and incentives and to the Japanese predisposition to associate with their own countrymen, so that they could fashion a mode of community life in their efforts to adjust to American conditions and to maintain certain traditional Japanese values. Prefectural associations were one of the chief means by which the immigrants adjusted themselves; they were also important in mutual-aid activities and in business affairs and in arranging marriages. They are one of the most important factors in the perpetuation of traditional Japanese culture and customs, and hence of the differences from the surrounding American world. The language school in its community activities is another way in which the American-born child was sensitized to Japanese activities and a Japanese world. Christian missionaries were active in getting the immigrants started in American life, and were of great assistance; in addition, Christian Japanese declare that Christianity has been a liberating factor facilitating adjustment to American life; instead of the Buddhist philosophy of resignation and acceptance, there is the feeling that they can do something about life on this earth. There are many church activities, essentially Japanese; the Japanese also feel that they are not wanted in the American churches.

In Japan, there are certain community responsibilities which are defined as obligations, the fulfilment of which establishes a family's reputation. Obviously the traditional system of duties and imperatives did not foresee the unsettled circumstances in which the immigrant Japanese found themselves in America, and the result was that what had not been an unreasonable burden in Japan here became often unbearable. In the static society of old Japan the system of gift exchange was based on the notions of equivalence and cooperation, but in America the competitive element has often sharply unsettled the balance of gifts and receipts. Other factors which tended to unbalance the score were the breakdown of the traditional system of control and the nonobservance of obligations by the more Americanized members of the community. Keen rivalry in the observance of these obligations has developed in the comparatively fluid social conditions of America. In the deferential framework of Japanese community life, the nisei have been looked upon as the group to whom least deference is due: they are the youngest; they have been considered socially inferior because they are not Japanese in the strict sense of that term. This system of deferential attitudes is one of the most significant factors within the Japanese family and community life. Other American institutions besides Christian churches which have introduced new ideas into the family and community life are: the public school, publications in the form of newspapers and books, and recreational institutions, including the moving picture theater and organized athletics, all of which have worked mainly through the Americans of Japanese ancestry.

Problems have been created chiefly by antagonistic attitudes of the Americans of European ancestry. The problems of occupational choice and the cultural differences between the two generations are complicated considerably as a result of discrimination; the problems are an integral part of Japanese family and community life. (Data follow with regard to the vocational problem and various methods of meeting it within the community.) There is probably no other experience in life with more potentialities for conflict with the parental generation than that of establishing families of their own, because the Japanese and American ways of setting up new families are so different. To carry out a marriage in traditional Japanese style is to express acceptance of parental and traditional authority. Getting married is one of many experiences in which the individual can see himself as a Japanese, an American, or a Japanese American. As the Americanization of the nisei has increased, the traditional go-between has become a focal point for major conflict between the first and second generations. Standards for husbands and wives are confused; the amount of discussion about nisei marriages indicates that accommodation and assimilation have developed to the point where there are several patterns of mate selection. It is generally recognized that the Japanese, even more than other peoples, tend to marry among themselves. At present the status of both men and women is in the process of change. The traditional matchmaker appears to be losing some of the importance which his office carried in Japan. With these changes in status, there is generated a personal conflict expressed in antagonism, bitter invective, and schemes for resolving the friction. Class differentiations were becoming evident among the nisei before the evacuation crisis developed. With improved incomes, control of land, and less impermanence in urban occupations, the young married couples were expressing their assimilation into American life by establishing better homes.

When the orders for evacuation were issued, there were no first-generation agencies to serve as a liaison group; with many of the issei leaders interned, the older nisei began to take over community leadership and to assume full responsibility for their parents and younger siblings. It thus appears that after a decade of friction with the first generation, the period of full family and community responsibility opened for the nisei with enforced migration and evacuation. Discrimination is a normal factor in Japanese group life, and it is a normal expectation which is incorporated into nisei expectations; the intensity of frustration is increased for a group which has a cultural heritage which also emphasizes status and prestige. It is therefore assumed that each nisei will experience feelings of inferiority; what is surprising is the amount of discussion among them about the "inferiority complex." This frank recognition and discussion of feelings of inferiority is certainly far removed from the traditional Japanese behavior. The issei are aware of their inferior status in American life, but any feelings about it are repressed and come to the surface only in a crisis. The lack of reticence displayed by their children is one more indication of their failure to establish Japanese perspectives in the second generation. The feelings of inferiority seem to develop into two basic types, which may be called the withdrawing and the compensating types — the first comprising those individuals who withdraw completely into the Japanese community, and the second those who make an effort to overcome the obstacles and have relations with other Americans. It is evident that the Americans of Japanese ancestry are marginal to the main body of Japanese culture. The most significant aspect of Japanese cultural heritage transmitted to the nisei is their general personality role of family membership. This basic role consists of at least three sets of attitudes: submission and recognition of authority and prestige of the parents, acceptance of family responsibilities, and maintenance of inviolate integrity of family status within the community, a higher level of conformance being expected than in European households. The individual who has become psychologically marginal is the person who has failed to acquire the techniques of managing frustration or conflict in a biracial and bicultural milieu; the critical periods for the emergence of psychological marginality appear to be at adolescence and at the time the person is expected to accept community responsibilities. The development of marginalism is progressive through the first and second generations, and perhaps through the third generation.

Conclusions. — 1. How long the Japanese family will continue to function as an economic unit cannot be predicted. If the nisei can follow the example of other young Americans and find work away from home and the parental business, the family firm or enterprise may be expected to dissolve. If, however, broader employment opportunities are denied to them, the nisei will find a place in some marginal occupation, and the family as an economic unit will continue to thrive [29].

2. The experiences of the kibei with other members of their families indicate that mere blood relationship is insufficient to overcome differences of training and experience. The expected formal behavior is not forthcoming [33].

3. The conflict over sex segregation is part of the community heritage of the Japanese Americans. The resolution of that conflict is one index of their "Americanization" [51].

4. The nature of the individual's compliance with any of the traditional family and community obligations is an important criterion by which the nisei are judged to be pursuing American or Japanese ways [64].

5. The system of deferential attitudes is one of the most significant factors. It involves behavior which nisei are unable to learn well enough to feel at ease in situations where much deference is involved; it cuts a deep, clear line between the American and the Japanese ways of life [69].

6. The Japanese and American ways of setting up new families are so different that what one does and says in this situation reveals in part the extent to which one is Americanized [109].

7. Since the go-between represents family control over the making of marriages, any change in his functions means that the individual is breaking away from the control of his family, or that new devices are being used by the parents to maintain their traditional position of authority and prestige [115].

8. The most significant factors determining into which of these categories (withdrawing or compensating responses to inferiority) a nisei will develop are probably his family's status in Japan, his parents' attitudes toward problems of Americanization, their feeling of whether or not their residence in America is permanent, and their ability to direct and support the adjustments of their children. If the child later approximates the achievement which is expected of him, the "inferiority complex" does not become a point of discussion and rationalization [170-71].

22. Leighton, Alexander H. THE GOVERNING OF MEN. 1945. Princeton Univ. Press.

Purpose or Problem. — 1. What are the general characteristics of human nature which gave rise to the breakdown of organization at the Japanese Relocation Center at Poston? Out of one particular episode (the general strike) could one extract a few particular constants of practical value [6] ?
2. We conceived the understanding of the community as being dependent upon knowledge of its patterns of sentiment and its social organization. We emphasized the interrelationship of the two and sought to learn how individuals are influenced by them and how in turn the patterns of sentiment and social organization are modified by contributions from individuals. The study of social organization in Poston was aimed at compiling a schedule of the standard behaviors recognized by the evacuees with especial emphasis on outlining patterns of leadership and followership and on defining the principal groups, cliques, and social levels of which the community was composed [383-87]. To what extent is the administrative program and the methods used by the administration to achieve its program realistically geared to what the community can do on the basis of its predominant sentiments and its social organization?

Definitions, Assumptions, and Hypotheses. — 1. In all the different peoples of the world there are universal, basic characteristics inherent in human nature [249].
2. There are profound differences in belief, sentiment, habit, and custom among the various communities, tribes, and nations which make up mankind [249].

Methods and Techniques. — 1. The appendix, entitled "Applied Anthropology in a Dislocated Community," contains a history of the research project, concepts and methods, etc. Methods of collecting data included: general observation, intensive interviews, records from all available sources, public-opinion polls, personality studies of a limited number of individuals.
2. After stating a basic postulate, the behavior of the individual human being will be considered. Following this, two sections will deal with the behavior of human beings acting together in societies. The first of these will set forth some facts about the nature and influence of beliefs held in common and the second some facts about the habits, customs, and ways of doing things which make up social organization. At the end will be a chapter of somewhat abstract, general suggestions [248].

Graphs and Charts. — Ten: Location and Temperature Range of Poston; Comparative Age Distributions; Organization of the First Temporary Community Council and of the Administration; etc.

Data. — Part I consists of the story of Poston, beginning with the evacuation of the Japanese from the west coast of the United States, with its consequent disturbing effects, both social and psychological, on the people concerned. The Poston Relocation Center was established in a hurry, suffering under many handicaps in lack of supplies, equipment, personnel, and organization. Nevertheless, policies embodied respect for the rights of aliens and American citizens of Japanese ancestry and were aimed at creating democratic self-management as quickly as possible. The evacuees consisted of many different sorts of persons, but could be roughly grouped into three important categories as Isseis (original immigrants born in Japan), Niseis (American-born and -educated), and Kibeis (American-born but educated in Japan). It was also possible to group the Administration into those who were "people-minded" and those who were "stereotype-minded."

In spite of many difficulties arising from outside the Center in matters of supply and co-operation, and in spite of grievances, lack of confidence, and antagonism from the evacuees, the fundamental physical needs of the community were successfully met. After the bare essentials of the Center became established, the Administration began to develop plans for creating economic opportunities and wholesome community life. The self-government formula established by the War Relocation Authority was in operation three months after the Center opened and resulted in actions which reflected the outstanding needs of the people. Gradually, what was at first merely a collection of many different kinds of people housed in one area began to assume the elements of social organization necessary for carrying out the business of living together. Groups formed, leaders appeared, actions were taken. Social disorganization, however, continued to be more marked than organization and its effects were felt everywhere, both among the residents and in the Administration, and there was a growing need for some sort of consolidation to appear. In the autumn the lack of heaters caused the Center residents additional discomfort and led them to collect around outdoor fires to brood over their grievances.

The disturbance for which the Center was already primed was set off by the arrest and detention of two evacuees under circumstances which many residents regarded as unfair and illegal. For a week, both the Administration and the evacuees held their ground, but behind the scenes on both sides there were many divergent opinions, some of which seriously threatened orderly and reasonable handling of matters. After a week, the strike ended peacefully through negotiation. The manner in which the strike was handled and the continuation of that same technique in other dealings between evacuees and Administration led to the establishment of effective self-government and considerable increase in the efficiency of operation in the Center. The Poston incident was the outcome of major themes that had been operating ever since the beginning of the project [232-41].

1. Many of the features of evacuation produced extensive mental and emotional reactions in the evacuees which in turn greatly affected the way they behaved in relation to administrative acts and new events.

2. Evacuation broke apart and reshuffled the society of the Japanese with the result that for some time most forms of collective activity, including those related to work, were unstable and inefficient.

3. Strong differences of opinion, often amounting to considerable antagonism, divided a number of groups among the Japanese and greatly affected their adjustment to the relocation program.

4. As a reaction to their feelings of insecurity, the evacuees struggled hard to achieve a sense of security.

5. There was a continuous struggle for recognition and supremacy on the part of individuals and groups of individuals.

6. The development of Poston was much affected by difficulties of achieving integrated actions by various government agencies and by the different departments of the local Administration.

7. A tendency on the part of many persons to think of people in terms of emotionally colored stereotypes and sweeping generalizations greatly modified the conversion of official policies into action and was an obstacle in the way of co-operation between the Administration and the evacuees.

8. There was great difficulty in the transmission of information concerning policies, attitudes, and ideas among the various people, groups, and organizations concerned in relocation both in the Administration and among the evacuees.

9. The effort to rehabilitate the evacuees and to protect their interests served to counteract many of the adverse influences insofar as this effort became recognized.

Conclusions. — 1. Individuals Under Stress: Types of stress that are disturbing to the emotions and thoughts of the individual are reacted to by three universal kinds of behavior: co-operation, withdrawal, and aggressiveness, all of which may lead to varying results. This is made specific in eight "principles," plus a ninth: "The members of an administrative body are human beings and react to stress along the same general lines as do other people." Principles 10 to 13 are subsumed under the heading, "Control of Reactions to Stress."

2. Systems of Belief under Stress: (1) All people everywhere have systems of belief which range from the deeply ingrained to the superficial. (2) Human groups cannot effectively carry out acts for which they have no underlying systems of belief. (3) Some of the outstanding differences between the various classes, tribes, and nations of men arise from different systems of belief and the attitudes derived from them. (4) Systems of belief influence the way people respond to stress. (5) People under stress are inclined to become more intolerant of belief systems which they perceive to be different from their own. (6) Related to this intolerance is the common belief system that persons who live by foreign belief systems are cut to one stereotyped pattern and are possessed of traits that are unaccountable, inferior, or repugnant. (7) In communities undergoing stress, it is common for belief sys-

tems to: become more emotional and less rational, increase in number and variety, increase in tendency to conflict, become plastic and changeable. (8) The longer and more intense the stress, the more extensive will be the changes in the systems of belief until some new equilibrium is established. (9) As systems of belief in a community under stress become more emotional, unstable, and conflicting, the community becomes less able to deal with its stresses. (10) Out of the confusion of a community under stress there is likely to arise a single radical system of belief which may or may not bring a new stability, but which will bring to a large section of the population a sense of at least temporary relief from stress. (11) After a period of stress, there is a drift back toward former systems of belief, but the return is rarely, if ever, complete. (12) The members of an administration, like any other group of human beings, have systems of belief, and these may or may not facilitate the carrying out of the administration's aims. (13) To be effective, all measures aimed at correcting stresses must be applied in accordance with the belief systems of both administration and the people administered, or else the belief systems must be altered. (14) The things which alter the systems of belief that people hold are: (a) Observation of fact and reasoned thinking; (b) contact with other systems of belief; (c) all types of stress; (d) new opportunities for achieving security and satisfying aspirations.

3. The Nature of Social Organization: (1) Except for very recent mixtures of unacquainted individuals, all people everywhere have social organization. (2) Differing patterns of social organization, like differing systems of belief, mark off from each other the various classes, tribes, and nations of men. (3) Human groups cannot carry out actions for which they have no established social organization. (4) Social organization influences the way in which people respond to stress. (5) Forces of stress alter the social organization of communities. (6) Social disorganization tends to increase stress in communities. (7) Communities undergoing social disorganization also show new organization; breakdown and repair take place simultaneously. (8) Where stress is severe and social disorganization is extensive, the breakdown-and-repair process is likely to take a violent form consisting in groups of people, each coalesced around a different system of belief, struggling with each other until one group dominates or until an equilibrium is achieved among several dominant groups. (9) The most stable part of the population is that portion in which the systems of belief and the social organization are most resistant to change. (10) The patterns of leadership in the social organization of a community greatly affect the way it reacts to stress. (11) Correlated with the appearance of multiple systems of belief and changing social organization in a community under stress is the appearance of numerous competing leaders. (12) Conflict between older and younger generations is characteristic of the organization of many societies and has important bearing on the patterns of leadership. (13) An administrative body is always part of the patterns of leadership and authority in the social organization of

the community in which it operates. (14) In-co-ordinations and disarticulations within the administrative structure increase the social and psychological disorganization of a community under stress. (15) Social disorganization may be detected in numerous, conflicting factions, breakup of family unity, multiple leaders, lowered ethical standards, and an increase in crime; and it may be surmised wherever there are numerous emotional and conflicting systems of belief, and where many people are showing the reactions of disturbed emotions and thoughts such as exaggerated compliance, apathy, poorly directed aggression, suspicions, attacks on scapegoats, and "pathological" rumors. (16) To be effective, all measures aimed at correcting stresses must be applied in some consonance with the social organization of both the administration and the people administered, or else the social organization must be altered. (17) The things which lead people to alter their social organization are: (a) Alterations in systems of belief; (b) perception of new needs or new sources of stress that are not adequately controlled by existing social organization; (c) interference with existing forms of social organization; (d) discovery of new forms of social organization that are more rewarding; (e) discovery that former types of social organization are more punishing.

4. A series of conclusions and recommendations dealing with the problems of the administrator follows, such as: Communities under stress, with their labile but intense emotions and shifting systems of belief, are ripe for change [6]. In producing remedial changes in a community, it is necessary to take into consideration the fact that people are more moved by appeals to the feeling man than to the rational man [8]. Communication from the people to the administration is no less important than the stream in the opposite direction [10]. The greatest promise, for men and their government, in stress and out of it, is in a fusion of administration and science to form a common body of thought and action.

23. Lesser, Alexander. THE PAWNEE GHOST DANCE HAND GAME: A STUDY OF CULTURAL CHANGE. 1933. Columbia Univ. Press.

Purpose or Problem. — The controlled consideration of the games in their changing forms has made it possible to consider the meaning of processes of change, and the inevitability of founding ethnological methodology on a metaphysic of history [x].

Definitions, Assumptions, and Hypotheses. — 1. Acculturation may be taken to refer to the ways in which some cultural aspect is taken into a culture and adjusted or fitted to it. This implies some relative cultural equality between the giving and receiving cultures. Assimilation is the process of transforming aspects of a conquered or engulfed culture into a status of relative adjustment to the forms of the ruling culture. In assimilation the tendency is for the ruling cultural group to enforce the adoption of certain externals, in terms of which superficial adjustment seems to be attained [ix].

2. Cultural understanding is a manifold and the more content we put into it, the profounder it becomes.

Methods and Techniques. — Field work; use of historical documents.

Data. — The first period of nineteenth-century Pawnee relations with the white man (ending with the treaty of 1833) was characterized by changes in the basic conditions of life of the Pawnee which were only to appear in their fullest effect in later periods. White emigration and settling of eastern Indian tribes west of the Mississippi resulted in an increase of population and a corresponding decrease of herds, along with greater conflict between the native tribes for control of the hunting range. The second period was characterized by an attempt to "civilize" the Pawnee by making them into an agricultural people. While they showed promise of becoming successful farmers more rapidly than other tribes, the farming operations were, in the long run, still a failure. The reason was that successful farming required the working of isolated plots, and meant the scattering of the people; this was to court death at the hands of the Sioux raiding and attacking parties. They were forced into a position where they became more and more anxious to make some further trade of land with the white man in return for a guaranteed sustenance, thus paving the way for the purchase of their lands and the settlement of the tribe on a limited reservation. An adjustment to this settlement was the redevelopment of village life, with some of the old tribal life continuing.

After 1881 agents were making a concentrated drive to get the Pawnee on individual allotments; this was opposed by the conservative majority content with band village life. The Pawnee had been accustomed to sedentary village life as far back as tradition could go. Their past experience inclined them to the belief that reservation life, based on farming, could be carried on successfully without the breakup of their villages. The greatest discouragement and check upon programs of a progressive nature were the physical unsoundness of the Pawnee tribe, showing a tremendous decline in population. The reservation period was characterized by a change from cultural maturity as Pawnee to cultural infancy as civilized men. They could no longer depend on their chiefs and leaders for guidance; the customs of paternal generosity which tradition commended to the chief was no longer possible. The disintegration of the old Pawnee culture which took place in the period from 1876 to 1892 was in part a correlative of the change in their economic and material life; in part it was stimulated by direct government attack upon specific customs and ways, as for instance in the long and difficult conflict with the medicine men, whose power the government was determined to destroy.

By 1892 the aboriginal Pawnee culture of a century earlier had been profoundly altered: a tribe of villagers had become a loose aggregate of people, dependent for their maintenance in part on plow cultivation of the land, and in part on the philanthropy of their overlords, the United States government. The hunt and the warpath were gone, and with them the activities of youth and early manhood, which, in terms of the tradition and beliefs of their race, gave value to the life of a man. The family relationships which had brought all the people close together were broken down with the substitution of frame houses on the farms for the old earth lodge. The arts and techniques which had been carried to practical perfection as their form of adjustment to the conditions of the world in which they lived, were broken down by the appearance of a new set of conditions in which they were no longer necessary or possible. The extinction of the buffalo and the complete cessation of hunting meant the elimination of all the arts which had centered around the handling of skins. This too was true of their ritual ceremonies and beliefs. The occupations which they were given to replace the old were essentially mechanical operations; on the intellectual side there was practically nothing to take the place of the old rituals and ceremonies, the old dances and social gatherings, the old traditions and songs. In 1892, after the best efforts of the Pawnee for over three generations to adjust themselves to living alongside the white man, the tribe had come to a cultural impasse, with nothing to look forward to and nothing to live by.

The Ghost Dance religion of 1890 arose in the visions of Wovoka, the Paiute Messiah; he sincerely believed he was a prophet with a divine revelation to impart. The rapidity with which it spread through the plateau and into the plains was in part due to the increased rapidity and ease of communication. In addition, those tribes who accepted the doctrine at once were, like the Pawnee, at a cultural impasse. The doctrines of Wovoka are clearly doctrines of peace; only among the western Dakota was it transformed into one of war, giving invulnerability in battle. To the Pawnee the Ghost Dance doctrine brought hope; it promised the coming of a new and restored Indian earth, on which the white man would be no more, on which the buffalo would roam again. Faith was an essential condition to participation in the benefits of the new order. The first tenet was to dance; a second tenet prescribed the casting aside of the white man's ways as an expression of faith. On account of the coming end of the world, and the uselessness of continuing work in the face of the expected changes which would bring back old times and the deceased relatives of the living, all those who became convinced of the Ghost Dance doctrine stopped work.

Of interest and importance is the fundamental way in which the Christ legends were fitted into Pawnee ideology. The traditional sanction for carrying out any ritual was that of having learned about it from ritual ancestors; the Ghost Dance altered the general view: where formerly it would have been sacrilege to have carried out a dance or ceremony to which one had not the right through learning and purchase, the trance vision now constitued a supernatural command that the performance be revived. The revival of Pawnee culture which began to materialize in the years of the Ghost Dance went back for its material primarily to three sources in the old culture: the bundles and bundle rituals, the societies, and the games. There were various concepts of the new doctrine, and some conflict between prophets. The Ghost Dance proved not only a force for cultural revival, but with a return to the past as an inspirational source and guide, and vision sanctions as immediate drives, the doctrine was an impetus to cultural development. The rapid development of the many Ghost Dance hand-game ceremonies were the most striking development and reintegration of the old and new.

With the allotment of lands in severalty, and the rapid increase of the lease system, the Pawnee found themselves no longer under absolute command of the Agency. The immediate results were that for the first time the Pawnee had plenty of money, and had to make no effort to support themselves. Along with the disappearance of all demands upon them to be self-reliant and self-maintaining, the Pawnee were stripped of their last outlets for self-management. Temporarily with their increased income, their living conditions improved. The conditions of idleness only served to reinforce the revival of the old cultural forms. They gladly leased their scattered allotments, coming together for a continual round of Ghost Dances, performances, games, and hand-game ceremonies. Stripped of their last vestige of responsibility, with no activities that were meaningful or satisfying, they turned to these with a kind of desperation. Under these conditions (combined with the government's policy) the cultural revival was doomed; it was based on no firm way of life. But those forms of life which had arisen in answer to their need for social gatherings remained, among these the continuing hand-game ceremonies, the major intellectual product of the Ghost Dance years.

The hand game is one of the guessing games of the North American Indians. Such a major development of guessing games is unknown from other primitive regions of the world so that the American Indian guessing games must be considered an indigenous development. The game was revived first as a game, and only later became of ceremonial significance. The concept of luck was important: winning was a sign of greater faith, just as the coming change could be attained through faith alone. In the old gambling game with its war-party tactics, women never participated. The participation of women in the new hand games must be traced to the elimination of the war ideology and the free type of individual religious participation permitted in the Ghost Dance wherever the religion spread. The general character of the transformation of the Pawnee hand game can be summarized by the statement that a gambling game was transformed into a Ghost Dance hand-game ceremony.

Three aspects of change must be considered: (1) The persistence of traits: these are for the most part those traits which are associated with the actual play of the game. In the old game the gambling was for definite stakes bet by individual members. In the Ghost Dance game there are as a rule no material stakes, but there is nevertheless a definite feeling about the value of winning and losing. It is now a matter of greater faith, and a sign of greater fortune. A major difference between the two forms is that losing or winning was an individual matter in the old game, while in the Ghost Dance game it is always a loss or gain by an entire side as a group. (2) Loss of traits: these are associated with two aspects of the old game—gambling and the war party simulation. For some of these we have substitutions of a peaceful nature—the round ceremonial fire, Ghost Dancing instead of war dancing, etc. (3) Accretion of traits: these can be traced to two general sources— ceremonialism and the Ghost Dance.

The games, as the Ghost Dances themselves, were cultural instruments for revivals. The ceremonial associations, because of the theology of the Ghost Dance, included Christian ideas, which still later become more predominant. Revivals of play were among the most important of the cultural revivals because play was missing from the life of the Pawnee in 1892. The hand games were thus the chief intellectual product of Pawnee culture in the last forty years. They called upon the originators for intensive creative effort within a formal style; they were reasoned and symmetrical "dances" of a high order. Continuing over four days, during which the whole gathering was camped at one place, there were many hours of the day for social intercourse. The scattering of the tribe on allotments made this a real need which the hand games could satisfy.

Conclusions.— 1. A general method or plan is indicated which applies to a treatment of any aspect of human culture when we are interested in the processes of change and their character. Over a period of time through which changes can be traced and controlled, and their meaning, sources, and stimuli disclosed, we plot a cultural institution or complex. The persistent core constitutes an analytic unit or constant against which the changes can be visualized [332].

2. This method makes clear that the total institution at any one time, viz., the core plus its analytically revealed associations, is a manifold which is not a unit system. The nuclear core is not merely a connected system of intrinsically related aspects, but also a combination of meanings which have tended to become associated [332-33].

3. It does not follow that that which is discovered to be an analytic constant in one given inquiry need necessarily prove to be itself composed of themes which are merely associated together. This leaves open the possibility of discovering systemic relations within culture which have the character of necessary or causal connection [333].

4. It is for the purpose of a definite inquiry that it is methodologically possible and useful to determine analytically a relative unit of culture [333].

5. Developmental or transformational changes come about by processes of associating and dissociating meanings to and from that which in the particular inquiry is analytically determined as a nucleus. The particular asso-

ciations which become attached to some particular persisting cultural core cannot be predicted or predetermined [334].

6. Linkages between themes or aspects may be either of different or the same weights. If of the same weights, we may be dealing with a system of "necessary" relations [335]. It is an inevitable part of such investigation to note the different modes and intensities of these functional interrelations.

24. Lewis, Oscar. THE EFFECTS OF WHITE CONTACT UPON BLACKFOOT CULTURE WITH SPECIAL REFERENCE TO THE ROLE OF THE FUR TRADE. 1942. AESM, No. VI.

Purpose or Problem. — To present a developmental study of Blackfoot institutions and to show, to the extent the historical material permits, the changes which occurred in Blackfoot economy, social organization, marriage, and warfare, following their contact with western civilization [5].

Definitions, Assumptions, and Hypotheses. — 1. Historical documents can be used to great advantage by anthropologists studying culture contact.
2. The fur trade was an important agent of culture change.
3. The Blackfoot tribes were subjected to two different sets of influences, the Canadian and American.

Methods and Techniques. — Examination of historical records — traders' journals, travelers' reports, records of fur companies, government papers, and secondary sources.

Data. — The Plains area is particularly suited to studies of culture change because of the rich history of movements of peoples. Early relations with the whites were friendly in Canada; the rivalry between the Hudson's Bay Company and its competitors led the former to abandon its old policy of keeping intoxicating drink from the Indians. Liquor soon supplanted other goods in desirability and became the most important single item in the trade, although it was dangerous as well as profitable. By 1830 the heyday of the Canadian fur trade was over. A tremendous expansion in the American fur trade occurred about this time, with the result that records there are much more complete.

Early misunderstandings with the American fur traders caused the Blackfoot to consider the whites as allies of their enemies, and to treat them accordingly. Relations improved when the American Fur Company began an extensive trade in buffalo hides, much of this friendliness being due to the influence of one of the company's agents. A further reason for the hostility toward the Americans was the policy of the early American fur companies of sending white trappers into Blackfoot country rather than depending upon the Indian supply; the Blackfoot considered them trespassers. The greater harmony of the relations of the Blackfoot and the Canadians as compared with the Americans was also due to the difference between a highly centralized and efficient organization, as contrasted with the rugged individualism and lack of organization of the newly developing capitalist economy of the Americans, in which massacres by irresponsible representatives could occur.

The displacement of the beaver trade by that of buffalo hides placed the Blackfoot in a strategic position, because of their control of the rich buffalo grounds, especially in the United States. The American trade supplied the Blackfoot with a market for buffalo robes; the Canadian trade with a market for provisions, horses, and small pelts—horses becoming an important item of trade very early for transporting supplies to the outlying posts. The presence of competing fur companies on both sides of the international line presented the Blackfoot with serious problems of adjustment. Differences in the three tribes were also of importance.

The effects of the fur trade on Blackfoot culture were characterized by expansion, the key to which is the transition from an economy which produced for its own needs to one which produced for an ever-increasing market. The changes are most discernible in their material culture, social organization, and warfare. When the fur traders first came to the Blackfoot, the Blackfoot were friendly, but aloof and independent, due largely to their economic self-sufficiency. Unlike the neighboring tribes, they never became subservient to the whites for their subsistence needs. The enlargement of the buffalo corrals and the increase in size of tipis were a direct result of the fur trade; the latter occurred shortly after the introduction of the horse, and is further related to the growth of polygyny which grew with the new demands on female labor.

Pottery was probably the first native item of material culture to fall into disuse; tobacco was another item for which the Blackfoot early became dependent upon the whites. Native clothing persisted, but from the beginning the Blackfoot adopted the clothes of the whites, which they regarded as superior to their own. The horse insured a larger and more regular food supply, lessening the contrasts between periods of plenty and scarcity; this could not have been utilized to the full, however, without the fur trade. Wives had to be paid for in horses, and the expansion of polygyny must therefore be related to the accumulation of horses and the growth of herding. This probably coincided, too, with an increase in the number of age societies, which were borrowed at this time as an ideal mechanism for expressing and channelizing the vertical mobility which came with the increase in wealth. The fur trade stimulated intertribal intercourse—tribes which had little contact with each other met at trading posts, resulting in much borrowing and spreading of culture elements. Of great significance was the effect of the fur trade on the authority of the chiefs: in periods of monopoly, the prestige and authority of the chiefs was increased; in periods of competition, their authority was weakened, accounting for much of the instability of bands in the middle of the nineteenth century. The Blackfoot were unusually shrewd in their trade with the whites; this commercialism was not limited to their trading practices but became characteristic of many aspects of their institutions — the buying of religious bundles, for example, was frequently a profitable investment.

Warfare of the later period was distinguished from the earlier by the new importance of equipment as over against numbers; the early religious motives almost completely disappeared. The horse and gun increased the use of the small raiding party to the point where it became the most characteristic type of Blackfoot warfare. The pre-horse motives of warfare, that is, vengeance and the defense and expansion of the tribal hunting grounds persisted, but were displaced in importance by raiding for loot. Warfare became an integral part of the new Blackfoot economy; in addition to their utilitarian and productive values, horses became a medium of exchange and the main form of wealth. The classical view of Plains warfare as a sporting game for honor, prestige, and scalps was ruled out by the dominating motive of loot, and the necessity for stealth. The prestige derived from the counting of coup and the ceremonial recitation of war deeds was in later years overshadowed by the prestige of wealth.

The accumulation of wealth, the manipulation of property, spending, buying, and selling dominated Blackfoot life. The ownership of horses became a major index of social status; they were also looked upon as a source of security in one's old age. The need for the new equipment put the poor at a distinct disadvantage, and was a check on vertical mobility. It also gave a new paternalistic role to the chief as a distributor of valuable goods.

The Blackfoot had already received a remarkable degree of political organization in pre-horse times, the effect of the horse being to bring about a decentralization in political organization and a fluorescence of individualism. Incipient social stratification on the basis of horse ownership developed, which resulted in internal disunity.

Conclusions. — 1. It was the fur trade, together with the horse and gun, which had a dynamic effect upon Blackfoot institutions [61].

2. It appears that at least three of our culture areas, the Northwest Coast, the Plains, and the Woodlands are recent historical products due in large measure to the role of the fur trade as an agent of diffusion [61].

3. This study demonstrates both the possibilities and limitations in the use of the recorded history of white contact toward constructing a developmental picture of Blackfoot culture. We have been able to show the general direction, but the specific processes are not always discernible; nor does the material shed light equally on all Blackfoot institutions [61].

25. Linton, Ralph. (ed.) ACCULTURATION IN SEVEN AMERICAN INDIAN TRIBES. 1940. New York: Appleton, Century.

Purpose or Problem. — A series of studies prepared in accordance with a single plan or outline for the testing of certain hypotheses, presented according to an ideal outline of the information which acculturation studies should contain, leaving gaps in those places where the desired information was not available [viii-ix].

To make available information on the acculturation process as it has gone on and still is going on in certain American Indian tribes; to take stock of what is now known about acculturation in general and to present certain conclusions which appear to be justified in the present state of our knowledge. It is hoped that these conclusions may serve as a basis for further investigation in the acculturation field [v].

Definitions, Assumptions, and Hypotheses. — Acculturation comprehends those phenomena which result when groups of individuals having different cultures come into continuous firsthand contact, with subsequent changes in the original culture patterns of either or both groups [501].

Methods and Techniques. — Material organized, as far as possible, according to the following outline, for any given tribe:
 1. The Aboriginal Community: A. Size and Density of Population. B. Economics. C. Social Organization. (1) Families and Kin Groups. (2) Other Social Groupings. (3) Patterns of Social Dominance. D. Political Organization. (1) Formal Organization. (2) Powers of Central Authority. (3) Techniques for Control of Individual. E. Supernaturalism. (1) Concepts. (2) Practices. (3) Functions. F. Mores. (1) Property Attitudes. (2) Sex Attitudes. (3) Respect Attitudes. G. Foci of Interest in Culture (Value System). H. Integration and Contemporary Rate of Culture Change.
 2. Influences from Other Aboriginal Groups.
 3. The Contact Continuum: A. Nature of Initial Contact. B. Changing Aspects of Contact. C. Agencies of Contact. D. Elements of White Culture Available for Borrowing. E. Active Cultural Interference by Whites. F. Outstanding Personalities. G. External Blocks to Culture Borrowing (Poverty, Lack of Opportunity, etc.).
 4. Noncultural Results of Contact: A. Changes in Population Size and Density. B. Personal Mobility. C. Changes in Economic Resources. D. Changes in Natural Environment (Territorial Removals, etc.).
 5. The Acculturation Process: A. Acceptance of New Cultural Elements. (1) General Order of Acceptance of New Elements. (2) Personal and Social Differentials in Acceptance. (3) Possible Causal Factors. B. Elimination of Old Culture Elements. (1) General Order of Elimination. (2) Personal and Social Differentials. (3) Possible Causal Factors. C. Organized Oppositions. D. Nativistic Movements. E. Changes in Accepted Elements. F. Changes in Retained Elements. G. Changes in Attitude toward White and Aboriginal Cultures. H. Changes in Value System.
 6. The Present Community: A. Population Trends (Vital Statistics). B. Economic Conditions. C. Social Organization. D. Political Organization. E.

Techniques for Control of Individual. F. Supernaturalism. G. Mores. H. Foci of Interest. I. Success of Cultural Integration.

7. The Modern Individual: A. Approved Personality Types. B. Personality Integrations. C. Maladjustments.

Data. — The volume consists of the following seven papers, plus a concluding theoretical section by Linton:

Elkin, Henry. The Northern Arapaho of Wyoming [207-58].
Goldman, Irving. The Alkatcho Carrier of British Columbia [333-89].
Harris, Jack S. The White Knife Shoshoni of Nevada [39-118].
Joffe, Natalie F. The Fox of Iowa [259-332].
Opler, Marvin K. The Southern Ute of Colorado [119-206].
Smith, Marian W. The Puyallup of Washington [3-38].
Whitman, William. The San Ildefonso of New Mexico [390-462].

Conclusions. — 1. The only constant phenomenon in situations of acculturation is the establishment, in the two cultures involved, of mutual modifications and adaptations which will enable the two groups to live together, if both groups survive.

2. It also seems that the more stable the conditions of contact and environment which the two groups have to adapt to, the more readily the adaptation can be made.

3. Lastly, everything indicates that the ultimate end of situations of close and continuous firsthand contact is the amalgamation of the societies and cultures involved, although this conclusion may be postponed almost indefinitely if there is opposition to it on both sides [519].

(See further discussion by Linton [463-520].)

26. Macgregor, Gordon. WARRIORS WITHOUT WEAPONS: A STUDY OF THE SOCIETY AND PERSONALITY DEVELOPMENT OF THE PINE RIDGE SIOUX. 1946. Univ. of Chicago Press.

Purpose or Problem. — The objective of this project was to investigate, analyze, and compare the development of personality in the Sioux with Hopi, Navaho, Papago, and Zuni tribes in the context of the total environmental setting, for implications in regard to Indian Service administration. The first field problem was to investigate the development of the personalities of a sample of about a thousand children, six to eighteen years old, selected by age groups so as to represent two or more communities in each of the tribes, in the context of the total environmental setting. The special interest of this study of personality has been in the effect of cultural change and present social conditions upon the Sioux. The nature of this change and the resultant disorganization of the society have profoundly affected the Sioux people and may fairly be assumed to be major determinants in their present personality adjustments [11-12].

Definitions, Assumptions, and Hypotheses. -- 1. Personality and individual development are the resultants of the interaction of a number of complex processes [12].

2. Any given overt behavior is a function of the entire personality organization rather than a simple reaction to a given objective stimulus [12].

Methods and Techniques. -- Field work from August 1942 to June 1943. Techniques drawn from social anthropology, psychology, psychiatry, and medicine; most of the data obtained from interviews and psychological tests.

Graphs and Charts. -- Children's Sample [11]. Children by Age [12]. Children Tested by Community [217].

Data. -- The wide range of Sioux behavior, the seeming sets of patterns within patterns, and the confusion of cultural values resulting in strong personal anxiety appear. In their recent economic and social change the Dakota have had neither much opportunity to contribute to their new life nor freedom of choice or education or understanding before acceptance of white life. Forbidden by circumstance to remain warriors and hunters, they have had to find new roles within the new economic and social order. They found in cattle, as they did in the gun and the horse, a means of making a living and adjusting to their new cultural milieu. But they lost their cattle during World War I, and, as a result, they became even more disorganized from this second loss of the foundation of their economy. The refusal or inability to accept the apparent fate of becoming socially and culturally white men has not prevented them from accepting many of the material aspects of white life. The conservative group has moved toward assimilation, embracing many elements of white life into their own. Living in much of the spirit and the vestiges of their old culture, they are on the fringes of both Indian and white cultures.

The first coming of the whites brought great material prosperity to the Indians. The period of acculturation actually began with acceptance of white material goods; this was stimulated by missionary activities. Three aspects of the dramatic period of change from Indian to white culture which followed are important to note: first, the suppression of Indian custom and authority; the education of the children in the techniques of white life; and Agency and other white pressures upon the adults to adopt white ways of making a livelihood. Today, adjustment is toward a cattle economy; there are traditions of the past and values in both the old culture and the adopted "cowboy culture" that give promise of successful transition from one economy to another.

The behavior of relatives today has been greatly modified by the changed economy and social life and the influences of the white social system. The modification seems to be toward the behavior pattern of the white family, but the Indian pattern has not been completely abandoned. The individual family has risen in importance, largely because it has become the essential economic unit in the livestock, farming, and wage-working economies which the Pine Ridge Indians have successively followed on the reservation. The individual family was also forced into greater importance because of the white man's administration, which dealt directly with these units. The present behavior between brother and sister is one of the most marked changes from the kinship pattern of the former culture. The old avoidance has disappeared, but mutual respect is still observed. The adoption of English kinship terminology appears to be a strong factor in breaking down the ties and behavior patterns of the extended family organization. Marriages are now made with little or no family sanction or symbolic expression of contract between the two families. The co-operation of a strongly knit, extended family, however, is still an ideal with much tension thus created. The band integration has also been weakened by the decline of Indian leadership and the passing of the functions of government to the Agency; the activities in the school are developing the integration of the district into a more functional unit. The Indians are merging to a greater degree with the lower than with the middle class of South Dakota whites.

The ceremonies and beliefs which were elaborated around the central theme of their religion have disappeared, but the basic belief in the need for power remains. It functions in minor native cults, the work of medicine men, and the Peyote cult, which has members in many of the reservation communities, and the orthodox Christianity introduced by missionaries. The process of religious change has been the dying out of the old native religion before the full acceptance of Christianity as the religion of the people. As long as there was a body of older people trained and experienced in the native rituals and led by the native priests or medicine men, the resistance to Christianity endured. The shifting from one religion to another of apparently conflicting concepts becomes more understandable when it is realized that there are certain elements fundamental in the native pre-Christian religion which are carried over into the contemporary religions. The first is the continuous seeking of divine power for strength and assistance in meeting the problems of earthly life. An adjunct is the specific use of this power for curing. The second is the seeking of social interaction and social participation, which give to the individual a sense of security and membership in a larger group not attained regularly in other institutions. The third is the sanctioning of a moral code.

People born in different eras of Pine Ridge history hold widely differing attitudes; the grandparent generation was trained in the old moral code. They accepted the cattle economy and made an excellent transition to the life of the white plainsman, which seemed attractive as represented by the cowboy. In the redevelopment of the cattle industry at the present time, therefore, it is the old people who are encouraging. Following the security and self-reliance of that period, the cattle and land sales resulted in poverty and sickness and a return to complete economic dependency on the government, bringing to them a sense of futility in following the white man's economy. The attitudes of the next generation differ to a considerable degree from those of their elders because the younger men had less training for Dakota life in childhood and as adults have not experienced the cowboy life or satisfactions of the cattle economy.

Since the sale and rental of allotments began, land has become property of intrinsic value to modern Dakota. It is not conceived of as a source of food or income but as potential cash, that is, in its possible sale -- the old premium on disposing of wealth is here evident. There is conflict between the developing individualism of the white man and the co-operation and sharing of the Indian; saving exposes one to visits from poor relatives and is against good Sioux behavior. The existence of such conflicting standards of behavior makes it inevitable that almost any action of the individual is out of line with the standards of some members of his community. The breakdown in family control and the failure of the child-training system have resulted in increasing sexual delinquency. There has been a marked change in the roles and status of women, whose position has risen with their function in the family, often more important today than that of the men.

The modern social structure, with its poverty, lack of adequate roles and cultural objectives, and social conflicts arising out of lost controls and changing attitudes, is strongly conducive to insecurity for the group and for the individual. Attitudes and values of the old culture still strongly affect the behavior patterns of the people, but some of its social institutions are gone or are only vestigial. The realization of cultural loss and being neither Indian nor white in any cultural sense adds to the Indian's insecurity and isolation in the modern world. This insecurity of the adults cannot help having repercussions on the children as they grow up. Today white methods are used increasingly by the more assimilated Indian families, but the stronger discipline characteristic of the training of white children comes chiefly from the schools on the reservation.

Conclusions. -- 1. The fundamental need of the Pine Ridge Dakota today is a way of life which will give them personal security and an opportunity for creative development.

2. The primary values of the Agency program are the restoration of cowboy life as an occupation around which sentiments and prestige have already been built, and the development of leadership and responsibility. The importance which the men play in this program is in keeping with Dakota tradition.

27. Mead, Margaret. THE CHANGING CULTURE OF AN INDIAN TRIBE. 1932. Columbia Univ. Press.

Purpose or Problem. -- A study of the tribal woman as she reacts in the present period of white contact [viii].

Definitions, Assumptions, and Hypotheses. -- 1. The complicated situation in which the tribe now functions might bear less heavily upon the Indian woman than upon the man [viii].

2. One set of similar conditions, whether they occur among the invading or among the invaded peoples, is in some measure sufficiently determinate so that general trends of culture conflict can be predicted and a detailed study here and there do duty as illumination and illustration of a wider social process [7].

Methods and Techniques. — Investigation, June to October 1930. The tribe was chosen because of the following considerations: must still preserve its group integrity; contact sufficiently prolonged so that English could be used; good ethnographic data available on the aboriginal condition of the tribe; the group had to be large enough to present variety and perspective and small enough so that the total situation could be envisaged and analyzed. The Indians were unaware of the investigation. Contact of the ethnographer was informal, but with individual informants carefully chosen.

An introduction presents the author's theoretical framework. Here is a general picture of tribal conditions, followed by studies of individuals.

Graphs and Charts. — Analysis of Household Organization [225-41]. Marital Situation [242-60]. Case Histories of 25 Delinquent Girls and Women [261-80]. Supporting Data, Notes on the Mixed-Blood Situation, Sample Conversations [281-304].

Data. — The Antlers are a Mississippi Valley tribe whose earliest contact with the white man was with French traders; the invasion of the white man was gradual and unaccompanied by bloodshed. They are living on a reservation which corresponds to part of the territory which was the most recent of their aboriginal habitats. With the disappearance of the buffalo and the influx of white settlers, the Antlers had to make a series of readjustments with pressure from government and missionary. The men were encouraged to farm, but this new activity had no old base upon which it could be grafted. The old system of prestige by which men attained rank (through giving gifts and feasts) and so could confer on their daughters the distinctive marks of rank was never properly incorporated into a rural agricultural way of life. The incentive for hard work was also removed. Women, however, were to do all the domestic gardening, and their way of life changed little. The Antlers made a second adjustment to white culture, partly expressed in the introduction of the Peyote cult. It was on this attenuated culture that the onrush of white settlement impinged, coincident with the end of the "period of trust." Life on the reservation and the towns around it is now characterized by a mixed population in continual contact, but without any sense of community of interest.

In ancient Antler economy the chief functions of wealth were to validate privilege; in the case of secular privilege, by accumulating merit ratings through the public distribution of wealth. The association of land with private property or inheritance was completely alien to them. These are the economic ideas which they retain today; for the situations which have resulted from white contact they have a separate ideology. Actual personal property is sometimes expended according to one set of ideas and sometimes according to the other. Conditions on the reservation have been getting steadily worse since 1920: leasing has increased, with resulting diminution of family incomes; the desire for American goods (especially the automobile) has increased. The new economy, introduced by the white man, was based on the ownership of land, with its incompatibility of recognizing a group of heirs and at the same time preserving the land in reasonable units. This has resulted in much friction in the tribe and continual pressure on the government to permit the sale of "heirship" lands. Selling their lands results only in lavish expenditure (as reinforced by the wealthy Oil Indians' example): for some sort of subsistence on the land is the only sort that is culturally recognized, and there are no rewards which he feels makes ordinary labor worth doing. A few weeks of absolute opulence have much more appeal. A new set of values has been evolved to meet the unprecedented situation—a pattern of aggressive economic indulgence, helped considerably by the automobile. In everything that does not relate to actual sums of money derived from land sales—in which he has taken over the white man's economic individualism—the Antler remains conservative and bound to the hospitality rule; in order to escape the continual exactions of relatives, he must either be rich enough to be accorded the right to spend his money as he wishes, or "go white." This last is considered to have happened when an Antler refuses to share his food, etc. It carries with it a good deal of social scorn and is difficult to bear when acceptance is withheld by the white man.

The old political organization of the Antlers was based on rank and wealth. Today their political existence is largely fictitious; their position is that of a child, lacking participation or obligations of any sort. All the feeling usually involved in citizenship and nationality is centered about the words "American Indians," as fostered by the white attitude. The Antler does not understand the premises on which the government acts, and so believes anything to be possible—a game of hopefully gunning for the government which is now the most engrossing occupation of many of the men who, having leased their lands, have no other occupation.

The kinship and gentile system have suffered severely from the scattered residence, boarding school, etc. Particularly well illustrated here is the Antler trait of learning the white values, as a separate set of ideas, but failing to incorporate them into the stuff of the culture. Joking and avoidance relationships are still in force, largely because they are so incomprehensible to the white residents that they do not know they exist. The grandfather's role is now very unimportant—the sense that the past is gone, never to return, has fallen upon the old men and paralyzed their interest in educating the children. Parents' authority in marriage choices have been undermined by coeducational schools and the state legislation against marriages by "Indian custom"; yet the stage of household organization is such that every individual has important stakes in the marriage of a close relative.

To the extent that tribal fetishes embodied the formal religious life of the Antlers, that life may be said to have vanished. By the first decade of the twentieth century, the Antlers were all nominally Presbyterians; there was no emotional value attached to their allegiance, no compulsion toward any particular form of behavior. They were ripe to receive some religious stimulation which would be germane to their older religious attitudes and yet conform to their nominal professions of Christianity, which would be distinctively Indian and yet not "old-fashioned." The Peyote cult fulfilled all these requirements. This cult is dwindling in importance due to poverty and the consequent difficulty of obtaining the expensive imported peyote; it still plays an important role as a cure for the sick and in the funeral service. The integration which has been achieved between the Peyote organization and these ceremonies is perhaps one of the most successful adaptations the Antlers have made.

The first serious attempt of the whites to share part of its tradition with the Antlers came when the old Mission was established. Some children were sent East to school, but their chance of becoming an influence with their tribe was marred by the fact that most were orphans or children of aberrant people who welcomed the coming of a new way of life, a bad start which militated against them. Attendance at the local schools today makes very little impression on the children, other than imbuing them with resentment. The best English on the reservation is spoken by a few old people with schooling in the East; from these there is a steady reversion downward of ability in English so that there are many young people of twenty who speak hardly a word. Coeducation is another feature of the Indian schools that has had particularly bad results: no new pattern has been developed for the Antler sex policy based on bringing up girls to be modest, frightened, shy in the presence of boys, but fair game when caught alone.

The vanished traits of the old Antler culture played a relatively smaller part in the lives of the women than of the men; the essential content of childbearing, child rearing, and domestic tasks cannot be as completely stripped of meaning. Their social, political, religious, and economic roles were limited; they were believed to be weaker and frailer. However, the proportionate role of men and women has changed radically as the culture has been shorn of its more distinctive emphases, because it was in the most intense cultural development that women had the least part. Today, the women have often as great a share in the past as the men, and are likely to be the ones who treasure the past more fervently. Economically, various factors have contributed to the conservation of the land owned by women, thus increasing their economic importance. They are now the core of Antler culture, still Indian in positive terms, in a multitude of details which bind mother to daughter and both to granddaughter; the men are Indian by virtue of blood, language, and a disinclination to accept the economic behavior and attitudes of white society, but characterized by a discontinuity in which each generation is careless of the preceding one, but without any active rebellion.

Conflict between Antler sex standards and present-day reservation sex laxity is the most important factor in producing delinquent women. The Antlers are essentially puritanical in their attitudes toward sex. With the old controls breaking down and no new ones taking their places, public opinion has not adapted itself to changing practice as it would in a less disorganized community. As long as the culture was a coherent, consistent whole, very few people would succeed for any length of time in flouting convention. Today, with every woman deviating from the code being disapproved of, the majority still deviate. This produces an essentially maladjusted society in which all are sinners and everyone points the finger of scorn. A part of the inevitable conflict between standard and behavior is solved by the myth that the white man is responsible for all of the Indian's sins.

Antler society as such no longer exists as a coherent social fabric; it has been replaced by a series of discontinuous, noncomparable, disunited Antler homes; the great divergence between theory and practice is so prevalent in different aspects of Antler culture as to be termed a trait of the society. The family setting is intensely important because every other type of setting for character training has vanished. The houses have now become mere places of shelter; the tendency to live by other means than agriculture is steadily increasing with extended leasing of land, so that it is reasonable to regard the nonfarming population typical. Adjustment to any new kind of life is very difficult, emphasized by the loss of capital and skills.

Conclusions. — 1. Divergent moral standards are continually being presented to the Antler young people in the form of (a) fixed moral theory accompanied by an almost universal breakdown in practice, and (b) the divergence between old-time, modern, mixed-blood Antler, other-tribal, and white practice [205].

2. Cultural breakdown and culture contact have forced on the Antlers a tremendous diversity of experience, removing all the old sanctions, leaving only a differentiated precarious family life as an educational background for the next generation [219].

3. In the problem of Antler women, these conditions which are making for increasing delinquency are of greatest importance in predicting their adjustment [219-20], which cannot be considered hopeful.

28. Mekeel, Haviland Scudder. A MODERN AMERICAN INDIAN COMMUNITY IN THE LIGHT OF ITS PAST: A STUDY IN CULTURE CHANGE. 1932. Ph.D. dissertation, Yale Univ.

Purpose or Problem. —(1) To develop a technique and an approach for the study of culture from the viewpoint of interaction, growth, disorganization, and other dynamic processes; (2) to study such processes in cultural as well as in psychological terms so that (3) data might be provided both for a more satisfactory administration of primitive peoples, and for handling forces at work in our own culture [1]. To find out what forces are at work facilitating or opposing acceptance of American culture [Summary].

Definitions, Assumptions, and Hypotheses. — 1. It is the writer's thesis that identification with functioning institutions creates and sustains an individual's life values. Some, like the family, may be more potent than others [150].

2. For a true study in cultural dynamics one should investigate the integration of culture traits for each person in a society. It would then be necessary to study the problem of the integration of these individual clusters to each other, in the formation of what we term a community, a society, or a functioning culture [176].

3. In spite of pressure from government and church certain ancient patterns still function—patterns which oppose community assumption of a white man's values and conduct. There still exists in the community, for the interaction of individuals, a mode for behavior which differs from that in a white community and which is maintained by sentiments of group solidarity [111].

Methods and Techniques. — Choice of tribe based on (1) a culture reasonably homogeneous and stable at the time of first European contact; (2) a relatively large population spread over a fairly extensive territory, thus affording opportunity for possible local developments.

Two summers with the White Clay Community, as a participant observer. Also use of historical documents. Historical background [12-83]. Personality fragments [176-88].

Graphs and Charts. — 1. Distribution of Teton Dakota by States [3]. 2. Distribution of Indian Tribes in South Dakota [3]. Maps: 1. Distribution of Dakota Tribes. 2. Reservations in South Dakota. 3. Pine Ridge Reservation, South Dakota. 4. White Clay Community. Appendix C: Statistics on Living Conditions.

Data. — I. Historical Background: A Study in Teton-White Interaction. From the white man's viewpoint there were found to be three periods: (1) Rising Action, 1700-1851: Fur trade, with interaction between Teton and white becoming more and more strained on account of white immigration. (2) Crisis, 1851-78: Warfare precipitated by white people who forced a way through the Teton Dakota hunting grounds and destroyed the game. The extermination of the buffalo and the collapse of the fur trade during this period played a large part in the military defeat and acceptance of reservation life. (3) Falling Action, 1878-1932: Provision of reservations for Teton Dakota hunting grounds, and beginning of organized acculturation. From the Teton Sioux standpoint there emerge five phases in contact with white people. (1) An acceptance of certain of the material elements of white culture, notably the horse, as well as articles of trade; these goods do not at first conflict with former habits but add comfort and convenience. Prosperity follows, with increase in population and territory. The invading white settlers disturb the game, leading to (2) struggle for sovereignty. (3) Acceptance of reservation life through military defeat and loss of subsistence. (4) Appeal to supernatural aid and rejection of white culture, in the form of revivalistic movement, especially strong. Suppression by the United States government, resulting in (5) passive acceptance of white acculturation.

It was not until the war of 1812 that the Dakota were directly involved in any inter-white conflict; this is one of the most important single factors in the history of their contacts with whites. Except in the early period, the three groups — government, economic exploiter, and missionary — are characterized by different, and often conflicting, interests, with the relation of the trader to the Indian the most natural and congenial. White contact in the form of trade gave the native economy a new emphasis, enhancing the material comforts without changing the principal cultural configurations or drives. Vitiating factors were: liquor, life about the trading posts, and economic dependence on the traders, which was sometimes abused. By the breakup of the fur trade through emigration and Indian wars, the Teton Dakota lost his closest and most intimate relationship with white men. The results of the war period left a great bitterness and depression with the Indian — partly from his treatment by the white people and more from the passing of the buffalo, on which the old life depended.

II. A Modern Teton Dakota Community. Relation by blood is the most potent single determinant for the behavior of one individual toward another, though signs of breakdown at certain points are becoming evident, even to cases in which the mother-in-law tabu is disregarded. The bands, too, betray evidences of breakdown; as the present chiefs in each band die off they are not replaced. The native U.S. Indian Service police have absorbed their functions. Exoteric institutions which in a sense "flow" into the community — school, church, police, boss farmer's office, general store — are important. Next to the white man married and living with the Indians, and the resident teacher at the Indian Day Schools, the trader can probably exert the greatest influence of any white man in the community.

For summary of "Getting A Living": see Mekeel, "The Economy of a Modern Teton Dakota Community" abstract. The woman's side of the picture is more difficult of analysis. Between the old life and the new there is the continuum of child rearing and food preparation. However, it does seem that even her primary tasks have changed meaning, with the women's institutions dead and none having arisen to take their places. It seems therefore that the women as well as the men have suffered from economic change.

A symbol of general breakdown in culture morale may be found in the amount of premarital license which is considered to have been uncommon in the older culture. Polygamy has been consistently frowned on by the whites and, under modern economic conditions on the reservation, would be an insupportable burden since a woman now is a liability rather than an asset. In ancient Teton Dakota society social recognition on the part of the men centered largely on bravery and generosity, defined by stylized forms of behavior in specific contexts. The society was individualistic and highly competitive. This applied also to the women, in whom were valued chastity, skill in certain tasks, close relationship to a man with many counts. Today, warfare, hunting, and the Sun Dance are gone; exhibitions of bravery are therefore ruled out as a sphere for competition and a criterion of a man's status. The police or soldiers' societies have thus been vitiated, as has the chieftaincy, which was never a hereditary office but depended on brave deeds accomplished. The office is becoming less of an honor as the older chiefs die off, and, as it is not recognized by the United States government, it lacks support from outside. A definite criterion for tribal leadership has thus been eliminated with the institutions fostering bravery going. The outlets for generosity have not all been cut off, but have in a way been intensified. The patterns for hospitality are still in force and often called upon by destitute families or lazy relatives.

Government schools and religious institutions offering educational facilities exist, as do such organizations as the Boy Scouts and 4-H Clubs; however, these have not yet been able to transfer the life values and drives possessed by the white community. Religion, for example (as in the instance of mourning presented by the author), strikes one as more Sioux than white. Leisure has never functioned as a social classifier in the older culture. Many situations (e.g., those connected with war) no longer arise for observance as a social occasion; others, such as death and marriage, do arise, and are socially recognized contexts for giving. There remain sufficient of these, along with extreme general poverty, to prevent much accumulation of property. Patterns such as hospitality and the Begging Dance reinforce this configuration. This is a society which chose release of wealth on which to build its values, and only gradually is it shifting. Leisure activities which consume much time are: social affairs (e.g., dances); feasts for such occasions as marriage, death, recovery from illness of a loved one; travel and the fetching of rations; gossip; illicit sex relations; games. Of these, the most outstanding in the minds of the Indian is the dance; dancing and traveling, however, serve a different outlet from similar behavior in the older culture, although to some of the older people both pursuits undoubtedly symbolize the older life. The automobile and radio also bode far-reaching changes; an increase in potential mobility as a result of the former might portend extreme reverberations in social life, with cars already being used for the meetings of the sexes. Little is known about music as a leisure pursuit; a few instruments—harmoniums, piano, cornet, victrola—were found.

Conclusions.— 1. The five stages of contact indicated by Mekeel are compared with Keesing's for the Menomini, and Firth's for the Maori: (a) Initial impact—enthusiastic adoption of new culture forms; (b) reaction against acculturation; (c) fresh and more deep-rooted adaptation and found to be comparable [82].

2. Such comparative evidence seems to establish the fact that peripheral societies struggle to maintain two things: their sovereignty and, more fundamentally important, their identity as a group distinct from all others. Incursions of white culture tend to break not only the distinctiveness, but also the very solidarity of the group. Consequently there is constant struggle for a peripheral group to reintegrate its culture and redefine the criterion on which is based its uniqueness among other groups [83].

3. A culture cannot be changed adequately just by educating each individual. It must be accompanied by a reformation or redirection of the institutions within that society [146].

4. For the purposes of a really scientific study of culture process the better method is to study specific behavior situations in one society; their variations from individual to individual, or group to group, both in regard to exciting and fundamental situations as well as to specific content; and the variations over periods of time [161]. Historical evidence is too meager, too vague, either to analyze all the elements in a behavior situation or to give an insight into the human mind at work in culture.

5. Travel proves to be an interesting problem for study in a modern Plains tribe like the Dakota. There was in the past a seasonal rhythm, alternating isolated sedentary life in winter with communal traveling in the summer. It would be interesting to determine what relation the present summer restiveness bears to the older rhythm. Changes from now on can be watched and the nature of the process itself recaptured [167].

6. Irrespective of specific context, there is a direct correspondence between the integration of this older set of values as presented to the Indian. There appears then to be a condensation of new and old in the new. Those who have arrived at this condensation would then reject the merely old form of traveling and dancing and see it in its new meaning as a disintegrative force among the younger generation, who retain few or none of the older sentiments connected with them [172].

29. Miner, Horace.   ST. DENIS: A FRENCH-CANADIAN PARISH. 1939. Univ. of Chicago Press.

Purpose or Problem. — The ethnographic description of the old rural French-Canadian folk culture in its least altered, existent form, the analysis of the social structure of the society, and the consideration of the factors responsible for culture change in the direction of urbanization and anglicization. The first two aspects are basic to the adequate diagnosis of the third [vii].

Definitions, Assumptions, and Hypotheses. -- 1. French Canada is a peasant society, in many respects resembling a primitive society, but differing in that it forms a part of the modern urbanized world.
2. French-Canadian culture was one which had a high degree of internal social integration based on a short-term adjustment to the environment [xviii]. The system, based on expansion into new lands, contained its own future problems.

Methods and Techniques. -- Continuous residence in St. Denis from July 1936 to June 1937; St. Denis being chosen as a long-established agricultural community which had maintained the old culture to a great degree. Field methods included writing up observed behavior, direct interviewing, and analyzing family and parish records.

Graphs and Charts. -- Lists of newspaper subscribers, number of members per family, children of school age, etc., appear scattered throughout the monograph.
Appendix I: Age-Sex Distribution of the Population of St. Denis (1936). II: Traditional Cures and Remedies. III: The Autobiography of an Habitant. IV: Old and New Traits in St. Denis.

Data. -- The unified background of the colonists gave to the pattern of life in the whole province the homogeneity which existed down to the beginning of the movements of the habitants to the towns and cities. Basic to the community are agriculture and religion. The church has stood between the changing world and the habitant, preventing the admission of elements which she condemns and interpreting admitted elements in accordance with the faith and with the local culture. There is an increasing loss of economic independence, requiring the farmer to use more land to produce cash crops in order to support his changed standard of living. The same amount of land, therefore, cannot support as many people as it formerly did.

Since the turn of the century, more importance has been attached to education, largely because it assists young men in securing positions in urban centers; literacy is increasing. Girls are more likely to receive supplementary education after finishing the local schools than are the boys, because of the older tradition of convent training and the lesser need for their services on the farm. The discontent of the rural youth with country life, which is already appearing, may well be increased by education which stresses urban culture and values. The rural Frenchman is usually apologetic about his speech, offering little resistance to the entrance of English words, as he has no basis for judging what is standard French and what is not. The outside contacts of both children and adults are extremely limited, despite a former movement to New England for work; those who returned to

St. Denis were largely those whose modes of life had changed but little. Travel still follows the family channels. A place where one has no relatives is particularly uninviting. The newspaper and radio have increased their consciousness of the wider sphere of life in the province; automobiles are not wanted, because of the upkeep. An oxcart drawn up by the gasoline pump outside the local store is a common scene, which characterizes the disparity between the old economy, with its dependence on farm animals, and the new special economic adjustments.

The unit of social life is the parish—those people who can go conveniently to a single church which they support. The real basis of rural life is the family. The whole social system and the family system upon which it is dependent are based upon large families and the eventual establishment of all the children, save one, outside the paternal home. To function properly there must be a continual outlet for this surplus. In France, whence came the system, the disappearance of the outlets resulted in decreased birth rate. In Quebec, most of these outlets are now closed, so that the surplus has little means of establishing itself—a problem complicated by the decreasing death rate. The family cycle has not changed; but the social structure of which it is an integral part has become altered so that children are no longer assured a full social life.

All the inhabitants of St. Denis are Roman Catholics. Lack of contact with persons of other convictions and the relative lack of functional problems in the mode of living mean that the particular native belief is rarely questioned. What lack of faith exists is the result of the recent changes in the functioning of the society itself. The new city values are in general attacked by the church. In those areas of control over nature, the general tendency is for the nonrational to be dropped. The direction of this shift originates outside of the local society but enters through channels held in high local regard; as a check to this shift stand the economy and tradition. "Superstition" has come to be construed to mean anti-Catholic or non-Catholic, nonrational belief because of the dominance of Catholic belief over the loosely knit, undeveloped beliefs which might have opposed it, as contrasted with the situation, for example, in Haiti, where they were not able to suppress the strongly ritualized black magic beliefs. Acculturation in St. Denis differs further in that innovations enter sanctioned by a church which is the most powerful force in the native community, and that the society is two centuries more advanced along the lines of Western industrial civilization. Support for the new ideas comes from within the parish, rather than from an entirely different type of culture—as is the case in the urbanization of most folk societies. It is therefore suggested that the sophistication of rural French Canada will take place more rapidly and completely than in these other regions.

Rural French-Canadian culture has changed more in the last forty years than it did in the preceding century, and in every phase of life. The social organization of rural French in Canada is losing its folk character. Many of the old culture traits are so closely allied to the thrifty, close-family economy that they have resisted change to a remarkable degree, but even for these there is often some complementary alteration of custom. The trends are toward industrialization and urbanization, toward the acquisition of city manners. Fundamentally the culture shift is toward increasing dependence of the local society upon the great industrial civilization of which it is becoming a part. This shift from a self-sufficient to a dependent economy is best understood in terms of the increasing land pressure. The changed land conditions have created problems in the society, which was based upon specific geographic requirements, and the society has had to change to meet the problems. The structural problems in the society, therefore, are due to the operation of the traditional system itself. Since good unsettled lands were rare, one way of placing children was to educate them or to buy farms from farmers willing to move to more marginal land. Both these possibilities necessitated capital in money, and thus implied basic social changes. Agricultural methods had to be changed in order to develop a surplus. Along with this has come an alteration of social values, as well as a separation into two groups of families whose interests are different, that is, the landed and nonlanded or day-laboring families.

The growth of literacy and the introduction of the newspaper, radio, and advertising have maintained and developed the consciousness of the value of the city manner of doing things, although the diffusion of these patterns has been restricted by the close-family economy. The loss of isolation through increased social mobility has set up the conditions of social contact through which cultural diffusion is possible. The forced change to a dependent economy has motivated the acceptance of new culture patterns which are altered to fit into the old culture pattern. Cultural needs are now usually met by borrowing. The industrial and class dominance of the English in the cities makes the adoption of their traits by city French desirable; this comes about through various channels and does not affect everyone in the community the same way.

Conclusions. — 1. In the study of cultural integration, not only must the degree of integration within the society be considered but also the degree to which the culture is adjusted to its habitat. Both are important as expressive of probable conflict and change [236].

2. The weakness of the territorial adjustment of French Canada has resulted in its attempting to integrate itself more adequately to its environment; in so doing, it has seized upon elements of American social environment, in contrast to the purely physical environment on which French-Canadian culture was once founded [237].

3. The diffusion of elements of material and nonmaterial culture from the cities to the country has been a feature of this growing dependence [237]. Loss of stability and change in values have ensued.

30. Nash, Philleo. THE PLACE OF RELIGIOUS REVIVALISM IN THE FORMATION OF THE INTERCULTURAL COMMUNITY ON KLAMATH RESERVATION. 1937. Social Anthropology of North American Tribes, 377-442.

Purpose or Problem. — The careful examination of a nativistic religious revival which took place between 1871 to 1878 on Klamath Indian Reservation, where, in 1864, members of three tribes were brought together. The main problem was broken down into two problems concerned with two classes of facts: (1) the problem of deprivation; (2) that of participation in the religious revival.

Definitions, Assumptions, and Hypotheses. — 1. Nativistic cults arise among deprived groups, They follow a shift in the value pattern, due to suppression and domination, and are movements to restore the original value pattern, which they do by the construction of a fantasy situation. The nature of this fantasy, which is basic to the cult, is a function of (1) the original value pattern and (2) the successive changes in the value pattern under white domination [377-78].

2. If the hypothesis is correct, those groups which participated most fully in the revival should be those which suffered most deprivation in their contacts with whites. Furthermore, the fantasy situation integral to the cult should be appropriate to shifts in the value pattern which had taken place in the formation of the intercultural community [378].

3. It was felt that acts of aggression committed or condoned represented potential sources of deprivation and indulgence. It was also felt that the introduction of new values, with attendant techniques for acquiring them, represented potential sources of deprivation and indulgence [379].

4. If the hypothesis is correct, the fantasy should express the restoration of the values denied its adherents, and the mode of participation in ritual experience should be appropriate. All the symbolic aspects of the revival were open to this kind of interpretation— doctrine, songs, face painting, ritual, and autisms in the forms of dreams and visions [379].

Methods and Techniques. — Library study of revivalism in three primitive groups, followed by careful examination of this nativistic religious revival.

Data. — The general area originally inhabited by these peoples (Klamath, Modoc, and Paviotso) embraced the lake district of southeastern Oregon and its extension in northern California. The circumstances under which these three Indian groups first met whites, and the degree of change introduced into their lives by contact with white culture vary widely.

The Klamath at an early date began direct trade relations with the whites which resulted in a shift in the social structure so that the more aggressive, younger men, with no previous background of wealth or social position, derived prestige and wealth through their contacts with whites. Trading was a well-established technique among the Klamath but it was greatly enhanced in the new situation. Thus the position of the shamans as the richest, most powerful, and prominent persons in Klamath culture was successfully challenged by a rising group of younger men; their decline in importance was increased through the application of an antishamanistic policy. Early in the reservation period, a similar division among the chiefs began to take place, with those younger ones who had learned to speak English given jobs at the agency, thus assuming the mediative roles between the administration and the Indians. By thus identifying themselves with the values and techniques of the white community, they estranged themselves to a certain extent from the Indian community but gained in power and wealth. A small portion of the new values filtered through to the "common" Klamath, who gradually absorbed certain aspects of the new technology. In terms of gain and loss, therefore, the Klamath as a whole were better off than either the Modoc or the Paviosto, since they never fought the whites and were not removed, but had the reservation built up around them. From the earliest days of white contacts, chiefs and slaves gained, shamans and commoners lost, the latter in the postwar period, when the one-family farms were introduced, only to be destroyed by frost. Ritual techniques were on the decline, while secular techniques were in the ascendant; at first, trading as a skill began to supersede shamanistic practice; later, the skills associated primarily with white culture were in the ascendant.

The Modoc as a whole suffered more than any other group in their contacts with the whites. They fought them at first, had their homeland taken away against their will, and suffered ridicule at the hands of their supposed friends, the Klamath. The earliest effects of culture contact reached the Modoc indirectly through the Klamath. Within the Modoc a division occurred after the first direct white contact. One group proposed making peace with the whites; the other, with three leaders, proposed active resistance. The primary difference between Modoc and Klamath, with respect to the deprivation or indulgence they experienced as a result of their contact with the whites, was the uniform character of deprivation and indulgence within the Modoc as a group. Among the Klamath there were wide individual differences in indulgence and deprivation; the character of the deprivation was also individual in nature (because of the policy of individualization — the breaking up of communities by putting individual families on their own farms). The economic changes which produced the basic shift in Klamath social structure were not carried so far among the Modoc. The deprivation the Modoc suffered was multiple: they lost their young men in the fighting, lost their homeland as a group, and were ridiculed by the Klamath; they were not given the opportunity to learn and apply those skills of individual enterprise in which some Klamath were conspicuously successful. The ways in which they suffered deprivation were those in which the group as a whole was jointly deprived, and in which the collective symbol "Modoc" was devalued in the eyes of both the white and the Indian community.

Both groups were united in opposition to the Paviotso. Those Paviotso who came to Klamath Reservation did so for protection, and were immune to change. They differed from the other Indians on the reservation in that they made no effort to become individual farmers during the entire period under consideration. With respect therefore to initial deprivation the Modoc suffered most, the Klamath least, and the Paviotso were intermediate; with respect to changes introduced through administrative policy and attendant deprivation and indulgence, the Klamath changed most, the Paviotso least, while the Modoc were intermediate.

The revival on Klamath Reservation passed through three phases, which correspond in a general way to those of the movement elsewhere, although each phase is successively more limited in its similarity. Among the Modoc, the doctrine was specific and aggressive toward both whites and unbelievers; it was attended by great excitement and autism. The dead appeared more prominently, and the collective symbol "Modoc" had a role here which similar symbols did not occupy among the other groups. Here the role of Doctor George as an innovator should be taken into account as one of the most powerful Modoc shamans. Among the Lower End Klamath, interest in the Ghost Dance was general, and excitement was minimal. No threats or promises were made, no visions were experienced, and the doctrinal emphasis was on the beneficent aspects of the expected change. The attitude of all the groups on the reservation had the common characteristic of mild skepticism except for the Tule Lake Modoc. As far as the Paviotso were concerned, the Ghost Dance was a religious revival in a strict sense: an increase in religious activity accompanied by the enhancement of well-established religious symbols and practices. The Klamath and the reservation Modoc responded in much the same way, emphasizing the joint or group aspects of the ceremonial. For neither of these people was the Ghost Dance a revival except in the loose sense; for the dance forms, the "message," face painting, and modes of participation were foreign to the ritual of both. Their participation implied no discernible anti-white feeling, merely a generalized apprehension about the future which was approached by the Modoc with some slight concern and by the Klamath optimistically.

With the progression from the Ghost Dance to the Earth Lodge cult, a shift took place in the character of revivalism. In doctrine, practice, personnel, and symbolic appeal the religious interest moved from the group symbol toward the individual symbol. Dreaming soon became more and more common, with people beginning to dream at home as well as at Earth Lodge dances. Among the Klamath, these performances conform closely to a single type in which the dreamer sees himself in some self-enhancing role. The dreams, and the ritual based on them, follow the cleavage in identification with white and Indian values, none showing real opposition to white values.

Conclusions. — 1. All the peoples who participated in the revival were in a preliminary period of change in which acceptance or rejection of white values was still tentative. Within every tribal group there was a division of opinion which was expressed in separate forms [435]. During this early and tentative stage of acculturation, these people were presented with a doctrine and ritual which they accepted and reinterpreted [436].

2. It will be seen that [441-42]: (1) Deprivation on Klamath Reservation occurred both as a result of initial attack and as a by-product of acculturation. (2) When both these aspects of deprivation are taken into account, it is seen that deprivation coincided closely with participation in the revival. (3) Deprivation through acculturation occurred primarily as an incongruity between values and the techniques for attaining them. Skills were introduced which brought no rewards, and values were introduced without appropriate skills for acquiring them. (4) Deprivation occurred, therefore, in groups which accepted, as well as those which rejected, the symbols of white culture. (5) Hence the basic fact of deprivation was the denial of satisfactions anticipated and sought for by resisting or accepting the symbols of white culture. (6) The groups which suffered the most aggressive attack initially accepted or produced ritual symbols which either (a) threatened aggressive retaliation against the whites, (b) named the agency of retaliation as an impersonal cosmic event, (c) protected themselves from destruction by the performance of ritual and belief in the doctrine, or (d) engaged in self-punishing ritual practices. (7) The only group which had extensively taken over white values and skills — the Klamath — produced fantasies which expressed (a) their acceptance of the roles defined by white administrators, and (b) their dissatisfaction with the benefits attached to their own roles. (8) The only group which had unequivocally benefited by identification with, and acceptance of, white skills and values — the Indian employees at the agency — not only took no part in the revival but attempted to suppress it. (9) The course of the revival as a whole followed a progression from enhancement of group symbols, group participation, and attention focused on doctrine to enhancement of personal symbols, individual ritual, and attention focused on the self.

3. The hypothesis set forth in the introduction should be modified as follows: Nativistic cults arise among deprived groups. Deprivation may occur within the framework of either acceptance or rejection of values and skills associated with white culture. Revivalism, however, is only one aspect of a total response to white culture. Revivalism is that portion of the response which expresses in ritual symbolism the basic attitudes of acceptance or rejection of white culture, feelings or loss or damage, aggressive retaliation in response to deprivation suffered, and self-punishing assertions and practices in proportion to aggressive retaliation [442].

4. The fact that abandonment of the doctrine among the Tule Lake Modoc coincided with a more direct and aggressive mode or response,

namely, fighting, suggests the possibility that in this situation the two responses were mutually exclusive [418].

5. Participants in the revival were people who in some measure had failed to derive the satisfactions they anticipated in following a particular course of action. In this sense they were deprived, and this, it appears, is the basic relation between deprivation and revivalism [439].

31. Opler, Marvin K. THE SOUTHERN UTE OF COLORADO. 1940. In Linton, 119-206; see Sec. 25.

Purpose or Problem. — See Linton.

Definitions, Assumptions, and Hypotheses. — See Linton.

Methods and Techniques. — Field work; otherwise not indicated.

Data. — Before the advent of the horse and subsequent consolidation into warlike bands, the Ute were peaceful and withdrawn. They were constantly on the move as a result of their hunting and gathering economy, entirely lacking techniques of agriculture. A central political structure for the entire tribe has always been absent. The band functioned as a cohesive social unit for only a brief period of festivity in spring. Major loyalties were directed to the extended family group which was accentuated by the actual isolation of the family over long winter months.

The nature of initial contact in the latter half of the seventeenth century was peaceful trade somewhat reminiscent of the barter they carried on in the early 1700's. A new item of trade was the horse, which furnished a convenient means of evading Plains Indians who overran Ute country constantly. Payment in Ute children sometimes took place, the child serving as shepherd and helping to bridge the gap between Ute and frontiersmen. The acculturation phase was thus, in its first phase of expansion, a process of cultural elaboration. The introduction of the horse allowed Ute bands to consolidate, to establish political leadership, to develop society organization and social mechanisms for the cohesive functioning of the band, and finally, to embark upon a career of raid and military glory.

The nineteenth century brought with it the full impact of white civilization, ushering in long years of defeat, of territorial loss, of utter disillusion, canceling the earlier gains and dislocating the culture at important points. The shrinkage of range was accompanied by changes in density of population, in band mobility, in the effective utilization of economic resources, and in natural environment. This shrinkage runs like a major theme throughout recent Ute history, underlying the gradual defeat of these people and determining their attitude toward white culture. The organization of military power was effectively broken by white contact, and today the function of band chiefs and tribal elders has become wholly civilian and has retained none of the meaning and content of former days. The present existence of progressive and conservative groups is important as indicating the role which particular personalities may play in the acculturation process.

To meet the new life, the Ute invented new dances and borrowed others from neighboring tribes. To the extent to which the Ghost Dance provided a means of cultural revival, it has been accepted. The Peyote cult has crystallized a number of older Ute conceptions and welded them into a churchlike organization able to compete with mission influence for the spiritual welfare of a rising generation. In its main emphasis, however, Peyote remains a Ute curing ceremony, with just enough of Christian symbology to bridge the gap between older religious values and a modern American environment.

At the root of the shift toward white norms among the Ute of Ignacio (the progressive group) is the increased reliance upon an individualistic economy inherent in farming, competitively organized. This change in economic organization has effectively destroyed band solidarity and has replaced a coherent aboriginal system of values with new interests. Towaoc is characterized by the rigid adherence to old beliefs and practices, the feverish quest after old cultural values in the Peyote cult and the Ghost Dance, and the backward-looking emphasis in the total adjustment.

Conclusions.-- 1. The whole transformation of the Utes into horse nomads shows how readily a culture can adapt itself to new elements in the absence of complicating external factors [205].

2. The present existence among the Utes of progressive and conservative groups is also important as indicating the role which particular personalities may play in the acculturation process.

32. Powdermaker, Hortense. AFTER FREEDOM: A CULTURAL STUDY OF THE DEEP SOUTH. 1939. New York: Viking Press.

Purpose or Problem. -- To apply to a segment of contemporary American society the training and methods of a cultural anthropologist and whatever perspective had been gained through field work in civilizations other than our own [ix]. To view a unit of southern American culture in terms of human beings who have inherited a historical situation and whose personalities are being constantly affected by the culture in which they live [ix]. An effort was made to select a place in which forces of the past and present could be studied, one in which the old plantation system still functioned beside recent developments [x]. The purpose was to study the living forces of a culture: their present functioning and their impact on the individuals who comprise the community [xii-xiii].

Definitions, Assumptions, and Hypotheses. -- The Negro lives in no isolated black community. To understand his life there must be an understanding of the whites who form so large a part of it [x]. The whites have been studied chiefly from the point of view of the interracial situation, which has been envisaged not as a separate phenomenon but as a social climate, pervading every aspect of life for every individual in the community.

Methods and Techniques. — Two visits, covering the seasonal cycles of a complete year; the work divided equally between the town and the surrounding area. Initial contacts through the State Department of Education. Ninety-seven colored informants interviewed; also constant participation. Living in a white boarding house; informal observation and interviewing of whites, supplemented by a questionnaire on attitudes among them.

Graphs and Charts. — Appendix A: Questionnaire on White Attitudes toward the Negro. B: Cotton Prices, 1890-1933. C: Sermon: "The Poor-Rich and the Rich-Poor." D. Homicides in Mississippi.

Data. — The background of all the Negroes in Cottonville, Mississippi (the town studied) is slavery. However, significant differences can be found between offspring of slaves of the aristocracy and slaves of small farmers; between house slaves and field slaves, with the latter being more numerous. Linked with this is the degree of intermixture in racial stock; mingling with Indians was confined to a very limited period, whereas mating with whites began as soon as the Negroes landed in America and still continues, though in a constantly diminishing degree.

The town itself is the county center, and in this study the surrounding countryside is included as an integral and interdependent part of the community. The white section of town is homogeneous, that is, suburban middle class; while "across the tracks" the only unifying factor is the fact that the inhabitants are Negroes. This segregation and the contrast between the two sections is the most striking physical feature of the community which extends into the social scene. There is, however, a complex interaction as well. Although the white aristocracy is not actually represented in Cottonville, their role and function there is unmistakable; the poor whites generally live outside the town, coming to Cottonville for purchasing supplies and for Saturday diversion, but have only slight contact with other whites and with Negroes. In general, social mobility is exceptional for the whites: the expectation, usually fulfilled, is that they will remain members of the class into which they were born.

White attitudes toward the Negro correspond to their own social class, with the poor whites most bitter because of Negro economic competition; all, however, share the same beliefs. Differences in attitude occur in different age groups; the younger generation has responded more to outside influences and generally does not have so strong an emotional attachment to these beliefs. It is evident that those who exploit most fully the opportunities for expressing dominance and aggression toward the Negroes are often the ones who are badly adjusted and unpopular within the white circle. The general belief is that the South needs the Negro as a laborer and that he is by nature designed to be a servant. Nothing the white offers to the Negro is more significant, in shaping the relations of the two races, than the respect he withholds (e.g., refusal to call the Negro "Mister").

The criteria for the Negro classes are not the same as those used for the whites. It is the mode of behavior and the degree of acceptance of white patterns which primarily indicate class to the Negro rather than occupation or income, the standards of both the latter being far lower than for the whites. Some indices of upper class status are: light skin (since they are likely to be the descendants of the relatively privileged house slaves); the code of sexual behavior, which corresponds to white standards of a generation ago, in the Negro upper class; education; occupation; and family background. In marriage forms, family life, and patterns governing sexual behavior, the middle class differs strikingly from the classes above and below it. Most middle-class marriages are of the common-law type, easily entered into and easily dissolved. The instability of family life and the relaxed sexual code in this class are in strong contrast to the Puritanism of the upper class, and to the conventions of the lower class, which makes no pretense to monogamy. Age groups cut across social classes, especially in the effect of age on the individual's conception of his place in the world and his relations to white people.

The community is agricultural, based on cotton. This one-crop system has played a large part in shaping the social structure and attitudes of Cottonville, and has provided the Negro with two conflicting white patterns to choose between: the example of extravagance in boom times and the Puritan ideal of thrift. The plantation tradition still exists, with the entire family of a tenant considered as an economic unit, and the division into sharecroppers and renters. For a colored person to be a landowner and employer is still a revolutionary development in the community, but one which has made a substantial contribution to the race. It is the closest possible approximation to the former position of the white master, and its significance is enhanced by the contrast to old times. While rising to the status of landed proprietor is similar to the process in most propertyless peasant groups, special elements assume significance because of the interracial situation. For some Negroes, the government has taken over the role of "good white folks." Vocational teaching is an occupation preferred to land ownership since it is away from the past.

There is little competition in town jobs between whites and Negroes except in recent occupations of unskilled labor, such as road jobs, with considerable hostility thus being bred as the white man is struggling to obtain work which until recently was considered beneath him. Negro women are expected to be employed as domestic servants although government activities here too have brought about some interrace rivalry which was previously not present. There is greater opportunity for employment among the women so that their earning capacity is superior, and in general it is the woman who is the chief breadwinner. The Negro domestic servant is thus important both economically and as chief liaison agent between the races. Members of the upper class are generally in business or in a profession, generally teaching.

The typical Negro family throughout the South is matriarchal and elastic, in striking contrast to the more rigid and patriarchal family organization of occidental white culture. This is partially a result of the background of slavery with the white man's right of access to any Negro woman, and the preferred position of house slaves, usually women. In the upper class, furthest from slavery and closest to white modes of behavior, the patriarchal family structure predominates. The source of support and the structure of the family show a consistent correlation: regardless of class, the economic head is looked upon as the administrative head, as in the white pattern. Licensed marriage, too, furnishes an example of a white pattern accepted in different degrees by different classes, and is regarded as an index of status.

For the Negro in Cottonville color is highly important socially, economically, and sexually: to make a "good" marriage means to marry light. Sexual relations between Negro and white continue, but in diminishing degree, with the white men and colored women who "have the run of both races" considered to have the advantage. Sexual rivalry on the part of the Negro male is thus complicated by the interracial situation. With the increasing irregularity of intra-white sexual relationships has come a marked decrease in Negro-white relationships, strengthened by increasing race pride and demand for respect on the Negro side.

In Cottonville, where the Negro family is so loosely held together, the role of children as an integrating force is more potent than that of the white children. The Negro woman in the middle or lower class concentrates her hopes and her efforts almost completely on them; often the desire for their education provides the main motive for her life. She may also view them as an economic asset. Because of the children, the frequent separations of husband and wife do not necessarily disrupt the home. Children are, then, the chief effective nucleus of the family life.

The Negro church is the one institution where the colored people of the community are in full control, even though their religion was originally taken over from the whites. The emphasis and ideology of Christianity have been transformed by the peculiar needs of the Negro, and in its functioning the church is free of white dominance. Historically, as the religion of the master class, Christianity was endowed with tremendous prestige, with most of the Negroes joining either the Baptist or the Methodist churches. Cut off from their country and their former tribesmen, it gave them a historical tradition, a literature, and a background all at once, catering to their deepest needs also by helping their adjustment. The chief differences between the religions of the two races today are in ideology, individual participation, and the manner of conducting the informal part of the service, due chiefly to the different way in which the Negro has modified the religion he received. Denominational distinctions have little significance among them. Benevolent mercy rather than stern justice is the chief attribute of the Negro's God. Among the young, religion is frequently of less importance; it has not kept pace with the general culture, in which they participate more fully than did their parents. In addition, the ministers, most of whom have had little education, can exercise little influence over those who have been to school. The religious services offer an expressive outlet far greater than is to be found in most white churches today. The church is also the chief pivot of social life for the Negro community, and provides an avenue for administrative and executive abilities which have little or no other outlet. It thus contributes to the sense of respect and esteem from others which is so consistently refused to Negroes by the white society which dominates most of their lives, with the church the only public institution which offers him a public field of expression. It has at the same time been a conservative force, tending to relieve and counteract the discontents that make for rebellion.

The faith of the present-day Negroes in education is much like the faith of the Americans who set up the public school system: illiteracy, poverty, social disadvantage, for them have fused into one picture. It is a new faith which recommends a means to better things on earth. The whites, however, must be reassured that the status quo will not be upset to their disadvantage. Schools to the Negro symbolize and are powerful mechanisms for him for induction into the white man's world, and for this the colored mother is willing to make many sacrifices. Higher education is primarily directed toward producing teachers. Books, newspapers, magazines, and movies also provide part of the Negro's education. In intellectual and physical gain, the fruits of the new faith are substantial. Literacy is making swift strides; with it has come a broadening of economic opportunity and well-being. In terms of satisfaction the advance, though very great, is less clear-cut and is attended by certain drawbacks. The younger generation are being nourished on intellectual fare much more like that of the whites, and accordingly are developing attitudes closer to those of the whites. The knowledge of Negro achievement increases the student's self-respect and gives him a respect for his race beyond anything the older generation had; it also enhances his own expectations and with this his demands. Accordingly, many who have acquired a college degree have lost the hope and confidence which made them work so hard to attain it. For these few, the new faith is already outworn; so far, they have found no substitute.

Negro attitudes toward white people are correlated roughly with age differences. In the oldest group, belief and behavior consistently acknowledge white superiority. The middle-aged group do not believe that the whites are actually superior, but in dealing with the white people they act as if they did: by dint of this accommodation they have been able to get along. The average white person in the community seldom realizes the extent to which this group questions his superiority. Among the younger generation of Negroes, however, resentment is keen and outspoken. The Negro preferred by the average white man today is the type his father preferred; the younger Negroes, however, do not prefer "good white folks," but those who will give them respect and courtesy as fellow men. Lack of such courtesies (as in the use of social titles) imposes on the Negro a constant need to keep guard over his feelings, and may be connected with serious acts of aggression by Negroes against Negroes. Always latent is the terror of lynching; while the actual outbreaks are comparatively few, the atmosphere which permits them is constant.

Conclusions. — 1. There often appears to be a relation between the insistence of the white upon the observance of such usage as courtesy terms and his own adjustment within his group [46].

2. A steady penetration of white-American patterns into Negro life has been under way ever since the Negroes first came to this country, and is at present accelerating. The manner and degree of acceptance vary. It is the upper class that has to the greatest degree taken over both form and meaning. The middle class has adopted fewer white patterns and it is in most cases the form rather than the meaning that has been accepted. The lower class follows the fewest, and most of these in the form merely [61].

3. Active (or primary) factors which combine to put a Negro into a certain class are modes of behavior connected with sex and family life, education, occupation. They all have direct bearing on the racial situation: all represent privileges that have been denied to the Negro, demonstrations of the Negro's capacity for assimilating patterns of white behavior. Wealth and the symbols of wealth are perhaps half-way between the active and the passive (or secondary). Whatever importance money has in terms of social status is derived from its connection with the active factors. Religion and social activities could be considered more passive or secondary elements; they too show a correlation with class [70-71].

4. The white attitude, that manual labor is degrading, is one which has not been taken over by the Negroes. Several factors have blocked the process of acculturation here. Physical work has been and still is woven into the very fabric of their life. Even among the town Negroes there is a feeling of closeness to the soil [113].

5. The form and focus of the family "before freedom" still survive; and a surprising number of the circumstances which determined its structure survive also [145]. These Negro households are sufficiently unlike those typical of white American culture to furnish data well worth further investigation [197].

6. The prestige value of light skin and "good" features seems to reflect a desire, conscious or unconscious, to identify oneself with the dominant group, as well as a wish to profit by the advantages to be derived from resembling it [180].

7. There may be some doubt how far there is a causal connection between the unfavorable position of the Negro man and the large amount of intra-Negro violence, but the material strongly suggests the presence of such a connection [194].

8. In general, shame attached to illegitimacy is a white attitude, and the degree to which a class or age group has adopted it is an indication of the degree to which it has assimilated white patterns [205]. This is why most individual variation is found among the young Negroes of the upper middle class who occupy the frontier area between the middle class, which on the whole conforms to Negro patterns of sex behavior, and the upper class, which has accepted those of the whites.

9. The accent in religion has shifted from hell to heaven, from retribution to forgiveness, from fear to hope. Such a shift could be accounted for by the urgent need to belittle present conditons, to hope for better things. It is possible that a secondary cause contributed to this change of tone and tenor: namely, the structure of the Negro family. While the Jews and early Christians were patriarchal, the Negro family, now and under slavery, has been chiefly matriarchal. Although, like the whites, the Negroes continue to call upon the Lord as Father, he seems rather to be conceived in the image of the mother [246].

10. The religion practiced in the community must have some appeal for women which it does not offer to men. The familiar psychiatric explanation is that for women the church provides a means of sublimated sexual expression which it apparently is unable to give the men. The striking point in this situation is that the colored women might seem to have less need of sublimation than the men; that those who indulge most actively in ecstatic religious behavior are among the least inhibited sexually. It may be simply that the people who are least inhibited in their everyday life are also least inhibited in church [272-73].

11. There is much to be said for the theory that the repressions caused by the interracial situation find relief in unrestrained religious behavior. Such an explanation is partial, however [273].

12. As acculturation advances, voodoo, which has no prestige value in white culture, will tend to disappear [296].

13. As a result of the differences between the roles of the two races, and of the various social strata in each, a curious inversion appears with regard to typical attitudes. The white aristocrats are the least, and the poor whites are the most, hostile toward the other race. Among the Negroes the upper class is the most, and the lower class is the least, antagonistic toward the whites. Again, the older generation of whites are the ones in whom most affect is roused by the interracial situation, while the younger generation is inclined to view the problem more casually. The reverse is true for the Negroes. Further, the Negro upper class and the poor whites each serves as agent for its race toward the other, taking actions and ex-

pressing sentiments to which the group as a whole is not ready to commit itself. Each of these two classes is set apart from the rest of its race, experiencing different conflicts and holding different attitudes, and each awakens in the other race a special hostility strongly tinged with fear [334-35].

14. The increasing numbers of educated Negroes enlarge the proportion of those who incline to resentment rather than to acceptance. It is their attitude that is spreading and the more passive one that is on the wane, as patterns of white American behavior and ideas of what is due the individual citizen penetrate ever more deeply into the Negro group [353].

15. Certain elements are common to any process of acculturation. One is lag, apparent between the patterns of the white group and those of the Negroes. It is especially visible today because the white culture itself is in a period of rapid change. The amount and noticeability of lag vary within the Negro group according to the social level and also according to the particular pattern of behavior. Lag and its gradations are perhaps most obvious in connection with family life and sexual standards. The upper class enforces strict Puritanical standards formed after the white model of a generation ago. In attitudes toward education, lag is also present [354-55]. The variability no less than the presence of lag between patterns taken over by the Negro and those current among the whites is a reminder that, while the Negroes are reacting to white behavior, the whites themselves are reacting to changes in local and general conditions; and that the Negroes are affected also by these conditions. The rate, selection, form, of taking over white patterns represent the resultant of a dual impact [355].

16. Another element invariably found in acculturation is the alteration of the patterns taken over. Such alteration arises from partial acceptance, from accepting the form without its meaning, from the new associations and symbolisms acquired by a pattern through transfer [356]. The process of acculturation takes a great deal of its individual character from the relative roles of the two groups involved.

17. Both the attitudes of the whites and the conditions under which the Negroes live impose a false homogeneity, overshadowing intragroup distinctions. This is reflected by the Negroes themselves, making for an equality of expectation which prompts immediate questioning of the superior good fortune of an individual. At the same time it acts in the opposite direction toward cohesion [359-60].

18. The Negro knows more about the whites than they do about him. He also appears to have a greater awareness both of the situation and of the conflicts to which it gives rise. This makes for greater realism in coping with many of his personal problems, and for greater sensitivity. Also, the Negro feels guiltless with regard to the racial situation, and deeply wronged (these are potential psychological advantages) [361-62].

19. The comparative newness of economic and educational opportunity for the Negro means that he is in a sense a pioneer as contrasted with the

whites. Possibly for this reason the younger Negroes of today may have suffered less than their white contemporaries from the effects of a prevailing decadence in religious and social belief. There is, in the sense of a cause which must be served, a potential integrating force [363].

20. To develop the capacity for present enjoyment at the expense of the more dreary virtues would seem a plausible accommodation to the conditions that have surrounded and dominated the Negro. The appearance of abandon and relaxation is, however, an index not fully to be trusted, since it depends so much on culturally determined habits of expression [366].

21. The process of acculturation in the community is and will increasingly be subject to the effects of forces from without, upon each group separately and on the community as a whole. Increasing efficacy of radio communication, increasing circulation of papers, magazines, books, have already brought Cottonville into closer touch with America and the world at large [371]. Specific agencies are stepping in to take an active and formative part in the course of local events. Northern interference has done much to stimulate and to implement the Negro's efforts in his own behalf [371].

22. It seems not unlikely that some form of political activity may prove to be the coming faith of the local Negro, despite his present lack of the franchise [372].

33. Smith, Marian W. THE PUYALLUP OF WASHINGTON. 1940. In Linton, 3-38; see Sec. 25.

Purpose or Problem. -- See Linton.

Definitions, Assumptions, and Hypotheses. -- See Linton.

Methods and Techniques. -- Field work; otherwise not indicated.

Graphs and Charts. -- Population Table [8-10].

Data. -- Prior to the advent of the whites, there seems to have been a good deal of intermingling with Sahaptin-speaking peoples who were infiltrating westward. Little is known about this, but it is clear that the two cultures differed radically on very few scores and that these were rather readily absorbed. The coming of the horse brought about a more spectacular change in culture. A class differentiation grew up between "canoe Indians" and "horse Indians," based on the greater mobility of the latter. The first white contact was with settlers— there was no introductory period when contact was only through traders— with the Indians being accepted on terms approaching social equality and many legal intermarriages. The only direct attempts to change the native culture were those connected with the abandonment of the communal houses and the introduction of Christianity, with the latter apparently in the hands of intelligent and sympathetic missionaries. The individualistic patterns of the native culture made it easy for certain Indians to take on white habits without waiting for the rest of their group to assume them. The result of all this was the rapid assimilation of the Indians into the white population. Later settlers, however, introduced attitudes of social discrimination. In addition, the sale of the Indian lands brought with it deadly results in the form of a sudden influx of wealth which the Indians had no patterns for dealing with, and resulted in degeneration and idleness as well as a decrease in population. Certain families whose acculturation had progressed far enough at the time have survived in a favorable condition; the complete absorption of the remnant of the population into the white population seems only a question of time.

Conclusions. — See Linton.

34. Spicer, Edward H. PASCUA: A YAQUI VILLAGE IN ARIZONA. 1940. Univ. of Chicago Press.

Purpose or Problem. — 1. To examine one village of Yaqui Indians in southern Arizona in an effort to isolate, on the one hand, some of the factors which are making for cultural stability and, on the other hand, some of those which are bringing about change [xiii]. A study of the nature and the processes of adaptation under conditions of acculturation [xiv].

2. The problem is one of determining the character of present integration between economic and other aspects of the culture [xvi].

Definitions, Assumptions, and Hypotheses. — 1. The belief that Pascua provided a very simple situation for the study of "culture contact" [xv].

2. "Economic assimilation" had to be defined in the light of the actual situation in the village. In the light of closer study it became apparent that these acceptances did not involve the acceptance of the values of the economic system from which they were taken [xvi]. Functional inconsistencies might therefore be expected.

3. The analysis of three types of facts were involved [xvii]: (a) The deliberate adjustments which the group, as a group, is making (or has made in the recent past) to the new economic adaptation; (b) the modification of Western concepts of economic life; (c) individual conflicts that center about or are connected with the economic life.

Methods and Techniques. — Residence in Pascua from July 1936 to June 1937. Establishment of a definite function in the village, with increasingly intimate contacts. In general, the program followed was to observe and record whatever events came to notice in the village and then to examine these in the context of the personalities who participated in them [xx]. No regular paid informants were employed. The immediate objectives of the field work were to obtain a complete record of the events which took place in the village during the year and to obtain life histories of each individual. Neither objective was realized [xx-xxi].

Graphs and Charts. -- Occupations of Pascua Males [30]. Activities of Pascua Males (April 5 to June 24, 1937) [31].

Data. -- Pascua is composed of persons who have come from different places in Sonora — their early experiences differ somewhat from the general pattern. They have come to the United States not with economic gain in view but as refugees escaping from an oppressive political regime.

The existence is wholly dependent on the establishment of relationships with individuals outside the village. Nearly all the males work for wages outside. They are entering American economic life at the lowest income level; characteristically their income and expenditure are extremely irregular. There is much financial assistance among relatives, especially for the expenses of ceremonies. There is no clear-cut sense of individual ownership of house or lot, a situation simplified by the absence of agricultural land. There is no co-operation in the production aspects of economic life. The fiesta is closely linked with other institutions by means of which economic co-operation may be effected. The values of the village are much more strongly centered about the ceremonial institutions than they are about wage labor. There results a conflict between the two patterns, generally resolved in the partial acceptance of both, except in the case of leadership, which requires that the ceremonial pattern be more highly evaluated. Here, instances of acute and unresolved conflict are apparent.

The present kinship system is a fusion of Yaqui and Spanish elements; the elementary family terms remain Yaqui, while those for more distant kin are becoming Spanish. The explanation given for this is that the elementary family has had continuous existence throughout the recent period of social change, whereas the more remote kin groups went out of existence and with them the Yaqui terms. With their redevelopment, new terms were needed and borrowed from the Spanish. The padrino system is a formal social institution based on ritual obligations which formalizes the relationships between groups already organized on a basis of blood. This system is universal in Pascua.

There are five male and two female ceremonial societies in Pascua which crosscut the other two important aspects of the social organization — kinship and ceremonial sponsorship. The significance of this system lies in its role as maintainer of those values which chiefly differentiate Yaquis from the surrounding population. In addition, the societies have important economic functions as ultimate insurance groups with village-wide resources, where individual economic surpluses do not exist. In this combination of functions they become the focus of what are perhaps the most significant conflicts in Arizona Yaqui culture today. The ceremonial societies, which together compose the church, provide what social and cultural unity the village of Pascua has. The concept of "pueblo" exists, but there is at present no social institution corresponding to it. Leadership is achieved only through the channels of the ceremonial institutions. This is explained in view of the noncitizenship of Pascuans, which precludes political powers from crystallizing around individuals.

The pascola dancers combine obviously Christian with non-Christian elements in their ritual. They are not closely integrated with the church, and in many ways are the object of conflicting attitudes. They are intimately connected with animals in many ways (e.g., the deer dancer). Aside from them, the two dominant men's dance societies are the matachinis and the fariseos. The dominance of each group divides the year into two ceremonial seasons. Both are closely tied up with the church. Their concern is with the dead (ancestors), thus giving continuity with the past and affirming the solidarity of Yaqui culture. The two other centers of interest are in the Virgin and Jesus, each being the "patron saint" of one of the main dance societies. It is the belief in their curing powers that lies at the foundation of the whole ceremonial organization, while there is a notable lack of any important connection with the economic life. There is, however, a close relationship between these beliefs and the social structure, with the ceremonial system providing the ultimate sanctions for the social system.

Pascua is a community organized basically along the lines of a primitive society, yet having its existence in the setting of a mobile, heterogeneous urban environment. It constitutes a closely integrated whole, except for the economic aspects of life there, and with the ceremonial society system integrating the society in its widest sense. The ceremonial system operates chiefly through the fiesta, the "periodic reintegration of the society." This occurs frequently, whenever there is an obligation as a result of crisis in an individual life and the fulfillment of that obligation with the co-operation of the whole village. The relationships of Pascuans with non-Pascuans, however, are not formalized along the lines of any of the three distinct systems of social interaction (kinship, padrino, and ceremonial society). Their relations instead, are changing, and specific to the situation. In that they operate to release persons from group controls, they are a disintegrating factor, although in cotton-picking time, for example, they serve equally to bring families together. The basic conflict is connected with the demands of the ceremonial and the job patterns. Here, the society itself is not providing a means for resolving the conflict; it is recognized only by the individual concerned. With the lack of dependence on the natural environment, animal gods are becoming contradictory, and are changing their character -- the deer dancers, for example, are gradually becoming simply entertainers. The emphasis on curing, in the guise of the matachinis and the Virgin, are becoming more important. This apparently represents an increasing sanctification along with the increasing secularization of the deer dancer, although there seems to be an attempt to adjust the pascola to the prevailing ceremonial pattern.

Conclusions. — 1. There are minor conflicts which are observable only in conflicting attitudes toward the performers. This is being resolved by the deer dance's passing out of the culture, with one of the associated institutions becoming associated with the new deities and remaining in the culture.

2. A functional inconsistency exists in the failure of the society of Pascua to adjust its primary conflict— that between leadership and jobs. The adjustment being carried on by individuals is chiefly in a process of moving out of Pascua society— which can result ultimately only in the extinction of the culture rather than in its reintegration on a new basis.

3. The difference in these two kinds of changes can be viewed as a distinction between "culture" and "society." While the culture continues to exist and even in certain respects to develop, its existence is definitely threatened by the gradual reduction of the society which finds the culture usable.

4. When a society is faced with a functional inconsistency, and a way is presented to resolve the crisis as it is manifest in the lives of the individuals by their withdrawal, either into the old system or out of the society there need occur no cultural resolution of the inconsistency— even though the disappearance of the culture results [306].

35. Spier, Leslie. THE GHOST DANCE OF 1870 AMONG THE KLAMATH OF OREGON. Univ. of Washington Pubs. in Anth., Vol. II, 1927-29, 39-56.

Purpose or Problem. — In this paper the author sets himself the problem of defining the character of the acquired dance, the conditions of its reception, and the modifications wrought by pre-existing habits.

Definitions, Assumptions, and Hypotheses. — It is possible to discover something of the process of acculturation of this dance complex among the Klamath. We can inquire what elements were foreign to pre-existing Klamath culture and how far the complex was in accord with Klamath patterns. In this way we may discover in some degree how far the Klamath made over the dance to conform to their existent habits and to what extent it was a novelty [53].

Methods and Techniques. — Firsthand information from informants (three) who were participants in the dance as children; included is a description of the movements of the cult through various tribes.

Graphs and Charts. — The Spread of the Ghost Dance of 1870 (Modified from Kroeber) [41].

Data. — Of the two great messianic movements that appeared among the western Indians toward the close of the last century, that of 1890 is best known for the extent of its influence. Much less is known of its predecessor of twenty years earlier. There can be little doubt that the new cult was encouraged by the chiefs as a check to the rival power of the shamans. The new cult brought priestly leaders, the dreamers, whose influence promised to rival that of the shamans. The Klamath thesis was the familiar one that the dead would return if the living danced in a prescribed fashion. The participants crossed themselves before they danced. Some put water on their heads when they rose in the morning. Spier's informant said this was not baptism. There was no other Christian symbolism; the cross used in the dance of 1890 had no place here. The sick were cured at these dances in the manner now characteristic of the pseudo-Christian Indian sect of Puget Sound, the Shakers. Several innovations were introduced by the slave, Pit River Charley; the whole situation seems to have distinctly favored whatever might be brought by this particular man. The end of the cult was the forcible act of the Indian agent.

Conclusions. -- 1. There seems to be an exception in the Klamath case to the general view expressed by Kroeber, that this messianic movement took hold among the Californians at this time because of the impending final destruction of their native life. For the Klamath had not as yet suffered seriously from the incursions of the whites. The Klamath dance must be looked on as merely another normal instance of the acquisition of a foreign ceremonial with the antecedents of which the recipients are not concerned [45].

2. Fundamentally the doctrine of the dream cult is foreign to Klamath thought. The insistence that dancing must continue over a long period in order to succeed in bringing back the dead is an old folk-tale theme. More important, because it more closely resembles their prior belief, is that the essential religious experience turned on acquiring a revelation and a song as an outward manifestation of it. But the older form of experience was never with the dead but with spirits. The form differed just as much; in contrast to the trance induced by the dance the older method was a solitary vigil [53].

3. Certain other features were interpreted in terms of antecedent Klamath notions [53]. The messiah was identified with the culture hero [54]. The curing of the sick by the prophets or dreamers during the progress of the dance was at variance with the ordinary practice. This was the province of the shaman, who was assisted by several individuals, but there was no dancing. Curing during the dream dance may have come as part of the dream dance complex [54].

4. What data exist from other tribes confirms some of these features as constant elements of the dance. Apart from the doctrine which was apparently the same in every case, many features such as the proselytizing, the leader's derivation of ceremonial procedure from dreams of the dead, curing as part of the dance activities, and the inclusion of both sexes appear in divergent settings [54-55].

5. In his study of the Sun Dance among the Plains Indians, the author

reached the conclusion that while extensive cultural borrowing had brought about a marked uniformity of regalia and ritual among all the tribes who had the dance, there was considerable tribal individuality in the manner in which the participants were organized and even more in the mythical-religious sanctions for its performance. This means that the motivation for rituals tends to become standardized in a group, however variable their form may be. The present case of the Ghost Dance of 1870 appears to be an exception, for here the doctrine is quite uniform. It must be recognized, however, that the two cases are very different. The revivalistic doctrine of the Ghost Dance is utterly different from the esoteric religious motives behind the Sun Dance. Its very revivalistic nature was the attraction, and conditions were ripe for the acquisition of the new doctrine. The new ritual was relatively immaterial in its very short span of life. No complex rituals had time to develop. This precluded any duplication of the cultural leveling effected by borrowing as seen in the Sun Dance. There is even a partial development of this to be seen. These then are familiar instances of the acceptance of ritual rather than doctrine among peoples with a richly developed ceremonial background [55].

36. Spier, Leslie. THE PROPHET DANCE OF THE NORTHWEST AND ITS DERIVATIVES: THE SOURCE OF THE GHOST DANCE. 1935. General Series in Anth., No. 1.

Purpose or Problem. -- 1. To show that the ultimate origin of the two Ghost Dance movements was not with the Paviotso but in the Northwest among the tribes of the interior Plateau area [5].
2. To show that it was the prior existence of the Prophet Dance which explains both the ready acceptance of Christianity at its point of introduction and its rapid spread [30].

Definitions, Assumptions, and Hypotheses. -- 1. The Northwestern cult appears in the ethnographic accounts under various names: dream dance, ghost dance, etc. In order to avoid duplicating a well-established terminology which reserves these names for complexes in other areas of North America, the author has coined the name Prophet Dance for it [5].
2. The Prophet Dance of the Northwest is strictly identical with the Paviotso Ghost Dance in doctrine and much like it in ritual, although there are some differences to be explained. It can be shown that the Prophet Dance was thoroughly at home in the cultures of the Northwest, which cannot be maintained for the Ghost Dance in relation to Paviotso culture [13].

Methods and Techniques. -- A distributional study, making use of the historical and ethnographic literature on the subject.

Graphs and Charts. -- 1. Map showing the distribution of the Prophet Dance and Derived Cults [4]. 2. Diagram of the Relationship of the Prophet

Dance, Ghost Dances, and Derived Cults [6]. An appendix includes information about the dance among several specific Indian groups.

Data. — Native accounts certify some antiquity for the complex, and also carry the additional implication that the performance recurred throughout the whole of the last century. The Prophet Dance complex, Spier attempts to prove, is old, clearly anterior to 1870, when the first Ghost Dance impulse spread north and west from the Paviotso. A distributional study is made, showing Northwestern origin for the Ghost Dance. It is shown that among the Northwest tribes there was an old belief in the impending destruction and renewal of the world, when the dead would return, in conjunction with which there was a dance based on supposed imitation of the dances of the dead, and a conviction that intense preoccupation with the dance would hasten the happy day. From time to time men "died" and returned to life with renewed assurances of the truth of the doctrine; at intervals cataclysms of nature occurred which were taken as portents of the end, each of these events leading to the performance of the dance with renewed fervor. Specific elements common to the Prophet and Ghost Dances are, for example, the notion that disbelievers will be punished by transformation and proselytizing, which is a most unusual characteristic for an Indian cult. Relations with the dead were a common theme in Northwestern cultures, integrated with several aspects of the culture. In the Great Basin, however, aside from the specific occasions of the Ghost Dance revivals, there is no such preoccupation with the dead.

There was contact with explorers and traders in the first decades of the nineteenth century, but Christianity had not yet arrived. Yet when their successors of the early thirties arrived they discovered elements of Christian ritual already present among inaccessible Indians. They assumed that the source was wholly Christian, that the pagan rites with which the Christian elements were integrated were unimportant aberrations. But it is important to recognize the Prophet cult in these rites. Such rites as the observance of the Sabbath, calendric holidays, and the posture in prayer are clearly Christian; on the other hand, fully half the ritual elements described as incorporated in the compound correspond to known native forms. It appears that the Christian doctrine reached them through Iroquoian arrivals from the east, which they amalgamated with their own rites rather than substituting for their own.

The Christianized version of the Prophet cult has current existence in modified guise as the well-known Smohalla cult and the Pompom religion. The Smohalla cult is almost certainly a direct offshoot of the cult of the 1830's. The Shaker religion, avowedly a Christian cult, was almost certainly affected at its origin by the Smohalla revival, although there is a somewhat remote possibility that some of its roots lie still further back in the original form of the Prophet Dance. So far as prophets and doctrine are concerned, the Smohalla cult was substantially the Prophet Dance. It differs, however, in its ceremonial forms, which it can be shown are probably derived from the Christianized version of the 1830's and not directly from older Prophet Dance rites. In addition to the great personal influence of Smohalla, a Columbia River Sahaptin, there were other prophets concerned in this particular cult, and it is clear that his doctrine and beliefs were temporally local expressions of the older complex. In this rendering, however, emphasis was laid on active animus toward the whites and their ways, quite comprehensible in the light of the drastic interference with native life then occurring (the 1860's). The Shaker religion is nominally Christian, but in actual practice is an extraordinary blend of old shamanistic performances with Catholic ritual and Protestant doctrine. Emphasis is on curing the sick rather than on relatively impersonal church services which seems to have been taken over bodily from aboriginal shamanism; there are also specific Smohalla resemblances.

Conclusions. — 1. It may be presumed that everywhere the concept of illness caused by soul-loss occurs, shamans attempt a cure in this manner, i.e., by shamans going to the land of the dead in pursuit of souls or spirits whose loss has caused their patients to sicken [14].

2. Christianity took so strong a hold upon these natives partly because of the prior existence of the Prophet Dance [30].

3. We unquestionably arrive at the conclusion that underneath the Christian guise there lay the prior Prophet cult. The doctrines are parallel; the rites are not in conflict. That they actually amalgamated rites rather than made a substitution is attested by the evidence. So far as the natives were concerned, the religion from the east was confirmation and stimulus to existing beliefs [35].

37. Thompson, Laura. CULTURE IN CRISIS: A STUDY OF THE HOPI INDIANS. (With a chapter, "Time, Space and Language," by Benjamin Lee Whorf) 1950. New York: Harper.

Purpose or Problem. — Out of the investigation of the Indian personality— have emerged a field theory of culture and a cross-discipline methodology for the multidimensional study of the acculturation process, not only in its technological and sociological manifestations but also at the psychological and symbolic levels. This book is concerned with a brief formulation of this approach and methodology and their application to the Hopi Indian situation viewed as a case study [xvii]. (By John Collier.)

The scientific problem to be investigated was initially formulated as an analysis of the development of Hopi personality in the context of the social system under varying degrees of pressure from the outside world. It was decided to make an intensive investigation of a representative sample of Hopi individuals from a sample of Hopi communities representing varying degrees and kinds of influences from the outside world. It was a practical problem in applied social research, stemming from a need felt by administrators to improve human welfare and community government by means of the findings of science. The research was initially conceived as an action-research project [5], in the course of which the selected communities would study themselves under technical guidance.

Definitions, Assumptions, and Hypotheses. — 1. Only by comparing the findings from at least two representative communities in historical and geographic perspective would the similarities and differences between them become apparent and the reconstruction of their common cultural heritage be possible. This could then serve as a base line by which to measure the kind and extent of deviation engendered by the various influences from outside in environmental context [3].

2. Acculturation problems are problems in the dynamics of culture structure (15].

3. This underscores and clarifies the close relationship between acculturation problems and practical administrative problems. Basically administrative problematic situations may be reduced to scientific problems in culture structure analysis requiring "structural insight" for their effective solution [15].

4. The significant problem of the present study is conceived as a structural analysis of the Hopi crisis in the context of the total pattern of human events in space and time relevant to it. For purpose of analysis the factors relevant to the crisis problem are conceived in five dimensions: ecologic, somatic, sociologic, psychologic, and symbolic [15]. (See pp. 15-17 for operational concepts and postulates.)

Methods and Techniques. — One of the projects of the Indian personality and Administration Research, a long-range, multidiscipline policy project. Scientists from several disciplines (chiefly social and cultural anthropology, psychiatry, psychology, pedagogy, public administration, linguistics, and ecology), working as a team, developed the methodology of the project experimentally as the research progressed. A total of fifty scientists worked either in the field, in the analysis of field data, in formulating the findings, or as advisors. Life histories and the emotional, mental, and physical development of selected children (ages 6 to 18) studied by means of participant observation, interviews, medical examinations, and a battery of eight relatively "culture free" psychological tests of the projective, guided-interview, and performance types. It was considered necessary to draw into the co-operative research enterprise not merely scientists, but also members of the communities being studied, both inside and outside of government service. Follow-up field work was also carried on.

Data. — The Hopi Indians are in the grip of a serious and far-reaching crisis. The roots of the crisis reach back four centuries to the first contacts with the Spaniards, which led to the introduction of new values, ideas, and techniques, and of new domesticated animals, plants, and diseases. The crisis was aggravated by the attempts of Franciscan missionaries to gain a foothold in the area and by predatory Indian groups, especially the Navaho, who gradually encircled the Hopi pueblos, leaving the Hopi tribe the actual use of only a fraction of their former land base. The Hopi crisis assumed acute proportions in 1943 when a boundary dispute of long standing between the Hopi and the surrounding Navaho Indians was settled by the Secretary of the Interior in such a way that the Hopi tribe was granted a land-use area only one-fourth the size of the original Hopi reservation.

Hopi traditional pueblo structure is correlative and equalitarian rather than centralized; biologically balanced, flexible, and mobile rather than "mechanical," rigid, and immobile; self-regulatory rather than regulated by forces from above or from without. Under exceptional pressures it can fissure and reconstitute itself into two or more complete units. In view of Hopi life circumstances, the functional adequacy of the pueblo fission "mechanism," with its balanced socioreligious base, is obvious. It underlies the remarkable strength and resiliency of Hopi pueblo life. The analysis suggests that the crisis in its sociologic dimension is characterized by: (1) a disturbance in the ancient pueblo organization expressed either by a disorganization or a breakdown in the ceremonial system which throws the whole social structure off balance, or by a solidifying of the ceremonial integrate which interferes with the dynamics of the whole social system and introduces a trend toward rigidity; (2) a structural limitation in the ancient but enduring social order, so far as its adjustment to the recently extended total environment of the tribe is concerned, that is, by the absence of traditional formal "mechanisms" for the promotion of tribal political solidarity.

In the face of constant and intense environmental pressures, the Hopi developed through time a social system which was apparently well adjusted to their needs in the indigenous setting. The complementary relationship between the female-centered kinship system and the male-centered secret society system gave a biological balance to Hopi society and tended to equilibrate the status of men and women. Social controls were diffused and internalized and they tended to extend inward to a group-structured individual conscience which reflected the group's ethical code, and outward to the farthest reaches of the Hopi natural and supernatural world. The Hopi developed a social system which apparently allowed and encouraged the development of their human potential to a high level of efficiency and intensity. Their culture is thus a delicately balanced, self-regulating type of structure, similar to that which distinguishes ecological "climax" types.

From the viewpoint of Indian welfare, the effects of the traditional Indian Bureau policy and program were highly injurious, creating in the minds of the Hopi a lack of confidence and a general negative attitude toward the government and increasing their sense of insecurity. The Hopi tribe, however, escaped some of the effects of traditional federal policy mainly through the following combination of circumstances: (1) the pueblos were located in the heart of a vast desert which lacks precious metals and was raided by predatory Indian tribes; (2) while adopting new traits which they found useful and suited to their needs, the Hopi showed remarkable cultural stability and resistance to out-group pressures; (3) the resistance of Third Mesa leaders to the federal land allotment program kept Hopi land free from fractionization and preserved therein the principle of group ownership of land. It should also be emphasized that, although retaining their traditional religion and most of their ceremonies and culture, the Hopi did not escape certain influences stemming from traditional American attitudes and values. Positive effects of the new policy on Indian welfare since 1933 have been marked.

Conclusions. -- 1. The Hopi crisis is a manifestation of critical disturbance, of considerable historical depth and scope, in Hopi traditional culture viewed in environmental context.

2. Although the present crisis has a tribe-wide spread in its ecologic, and somatic dimensions, it has reached acute proportions in its sociologic, psychologic, and symbolic dimensions only in certain Mennonite-dominated communities where the traditional ceremonial and social system has broken down under white pressures, and in ultraconservative communities where it has tended to petrify under white pressures. The evidence viewed as a whole leads to the conclusion that the core of the crisis is ideological [179].

3. In "optimum" or "climax" types of human communities, wherein an ecologically balanced and self-regulatory type of structure and a high degree of organic and logico-esthetic integration with the total indigenous environment has developed, new cultural elements and patterns may be added and many of the accouterments or so-called "content" of the culture may change and/or even disappear, but under favorable circumstances the ancient culture structure will endure. Culture crisis is engendered not so much by changes in culture "content" as by disturbances in culture structure which engender a condition of imbalance in one or more essential dimensions of the culture and generate thereby a strain throughout the whole structure [180].

4. The findings suggest that, in an acculturation situation, aside from extermination or forced dispersal of the culture group, the factors most deeply disturbing to the balance of a "near-climax" type of culture are intrusive influences which throw "out of kilter" the logico-esthetic integration of the symbol system with the total environment. Next in importance as radically disturbing to such a culture type are attacks or influences which bring out a severing of the bond between the culture group and its geographic environment. Somewhat less radical in effect are alien influences which throw the structure of the sociological dimension out of balance by attempting to superimpose thereon alien, structurally incompatible political and economic systems [180].

5. An integrative community administration and social action research allow indigenous solutions, indigenously structured [181].

38. Vogt, Evon Z. NAVAHO VETERANS, A STUDY OF CHANGING VALUES. 1951. Papers of the Peabody Museum of American Archaeology and Ethnology, Harvard Univ., Vol. XLI, No. 1; Reports of the Rimrock Project Values Series, No. 1.

Purpose or Problem. — 1. To determine in what ways and to what extent the Navaho veterans were changed by their service experience, and to what extent these acculturated veterans are changing Navaho culture [3].

2. Under what conditions and by what processes do significant changes in individual Navaho value systems tend to occur in culture contact situations [4]? Seen against this broader analysis of the conditions and processes of acculturation, what part did the culture contact experienced in service play in bringing about crucial shifts in individual Navaho value systems [4]?

3. In the present acculturation situation, which aspects of individual Navaho value systems tend to change more readily; which aspects tend to be resistant to change [5]?

Definitions, Assumptions, and Hypotheses. — 1. The veterans would reject the curing and mythological aspects of Navaho religion, but would retain certain of the deep-seated witchcraft and ghost beliefs of the old religious system [3].

2. Veterans would be leaders in Navaho society in the adoption of elements of white material culture, in the promotion of schooling for Navahos, and in the promotion of white medical treatment for the curing of illness [3].

3. The veterans would represent a well-crystallized group in Navaho society that would be hopelessly caught "between two worlds," Navaho and white [3].

4. A value is a conception, explicit or implicit, distinctive of an individual or characteristic of a group, of the desirable which influences the selection between available modes, means, and ends of action [5-6]. A "value-orientation" is a generalized and organized conception, influencing behavior, of nature, of man's place in it, of man's relation to man, and of the desirable and nondesirable as they may relate to man-environment and interhuman relations [7].

5. A greater degree of value change can be anticipated in cases marked by personal conflict and insecurity, and by social deviation from the traditional patterns of Navaho society [4].

6. It was anticipated that those veterans who had previously undergone a process of personal and social deviation from Navaho ways and who had acquired sufficient knowledge of white culture to adjust readily to roles assigned them in the white military system were more significantly changed by their service experience than those who had had little previous experience in the outside world, spoke little or no English, and who were so unfamiliar

with white culture as to be unable to make ready adjustments to the military situation [4-5].

7. It was anticipated that value-orientations toward material culture would be relatively susceptible to change whereas orientations toward religion and ceremonialism (especially the ghost and witchcraft patterns) would be highly resistant. This differential value change could be accounted for by (a) the distinctive patterns of Navaho culture which place emphasis upon change in material culture and upon adherence to tradition in the realm of religion and ceremonialism, and (b) the difference in the phenomena in more general terms, to wit, that instrumentalities or means (technology) are generally more amenable to change than the ultimate values of a people, which are typically given expression in the religious system [5].

8. Two fundamental premises are: (a) the explicit recognition that science itself rests upon certain assumptions which involve value elements; (b) that values are, in their own right, legitimate data for the social sciences [5].

Methods and Techniques. — Field work: June 1947 to March 1948. (For details of field methods see pp. 28-31.) Life histories, projective tests, etc. (data appended).

Graphs and Charts. — Eleven family charts. Three tables: Degrees of Change [86]. Ceremonial Participation [107]. Summary of Social, Cultural, and Personal Factors in Value Change in Each Case History [103-4].

Data. — The Rimrock Navaho group has had long and intimate contacts with other societies in the area, but full-scale acculturation has been limited by the linguistic barrier, by the geographical situation, and by the cultural patterning of the interrelations between the Navaho and the other groups. The intercultural contacts which occur are limited to specific types of situations involving particular segments of Navaho life, thus placing the Navahos under varying types and degrees of pressure in the acculturation process. Contacts with the Pueblo are: co-ordinate in structure (trader-friend and rodeo contestants) and hierarchical in varying degrees (employer-employee, host-spectator at Pueblo ceremonials, and Pueblo men– Navaho women marriages). The patterned roles found in Navaho-Spanish American relations are: co-ordinate (visiting, bootleg liquor sales, and rodeo contestants); hierarchical (employer-employee, host-spectator at the fiestas, and sexual affairs involving Spanish-American men and Navaho women). The Navahos clearly recognize that the Pueblos possess a superior technology and a more sophisticated and elaborated ceremonialism; their attitude toward the Spanish Americans is a common recognition that both are "depressed" groups in the local social structure and a tendency to feel "easier" in their relations with them. In contrast, their roles with the Mormons are strongly subordinate in the acculturation situation. The Mormons are traders, employers on farms and ranches, and missionaries; the Navahos are customers, employees, and "potential" converts. The Mormon roles of economic exploiter and missionary conflict. The attitude of the Navahos toward them is one of strong ambivalence. Relations with the Texans are: Navaho employees and customers subordinate to Texan employers and shopkeepers; more co-ordinate relationships in rodeos and in bootleg liquor situations. Other groups with which there is contact are the Galilean (or Fundamentalist) sect, which presents an uncompromising stand against Navaho ceremonialism in any form; a few Anglo families in the vicinity; anthropologists; and the Indian Service. In this study, the Navaho-white dichotomy is utilized as the major dimension of acculturation.

Case histories of individual veterans follow. The following four "stages" in the transition from Navaho to white-American ways of life are suggested: (1) Minimal contact with whites, with the individual Navaho manifesting the characteristics of the traditional Navaho value system. (2) Increased effective contacts with the dominant white culture bring about an imitative "stage" in which selected value patterns of the dominant culture are imitated but not internalized. The patterns learned are not related significantly to their lives but are merely incremental items of behavior which are carried out only in face-to-face contacts with whites. (3) At a much later period and after years of sustained white contact, a more fundamental shift occurs in which white value patterns begin to be internalized. These values come to be integral parts of their motivational systems. (4) In a final possible "stage" the acculturation reaches the point where the residuals of Navaho value-orientations are lost and the individual Navaho is culturally indistinguishable from whites of the same age and sex. In the present series of case histories there are no individuals who are entirely in the first and fourth theoretical "stages." The majority seem to be still largely at various points in the second or imitative "stage" of acculturation.

A problem to be considered is the structure of the "social orbits," the position of the individual Navaho within these orbits, and the relationships of these social facts to relative conservatism or change in values on the part of the individuals involved. One of the most important considerations in this respect is the disruption of the typical Navaho family of orientation by loss by death of parents or other close relatives. Another is the sibling position of the individual Navaho within the nuclear family; a third is the size and structure of the family of orientation. Two general aspects of the "cultural context" appear to bear important relationships to the degree of acculturation. The first is the level of acculturation found in the family and/or "outfit" of orientation as a whole. A second is the relative presence or absence of culturally "deviant" or culturally "conforming" relatives within each of the families of orientation, especially the father and the mother's brother. There is a high degree of correspondence between the quantity of white contact and the degree of value change manifested; but many of the cases deviate markedly from this simple scheme, and it is clear that sheer amount of white contact is not the only determinant of acculturation to white values, nor is the knowledge of English.

There are three general types of contact situations outside Navaho society which have been of significance in the acculturation of young men from the Rimrock community: boarding-school experience, wagework in white-operated enterprises, and service experience. The first important exposure to white values and patterns occurs when the children were taken away to Indian Service boarding schools; the effectiveness of this formal schooling in the acculturation process depended upon three factors: the number of years in school, the age at which the child started school, and the type of adjustment made to the school situation. The importance of wagework to the acculturation process appears to hinge upon two major considerations: the structure of the work situation and the command of English a given Navaho has. In the years before the war practically all of this wagework was done in the immediate Rimrock area, while during the war there were many opportunities in other parts of the United States, a situation potentially more effective for change. This type of contact situation is also closely related to economic differentials within Rimrock Navaho society in that the members of families with large holdings of land and livestock almost never do wagework, whereas members of families in lower economic levels do a large amount of wagework each year.

For most of the veterans, their service was the first period of sustained white contact they had experienced since they left Indian Service boarding schools. Almost all reported that the whites they met in the army were more friendly to them than the whites they had previously known at home. They seem to have been placed in inferior positions in the army rank system not because of their physical characteristics, but more because of their cultural characteristics. There were a number of special problems of adjustment resulting from certain features of Navaho culture, for example, concepts of modesty, differences in types of food, fear of the dead and ghosts, the marked differences between the informal, nonhierarchical nature of Navaho social organization and the formal, hierarchical nature of the army. As far as the idea of war itself is concerned, there is some evidence that traditional Navaho values carried over to the present in that the Navaho veterans gained some prestige in the Rimrock community because they fought in the war.

In a few respects the veterans as a whole show some important and highly crucial shifts in orientations that were not so clearly defined in the nonveterans. (1) There is a strong cognitive realization on the part of the veterans that the Navahos are an integral part of a larger social universe which is controlled by various kinds of "white people." (2) There is also a general realization on the part of the veterans that white people outside the local scene of the Southwest are friendlier and treat Indians with more respect than do the local whites. (3) In the cases of the more acculturated veterans, shifts from the Navaho to the white-American profile with respect to orientations toward "nature" and "time" were greatly stimulated by their service experience.

The most important features of the postwar situation with reference to change or conservatism in value systems are: (1) the marriage of the veterans to unacculturated Navaho women in the community, which has a conservative influence; (2) the tendency to patrilocal residence on the part of the more acculturated veterans; (3) the influence of affinal relatives upon the veterans; (4) the ambivalent attitudes held by the veterans toward local whites; and (5) the present economic situation in which veterans are temporarily receiving subsistence checks for attending G.I. schools, but in which there are few long-range alternative occupational roles for veterans who wish "to go the white way." The more acculturated veterans find themselves in the anomalous position of being attracted to white values and patterns but of being rejected as social inferiors by the local carriers of white culture. The G.I. training is also a force for continuing acculturation in that it brings the Navaho veterans into weekly face-to-face contact with the white veterans in the area and in that the agricultural instructors are bringing pressure to bear upon the Navahos to "improve" their farming and herding methods.

It is evident upon close examination of the cases that a few crucial features of personal adjustment do bear some relationship to acculturation with respect to values. There are two significant uniformities in the cases: (1) Embedded in the character structure of all the Navahos in the series is a strong fear of whites. (2) Anxiety about health is manifested in all the cases. There appears to be a relationship between degree of acculturation and extent to which the individual Navaho manifests a lack of satisfying affective ties with other people or the extent to which his life is characterized by personal conflict and/or insecurity. (a) The Navahos who have most generally accepted white values tend to be characterized by a lack of satisfying affective ties with other people; those who retain Navaho values tend to be characterized by close and warm personal relationships with other Navahos. (b) The Navahos who have most generally accepted white values tend to be characterized by stronger personal conflicts and/or greater personal insecurity; those who retain Navaho values, by less conflict and greater security.

The dispostion of the Navahos to accept elements of material culture from other groups with whom they have been in contact has deep roots in Navaho history. From the time they first entered the Southwest as a hunting and gathering people, they have borrowed successively from the Pueblos, the Spaniards, and the Anglo-Americans. Their technology has shifted rapidly from hunting and food gathering to the present subsistence pattern of farming and herding supplemented by silversmithing, weaving, and wagework for the whites. In almost all of the fifteen case histories there is marked receptivity to items of white technology and material culture, even when there is little or no change in other aspects of the value systems. One of the most important limiting factors to this borrowing is the lack of economic resources. A second is the fact that cultural borrowing is always selective. The current change in house type to white-style cabins is not a more efficient adaptation to the environment; the motive for building them apparently springs from the desire to live in a house in the manner of the white people— to the Navaho families in the area the fact that a certain family lives in a house rather than a hogan is a symbol of acculturation. Most families who live in houses also maintain a near-by hogan for ceremonials. This is an important instance of the persistence of an aboriginal item in ritual context. Another good illustration of Navaho borrowing of white technology is found in the veterans' current enthusiasm for farm machinery, as compared to the ritualistic resistance encountered in Pueblo.

The adoption of white styles of clothing by Navaho men is continuing; by and large, they resemble that worn by the white farmers and ranchers in the vicinity. The type of clothing worn by the Navaho women, however, has not varied from the style of the 1860's. It is significant that Navaho men (even the most acculturated veterans) feel strongly that the women should continue dressing in the old-style clothing. Food habits tend to be somewhat more resistant to change. While there is little resistance to white cleanliness habits, the objective conditions of Navaho living continue to present such serious obstacles that it is doubtful whether fundamental changes will take place along these lines in the present scene. The lack of radios, too (of which there is only one), is not due to any formal resistance, but rather to economic and cultural facts: electricity is not available; there is a general lack of knowledge of English, etc.

The data strongly suggests that the following aspects of religion tend to undergo change before basic shifts in orientations to social relations occur: loss of belief in the efficacy of the chants; adoption of the belief in germs as the cause of, and white medicine as the cure for, most illnesses; infraction of some taboos; and even genuine conversions to Christianity. Relatively persistent orientations toward social organization, such as strong adherence to the incest taboos, participation in the Navaho respect and joking relationships and the use of kinship terms, the tendency to think and behave in "familistic" rather than in "individualistic" terms, would seem to be related to (1) the manner and order in which the Navaho child is exposed to kinship and religious patterns in the socialization process, (2) the present basic economic and social conditons of Navaho life, and (3) the nature of the current acculturation situation. It is clear that the Navaho child is exposed to and thoroughly trained for participation in the kinship system long before he participates in ceremonials or knows much about religious beliefs. It is therefore not surprising that individuals have deep-seated orientations toward their kinsmen and that these are less susceptible to change in an acculturation situation than the orientations to religion and ceremonialism. In addition, Navahos still lead a precarious existence in widely scattered small groups in which co-operation with kindred is essential for survival of the individuals. Other than the efforts made by the Indian Service to superimpose the formal tribal council organization and the pressure of the missionaries against polygyny, the whites have made few attempts to alter the Navaho social system. The Navahos, on the other hand, have learned little about white social organization beyond such matters as the fact that white people do not avoid their mothers-in-law and do not practice polygyny; it is quite likely that the mother-in-law taboo has been the first important element to change largely because it does differ so obviously from the white pattern. With respect to the aspects of the religious system which are more resistant, the belief in and fear of Navaho ghosts and witches survives even in the cases of the most acculturated veterans. It is suggested that these elements tend to persist because they are among the most deeply ingrained elements of the Navaho religious system (one of the first features to which the child is exposed), and because they are related to a number of the psychological tensions in Navaho life. They still make contributions to the maintenance of personal equilibrium for these veterans who are still living in and must adjust to the present structure of Navaho society. It is suggested that divination is so persistent because it provides a means of knowing the unknown in an uncertain and perplexing world. There is evidence that certain aspects of the Navaho value system which may be designated as implicit are the most resistant to change in acculturation situations. Since they are matters of which the Navahos are minimally aware, it follows that most whites are completely unaware of them. Correlatively, the premises of white culture are matters that whites take for granted, and it is impossible for a Navaho to learn about them as he does some concrete activity.

Conclusions. -- 1. The problem of changing values is viewed as a dynamic process in which the value system of a subordinate society (Navaho) is changed and gradually replaced by elements of the value system of the dominant society (white American) via face-to-face relations between the individual carriers of the two value systems. The essence of the process is a succession of gradual and often subtle shifts in individual values over long periods of time. The process is seen as a complex one involving stages of (1) imitation and (2) internalization of white values [117].

2. Conditions crucial to significant value change are: (1) a background within Navaho society in which the individual is not effectively socialized to conservative Navaho values. This may involve two sets of determinants: (a) the structure of the "social orbit" and (b) the nature of the "cultural context." (2) Intimate face-to-face relations with whites in contact situations outside of Navaho society: schooling, wagework, and service experience. (3) A type of personal adjustment which tends to be characterized by a lack

of satisfying affective ties with others and a great deal of personal conflict and insecurity [117-18].

3. Service experience not only had an important effect in the further acculturation of those veterans who were maximally acculturated before the war, but also usually had an important effect upon those who were minimally acculturated before they entered the armed services [118]. (This is a restatement of the original hypothesis.) Effectiveness depended on (1) the command of English and the amount of cognitive knowledge of white culture; (2) the nature of the social orbit in which a given veteran was placed in the military situation. The service experience usually resulted in a more positive attitude toward white values and patterns when they served in military units with other Navahos. This led to the formation of a small Navaho social group with its own subculture, which decreased the number of contacts with white soldiers but provided them with a cushion against the abrupt transition to the military situation. (3) In some of the cases personality factors appear to have been critical determinants.

4. The orientations to nonmaterial culture tend to be generally more resistant to change than the orientations to material culture; in the realm of nonmaterial culture the values governing social organization tend to be more resistant to change than many value aspects of the ceremonial and religious system; implicit values tend to be the most resistant to change in contact situations [119].

5. The finding that certain value aspects of social organization are more resistant to change than many of the religious orientations was not anticipated. The previous lack of consideration of this problem may in part stem from our own American value system, in which it is assumed that a person's religion is the very core of his personality and hence the most persistent aspect of character structure in situations of change [119-20].

6. In general, it can be said that the problem of change and resistance to change of Navaho values toward values held by the other societies is both a matter of relative articulation or lack of articulation between the cultural traditions of the Navaho with the other societies and a matter of the nature and range of alternative roles which are open to Navahos in this larger social system.

7. Women seem to be a force for conservatism in the series as a whole, and it is suggested that Navaho acculturation takes place overwhelmingly via the males in the society.

8. Perhaps the most significant finding concerning the relationship of personal conflict and insecurity to acculturation is that such conflict and insecurity do not necessarily lead an individual to promote changes in the patterns of Navaho society and to accept the values and patterns of white society; this is only one type of response to personal conflicts and insecurity. It is the writer's hypothesis that the type of response selected is largely a function of the "stage" a given individual has reached in the transition from

Navaho to white values; when a Navaho reaches the point in the acculturation process where he has rejected most of the fundamental Navaho values and has interiorized many white value-orientations, his response to personal conflict and insecurity is most likely to be a further movement in the direction of white ways of life. While we can say that deviance from the traditional roles in the Navaho social system, departure from the traditional patterns of Navaho culture, increased personal conflict and insecurity, and sustained white contacts tend to lead to changes in individual value systems, it is also true that changes in values tend to stimulate changes in the social, cultural, and personal adjustment of the individual Navaho.

39. Whitman, William. THE SAN ILDEFONSO OF NEW MEXICO. 1940. In Linton, 390-462; see Sec. 25.

Purpose or Problem. — See Linton.

Definitions, Assumptions, and Hypotheses. — See Linton.

Methods and Techniques. — Residence in San Ildefonso in the summer of 1936, winter and spring of 1937. Extensive ethnological research in other Rio Grande pueblos.

Data. — The early Spanish contacts do not appear to have greatly disturbed the pueblo way of life. The two cultures were not at heart opposed. The Spaniards who came to farm the neighboring fields introduced new crops and new techniques, but they too were agriculturalists and on much the same economic level. On the whole the Spaniards broadened the pueblo horizon without disrupting the culture to any great extent. Military pressure was not necessary in order to keep them at least acquiescent except in religious activities. They gradually accepted those aspects of the new culture which appealed to their sense of economy and did not violate their sense of propriety, such as foods, textiles, and those techniques that were economically productive and useful to the village.

Within the last twenty years there has been a second period of change which is affecting the pueblo much more profoundly and rapidly; a reaction to the modern life in the United States. The fundamental integrity of the pueblos as a group is being undermined; the dollar is taking the place of exchange; co-operation is giving way to competition; pottery is upsetting agricultural values, and women potters are beginning to dominate pueblo policies; government schools and colleges are unsettling the young. Already the pueblo has split into two hostile factions, and the schism is widening rather than healing.

Although San Ildefonso was in frequent contact with other Indian groups, the people were slow to acquire new traits, and there is comparatively little in their culture today that appears to have been borrowed from non-pueblo peoples. No modern concepts of medicine and sanitation have been halfheartedly accepted. The traits that have been lost since the conquest are chiefly those that have been displaced by the acceptance of new ones. Old agricultural methods have given way to new; the household economy has been altered by the introduction of new white commodities. The hold of native religion has been weakened to some extent; cult practices favored by the medicine societies, etc., have begun to disappear. Such fundamental attitudes as co-operation in relation to competition are much affected. The world of the pueblo is becoming increasingly competitive due to the economic change brought about by the sale of pottery to tourists, and by government work. There is no organized opposition to the adoption of white ways, nor are there any nativistic movements, especially since the idea of dominating guidance is foreign to them. There are few external checks to culture borrowing; the people of San Ildefonso are not poor and live close enough to the city to visit it whenever they wish. On the whole, such checks to culture borrowing as exist are within the culture itself. The dispute which has separated the pueblo into two factions is generally thought of in religious terms; actually it sprang from numerous causes, among them the desire of one group to be independent of the established religious authority of the other. This was aggravated by economic pressure and the rise of the woman potter into power.

Agriculture is still nominally the basis of pueblo economy, but within the last twenty-five years it has slowly dwindled in importance. Stock does not flourish in the pueblo and little interest is taken in animal husbandry. Government employ is eagerly sought and is helping to break down the old co-operative structure, with men thinking in terms of a daily wage. Today pottery is of the greatest economic importance to the village. Because the making of pottery is primarily women's work, it is giving women an economic and social importance that they never had before. It is a unique example of a craft renaissance. With the exception of ceremonial bowls, San Ildefonso pottery is made solely for sale to tourists. Painting is an auxiliary source of income rather than a fundamental one. The other native crafts have all declined in importance to a point where they no longer affect the village economy, mainly since they do not offer a sufficient return when compared with government work; there is also no market for native crafts within the pueblo and, in comparison with other Indian groups, little market outside.

Within the last few years there has been a slight shift of emphasis in patterns of social dominance. All individuals were said to possess equal status, but an increasing respect is being shown to the wealthy at the expense of the religious or cult leaders. Differences in wealth are tending to increase intravillage resentment and jealousy. What was formerly communal property is now considered to be the property of individuals who are said to have rights of disposal and transmission. Today white concepts of love affect the marriage choice. Where before the chief focus of interest was in agriculture, there has been a gradual shift in values. For the women, life is almost completely centered in the making and sale of pottery. The men's adjustment to new values, many of them introduced by the successful sale of property, has been less complete. Where before men were glad to raise good crops, they now struggle to earn money. The desire to earn money, however, is not so strong that it has driven men to seek a livelihood outside the pueblo, but it has tended to be reflected in a decreasing interest in agriculture.

Conclusions. -- 1. San Ildefonso must still be considered a well-integrated community in spite of the dispute between the two factions. There is a high degree of solidarity and unanimity of opinion within each part [458].

2. The impact of white culture has been oblique in the sense that there have been no territorial removals, no change from one type of economy to one radically different, and no behavior patterns in one group that were intolerable to the other, so that adjustment was possible without violence (in the nineteenth century). Whether the culture can remain integrated under the new pressure of rapid change in basic economy remains to be seen [458].

3. The Spanish contact offers a situation in which the results of directed acculturation backed by force can be perceived with few complicating factors. The Spaniards attempted to introduce Christianity and a new type of village governmental organization and to eliminate the native religion. They succeeded in both introductions as far as the outward forms were concerned, but in both cases these forms were reinterpreted in the light of the previous culture and were adjusted to it. This integration was successful enough so that the forms survived even when all external pressure had been removed. The attempt to eliminate the native religion failed completely; it was met by the development of techniques of reticence and concealment which have also survived long after the necessity for them has disappeared. Although we have no direct information on this point, it seems probable that the Spanish attacks on the native religion actually heightened the group's attachment to it, giving it new symbolic values.

4. The whole program of directed acculturation seems to have had much less effect on native life than has the destruction of natural resources or elimination of aboriginal activities.

5. The encouragement of native pottery making and painting is an almost unique phenomenon of the direction of culture development by the dominant group.

Part Three
JOURNAL ARTICLE ABSTRACTS

JOURNAL ARTICLE ABSTRACTS*

1. Adair, John J., and Vogt, Evon Z. NAVAHO AND ZUNI VETERANS: A STUDY OF CONTRASTING MODES OF CULTURE CHANGE. AA 51, 1949, 547-61.

<u>Purpose or Problem</u>. — Objective in this paper was to describe some of the varying modes of response of the Zuni and Navaho to the war situation, especially with reference to the departure of veterans; to suggest how these responses are related to the historical development of the two tribes and to contrasting patterns of Zuni and Navaho culture at the present time; and to delineate some of the mechanisms of cultural dynamics revealed by a comparative analysis of the two cases [547].

<u>Definitions, Assumptions, and Hypotheses</u>. — 1. Returning veterans have been accepted differently among the Zuni and the Navaho [547].
2. Some of the processes whereby Zuni veterans were reintegrated into social frameworks were gossip, rumor, and ridicule [550].
3. Many of the most "progressive" veterans of the pueblo have left the village [551].
4. Literacy is greater among the Zuni than among the Navaho [553].
5. Pressures for conformity are less among the Navaho than among the Zuni [554].

<u>Methods and Techniques</u>. — Paper based on field research by Adair at Zuni (June 1947 to January 1948), and by Vogt in the Ramah Navaho area (June 1947 to March 1948). The data come from life histories of thirteen Navaho and six Zuni veterans (not included), from interviews with older Navaho and Zuni leaders, and from daily observations [547]. A section on tribal histories contributes to the meaningfulness of the article.

<u>Data</u>. — The Zuni Veterans: Between February 1941 and March 1946, 213 Zuni men went into the service. The village objected to the number of men being drafted and quotas were cut. Young men were deferred in great numbers as religious students. Among the Zuni, religious activities were increased greatly during the war years. The months following the discharge of Zuni men were dysphoric. Anxieties among veterans were manifested in drunkenness and restlessness. Some degree of social reintegration was occurring by 1948.

The Navaho Veterans: There was no disinterest or reluctance to go to war as among the Zuni. Many volunteered at the declaration of war. No efforts were made by Navaho officials to secure exemptions for young men. Navaho soldiers showed less tendency to carry over religious patterns into

---

*The abstracting procedure employed with the journal articles is the same as that for monographs, (see footnote, p. 19).

the war situation. Purificatory rites were staged by both groups on the veteran's return, but the philosophy behind the rites differed.

Conclusions.— 1. Differing historical developments and sociocultural systems account for the differences in the treatment of returning veterans in the two tribes [555].

2. Historically the Navaho have been more exposed and receptive to acculturative pressures than have the Zuni [557].

3. Historical experience for adaptation rather than resistance to new patterns is the main reason for the Navaho attitude toward the returning veterans [558].

4. The Navaho settlement pattern is more widespread and consequently social units are smaller and more localized and social organization is more loosely knit. Social control is less easily achieved than among the Zuni [558].

5. The traditional Navaho and Zuni patterns of warfare governed the attitude toward the veterans [559].

6. Dispositions toward the outside world differ in the two groups [559].

7. The contrasting modes of change that have taken place in the two societies ("acculturative" and "nativistic") provide an instance of Keesing's "factor of adaptability" [560].

2. Aginsky, Burt W. and Ethel G. THE PROCESS OF CHANGE IN FAMILY TYPES: A CASE STUDY. AA 51, 1949, 611-14.

Purpose or Problem.— To investigate the differences in role and status of Pomo women (of northern California) who are married to Filipino men from those married to Pomo men [611]. A reappearance of the pattern of domination by the men in very recent years.

Definitions, Assumptions, and Hypotheses.— (Implicit.) The influx of Filipino men has served to create a new pattern of male domination, side by side with the older Pomo pattern (which has itself recently undergone considerable change).

Methods and Techniques.— Short essay. Incorporating research carried on intermittently since 1932.

Data.— During the war years a large influx of Filipino men into the Pomo territory resulted from the need for harvest hands. They have remained in the area, some marrying Pomo women. They work conscientiously and constitute a close-knit group. They are considered by the Indians as intruders who have encroached on their rights. The Pomo feel them to be of a lower social order, and are ashamed when their women marry Filipinos. There are thus two patterns of family life existing side by side in Pomo society today. The first is of longer standing, and under it we find the Indian man married to the Indian woman, where the woman, culturally speaking, is the mainstay of the family. The second pattern, of more recent development, is that of the Indian woman married to the Filipino man where the woman lives a life of relative ease with few responsibilities. It is to be especially noted that the re-emergent culture with male domination places more power in the hands of men than any which they are known to have had in aboriginal days.

Conclusions. — 1. There is present in every population the possibility of more than one type of social organization, and both of these, or some combination of them, can fuse into a functioning system [614].

2. The data do not permit prediction of developments out of this situation because only a few cases of intermarriage have as yet occurred, and these have taken place only during the past few years.

3. This is interesting to observe as a change in a different direction from that of only a few years ago.

3. Albrecht, Andrew C. INDIAN-FRENCH RELATIONS AT NATCHEZ. AA 48, 1946, 321-53.

Purpose or Problem. — To demonstrate the existence of extensive and significant culture contacts, other than mere conflicts, and to describe the changing relationships of the two peoples in terms of the manifold forces — geographical, social, and religious — that were operative. To show the way in which one contact situation was transformed into another and to determine the particular forces which brought about these changes [322].

Definitions, Assumptions, and Hypotheses. — The various contact situations which arose from contact with the French at Natchez represent a certain developmental stage which was common wherever European explorers and colonists come in contact with native peoples [322].

Methods and Techniques. — Essay based on extensive use of historical documents.

Data. — Six stages of Indian-French relations are traced (1682-1730). These are characterized by (1) peaceful contact with explorers, (2) resentful contact with missionaries, (3) factional reaction to the establishment of a company trading post, (4) incomplete military subjugation. (5) Both friendly and hostile relations reached their culmination during French farm immigration (between wars adjustment was good). Finally (6) conflict became inevitable with increased agricultural expansion of the French. Ill-considered action by new colonial officials precipitated the terminal war.

Friendly contact between the groups was chiefly through trade. Fraternization was not discouraged, personal friendships united French and Indians. The latter accepted many new items of material culture, especially firearms, but remained conservative with respect to food, clothing, house types, and social organization.

Conclusions. — The history of French-Natchez contact reveals many instances of benign ethnic relations as well as the conflicts too often stressed. Acculturation was minimal, and affected only the Indians [353].

4. Altus, William D. AMERICAN MEXICAN: THE SURVIVAL OF A CULTURE. JSP 29, 1949, 211-20.

Purpose or Problem. — (Implicit.) To study the persistence of the linguistic aspects of Mexican culture in American citizens of Mexican ancestry [219].

Definitions, Assumptions, and Hypotheses. — 1. Sharp differences must exist between the non-English, Spanish-speaking trainee who had lived all his life in the United States and those who were non-English but who had been in the United States a comparatively short time [211].
2. The fact that a person can live all his life in his native country and never learn its language would appear to be prima facie evidence of low learning capacity, though dullness, per se, is not the most important etiological factor [212].

Methods and Techniques. — A check of personnel cards of "functionally illiterate" (by Army standards) newly-inducted soldiers who were Spanish-speaking [211]. Based on the Performance Tests of the Army Wechsler Scale (especially Digit Symbol subtest), an oral adjustment test shown to have high validity. Use of statistical techniques.

Data. — Tests indicated that the native non-English Mexicans were duller than the foreign-born non-English, Spanish-speaking trainees. This statement is true of averages only; in individual cases the relationship does not hold, since some native non-English Mexicans are relatively bright. There was more maladjustment among the American-born and American-reared non-English Mexicans than among the corresponding group lately arrived in the United States, maladjustment being equated with test score on the oral adjustment test used.

For certain Mexicans, their cultural heritage in terms of language not only survives, but survives to the exclusion of the national language of their native country. Spanish also survives, though to a lesser degree, as a written language. Data for the non-English trainees who were born in this country and had never left it, and who had no literacy in English, indicated that 9 percent were fully literate in Spanish and 39 percent had some literacy in that tongue. Yet these men had gone, on the average, about three years to American schools, had not studied Spanish in school, and their written and oral knowledge of English was nonexistent.

It may reasonably be suspected that Spanish persists with greater hardiness among the American Mexicans than does any other non-English tongue among comparable groups of American citizens.

Conclusions. — 1. The native-born and -reared non-English Mexican has been shown to be more maladjusted and less intelligent than the non-English, foreign-born, and educated Spanish-speaking trainee [219].

2. Possible explanations for the persistence of the Mexican culture are: propinquity to Mexico, permitting a constant renewal and revivification of the mother culture in a manner afforded to no other minority group; the tendency to follow unskilled occupations in company with other Mexicans, especially seasonal and itinerant agricultural labor, so that the education of their children suffers; differentiating cultural hallmarks such as religion and diet; the presence of Mexican movies and newspapers; the familial structure in which grandparents live with their children; antagonism on the part of the majority; memory of former Spanish possession of the land.

5. Barber, Bernard. ACCULTURATION AND MESSIANIC MOVEMENTS. ASR 6, 1941, 663-69.

Purpose or Problem. — To describe and analyze the conditions under which some of the fundamental myths of the North American Indians have become the ideological basis for messianic movements [663].

Definitions, Assumptions, and Hypotheses. — 1. Primitive messianic movement is correlated with the occurrence of widespread deprivation and is only one of several alternative responses [668]. It is defined as the ushering in of a "golden age" by the messiah in the immediate future.

Methods and Techniques. — Theoretical paper.

Data. — Twenty Messianic movements were recorded in the United States alone prior to 1890; the doctrine is essentially a statement of hope, anticipating a happy return to the golden age; traits and customs which are symbolic of foreign influence must be put aside; all members of the community must participate, and must adopt special ritual practices until the millenium arrives. The general sociocultural situation that precipitates a messianic movement has been loosely described as one of "harsh times." Its specific characteristic is the widespread experience of "deprivation" — the despair caused by inability to obtain what the culture has defined as the ordinary satisfactions of life. The stabilizing function of the messianic movement is illustrated in specific cases, e.g., the 1890 Ghost Dance; data of Nash on the Klamath reservation; Navaho reactions. The Peyote cult, like the messianic movement, was an "autistic" response, but the essential element of its doctrine was different. Whereas the Ghost Dance doctrine had graphically described a reversion to the aboriginal state, the Peyote cult crystallized around passive acceptance and resignation in the face of the existing deprivation. It is an alternative response which seems to be better adapted to the existing phase of acculturation.

Conclusions. — The primitive messianic movement is correlated with the occurrence of widespread deprivation and is only one of several alternative responses. There is a need for further studies, especially in regard to the specific sociocultural conditions which produce each of the possible responses [668].

6. Barker, George C. SOCIAL FUNCTIONS OF LANGUAGE IN A MEXICAN-AMERICAN COMMUNITY. AcA 5, 1947, 185-202.

Purpose or Problem. — An inquiry into how language functions in the life of a bilingual minority group in process of cultural change. The central problem may be stated as: "How, if at all, may the linguistic behavior of members of the bilingual minority group be related to other aspects of their social behavior?" Are variations the result of unrecognized uniformities in the way language functions in the lives of these people [185]?

Definitions, Assumptions, and Hypotheses. — 1. The language of any human society may be studied not only from the standpoint of its content and structure but also from that of its functions in the society [185].

2. The concept of the linguistic behavior pattern rests on the postulate that the linguistic behavior of any given individual exhibits a systematic patterning which can be defined objectively in terms, first, of the limits of the system; the second, of the parts of which it is composed; and, third, of the relative frequency of use of the various parts in standard situations [201].

3. Hypotheses regarding the division in linguistic function, where two languages are involved, are: (1) for individuals both inside and outside the ethnic group, the ethnic language comes to symbolize the group and its cultural background, or, in terms of its social function, to identify the group as a group (cf. Redfield); (2) that the individual's skill in using the language of a second or adopted culture comes to symbolize his status in the new society (cf. Bossard) [186-87].

4. The fact is apparent that in any given situation, members of a bilingual group have the opportunity of a choice between two or more alternate languages and dialects. It thus becomes possible to describe the linguistic behavior of any given bilingual individual in terms of patterns of usage and response to both languages, and to see precisely what relation may exist between these patterns and the nonlinguistic behavior of the same individual with respect both to his own group and to outsiders [188].

5. Since the subjects of this study are individuals of Mexican descent living sixty miles north of the Mexican border, the type of cultural change involved would seem to be both acculturation, involving the continuous first-hand contact of representatives of two different cultures, and assimilation, involving the gradual engulfing of representatives of one culture, and their absorption into the dominant group [185].

Methods and Techniques. — Selection of a number of individuals in one ethnic community (Tucson, Arizona) representing (1) a cross-section of the community's social system, and (2) a proportionate sampling of the community in terms of length of residence. Tucson was selected because of the wide range of social positions occupied by the town's Mexican-American population and availability of basic data on its social structure.

Six months' field work, including data on more than one hundred individuals, 1945-46. Informal observation, interviews, and questionnaires used.

Data. — Approximately one-fourth of Tucson's total population (or 20,000 persons) are of Mexican descent. The most striking feature of the social structure is the division into Anglo and Mexican, with the lower class being drawn almost exclusively from the Mexican population. In terms of socioeconomic class, at least five groups are represented in the Mexican community, ranging from the wealthy "Old Families" of Mexican descent to unskilled migrant workers. Two other important divisions are those of age group and national origin: about half of the Mexican residents of forty years of age or older are immigrants from Mexico. Four main variants of Spanish may be distinguished in Tucson: (1) the Southern Arizona dialect of Spanish; (2) standard Mexican Spanish; (3) the Pachuco dialect; (4) the Yaqui dialect of Spanish. The first is by far the most widely used.

Conclusions. — 1. In a bilingual minority group in process of cultural change, the functions originally performed by the ancestral language are divided between two or more languages with the result that each language comes to be identified with certain fields of interpersonal relations. In the Tucson Mexican-American group, four such linguistically identifiable fields of interpersonal relations readily may be distinguished: (1) the field of intimate relations (where Spanish is almost universally dominant); (2) informal relations (with rapid shifting from one language to another common among the younger people); (3) formal relations (with English widely used); (4) Anglo-Mexican relations (where English is the standard language) [195-96].

2. For each bilingual individual, the languages he speaks take on different symbolic values which vary according to the individual's social experience. The character of this experience depends on: (1) the position of the minority group in the general community; (2) the relation of the individual to the minority group; (3) the relation of the individual to the general community. The different values resulting are expressed in correspondingly different linguistic behavior patterns [196]. We find that the position of each individual on the cultural continuum is roughly paralleled by his position on the linguistic continuum [198].

3. The basic conditions of acculturation in the Tucson area indicate psychological as well as social subordination of the Mexican population as indicated by: (a) reticence of many Mexicans to speak Spanish with, and in

the presence of, Anglos; (b) identification of the term "Mexican" with lower-class status in Tucson, and corresponding substitution of the term "Spanish American" for Mexicans having higher status; (c) lack of informal interpersonal relations between Anglos and Mexicans as indicated by lack of informal linguistic categories common to both. Cultural, as well as physical, segregation of the Mexican population is indicated by: (a) inability of many young bilinguals to free themselves of "Spanish accent" in speaking English; (b) inability of many young bilinguals to translate freely from one language to the other; (c) dependence of American-born bilinguals on Spanish in certain fields of interpersonal relations (i.e., family life and close friendships); (d) use of pochismos and other hybrid linguistic forms. Divergent types of cultural orientation, and correspondingly divergent social goals, in the Tucson Mexican population are indicated by the four main types of linguistic behavior patterns found among members of the minority group [200].

4. Advantages of linguistic analysis of behavior are: (1) it does not consist of rationalizations of attitudes (as is frequently the case in formal interviews and questionnaires), but with how the individual uses and reacts to the linguistic symbol systems at his command; (2) it offers a means of obtaining an independent check on other sociological data. Since the linguistic system of an individual or group functions as an autonomous, self-contained system, this system may be analyzed and reported on independently of other cultural data. A high degree of objectivity is possible in the analysis of interpersonal relations from the data of linguistic behavior [201].

5. There is a need for extending this type of research to other frontier areas. We may predict that similar problems will exist wherever political boundaries are established between contiguous cultures having different languages. We may also predict that in any such area there will be a large number of bilinguals, and that these will tend to develop a hybrid culture and language of their own. In the long run, the assimilation process in such areas would seem to consist not so much in the engulfing of a minority group by a majority group as the fusion of the two to produce something new [202].

7. Barnett, H. G. PERSONAL CONFLICTS AND CULTURAL CHANGE. SF 20, 1941, 160-71.

Purpose or Problem. — To analyze the factors and processes involved in the acceptance of new objects, institutions, and behaviors introduced by the whites [160].

Definitions, Assumptions, and Hypotheses. — 1. Since cultural responses are in the last (or first?) analysis personal ones, the case history method has special merit in giving the problems sharper definition [160].

2. The misfits, the maladjusted, and the underdogs are in the vanguard of cultural innovation [163]. There is a positive correlation between eminence (not notoriety) and cultural conservatism, and eminent individuals

who do make radical departures from the accustomed modes and standards are more likely to be repudiated than followed by members of their society (cf. Linton) [167].

Methods and Techniques. — Case history method: "recording a large number of concrete responses to well-defined situations." Based on previous work in northwestern California, and among the Tsimpshian Indians of British Columbia.

Data. — A brief review of Tsimpshian contact with white culture is presented with emphasis on the militant Christianity of William Duncan. Removal to the model village which he founded meant an unqualified and voluntary renunciation of Indian customs. The motivations of several natives for going with him are then discussed.

Conclusions. — 1. It can hardly be doubted that it was the embroilment resulting from a personal conflict with the old system of values which stirred these prominent men to abandon the system and to seek an escape from its intolerable complications. An esteemed social status, while a good index, is no certain criterion of a completely successful cultural adjustment. If this case material proves anything, it indicates that personal difficulties and incompatibilities are one stimulus, if not the stimulus, to cultural change, the acceptance of new patterns and standards being the means of relieving personal strain or dissatisfaction [167].

2. It is impossible at this date to make any statistical estimate of the character of the responses to the renegade behavior of the chief(s). But the impression persists that they were condemned more frequently and vigorously than they were defended. The very fact of their high position made their apostasy more flagrant and incomprehensible [167].

3. The conclusion is that the disgruntled, the maladjusted, the frustrated, and the incompetent are preeminently the accepters of cultural innovations and change. It is not sufficiently appreciated that the members of the submerged elements of a population are rendered susceptible to subversive promises and ideologies of all sorts by their discontents [171].

4. To put a finger on the ultimate source of all cultural change, it is not unreasonable to suggest some kind of personal conflict as the primary motivation for invention [171].

8. Caudill, William. PSYCHOLOGICAL CHARACTERISTICS OF ACCULTURATED WISCONSIN OJIBWA CHILDREN. AA 51, 1949, 409-27.

Purpose or Problem. — 1. How closely related are personality changes and different stages in an acculturation process? Is there sometimes a lag in acculturation and the actual degree of personality change [409]? Is there a basic continuity of personality for two groups of Ojibwas that differ greatly in their outward manifestation of acculturation to western ways?

2. This paper presents personality data on the highly acculturated Ojibwa Indians, to be compared with Hallowell's previous observations of the culturally related but less acculturated Indians of the Berens River, in order to measure the variability in personality structure among Indians with the same aboriginal background but who represented different levels of acculturation.

Definitions, Assumptions, and Hypotheses. — The data for the establishment of a base line comes from extensive ethnographic and psychological material collected by Hallowell from one of the most remote branches of the Canadian Ojibwa. Extremely close and significant parallels exist between the psychological characteristics of the Berens River Indians and those which can be inferred from the accounts of contemporary observers of the Northeastern Indians in the 17th and 18th centuries [409].

Methods and Techniques. — Use of Hallowell's material as a base line; use of Rorschach and TAT.

Graphs and Charts. — Six charts showing types of TAT responses.

Data. — Analysis of the children's TAT series is made with some introductory statements explaining the method and terminology developed by Henry. These are then compared with the results of the analysis of the Berens River Rorschach material. The aboriginal Ojibwa and the relatively unacculturated Canadian Ojibwa of today are found to have in common: a detailed, practical, noncreative approach to problems; a high degree of generalized anxiety; an emphasis on restraint and control; an emotional indifference to things; a lack of warm interpersonal relations; a wariness and suspiciousness; and a great deal of aggression and hostility covertly expressed through sorcery. In the highly acculturated Flambeau Ojibwa, we find almost the same picture; here, however, the Ojibwa social structure, always weakly held together, seems to have broken down completely, with the result that aggression once expressed in sorcery is now expressed overtly in physical violence. Even this does not seem to be due entirely to acculturation since there were predisposing factors in Ojibwa social organization tending toward the open expression of violence once inhibitions had been released by alcohol.

Conclusions. — 1. There is a strong persistence of Ojibwa personality over a long span of time, despite the effects of western influence on Ojibwa culture, an example of the persistence of personality in the face of culture change that has wide implications for general culture-personality theory [425-26].

2. In Flambeau, the main effect of acculturation seems to have been negative: the old social structure has been destroyed, what integration there was is gone, along with the old roles and goals held out to the individual. The society is but an aggregate of individuals clustered in unstable family units for which the early culture was predisposed.

3. The women are able to make a more satisfactory adjustment to conditions of acculturation than men. Even this finds its roots in the aboriginal culture, where women carried a less heavy load of individual responsibility and prestige and were less anxious and vulnerable.

9. Collins, June McCormick. THE INDIAN SHAKER CHURCH: A STUDY OF CONTINUITY AND CHANGE IN RELIGION. SJA 6, 1950, 399-411.

Purpose or Problem. — To account for the acceptance of the Shaker church and the influence which it wielded during the last sixty years [399].

Definitions, Assumptions, and Hypotheses. — The argument here is that the success of the church was due, on the one hand, to the parallels between it and pre-white religious practices and, on the other hand, to the resemblances between it and Christian churches of the whites [399].

Methods and Techniques. — Field trip, January to March, 1942

Data. — About 1881 a group of Coast Salish Indians in western Washington founded a religious movement called the Indian Shaker church, so-called because members of the cult in their rituals engage in shaking movements of the body. After spreading northward and southward, it apparently reached the zenith of its influence and had begun a decline. It seems to have been an outgrowth of the Dreamers cult, headed by Smohalla, which became prominent in 1870 and, with the belief that dead Indians were to be resurrected and the whites swept away, incurred white antagonism. When white surveillance made the ceremonies impossible, new developments in religion resulted; among these was the Indian Shaker church.

Belief in guardian spirits for each individual formed the basis of the indigenous religion, the owner usually acquiring his spirits during a period of fasting in isolation. The need for the assistance of guardian spirits did not end with the arrival of the whites in the area; thus, such new developments as the Shaker church arose. The doctrine provides continuity between the old spirits and the new source of supernatural power, with heavy borrowing from Christian churches in theology, ritual, and material traits.

Conclusions. — 1. Today the main split is between those members of the Shaker church who wish it to resemble Christian churches more closely and those who cling to the older ways. But the two factions are not divided in the same way in other areas of acculturation, so the Indians adhering to the older Shaker procedures are not the most backward in taking over white material traits or familial patterns. About the same ages are represented in both, since membership follows family lines and does not cut across them [410].

2. Formal recognition of this division has recently been made, with persons who prefer the white church ways having left the Shaker church and become members of a new church. Participants in this new church still

"shake" and perform cures. It seems possible that these old features will disappear in time as younger generations come to have less understanding of the guardian spirit counterparts [410].

3. The Shaker church, by reason of its basis in guardian spirit belief on the one hand, and of its resemblances to white churches on the other, has provided a transitional step in religion for Indians who have accepted it [410]. The structure of the old Shaker church has proved sufficiently elastic to permit the new deviation (noted in 2 above) to be modeled on the old rather than necessitating a complete departure.

4. The Shaker religion was accepted by the Indians of Puget Sound for the following reasons: (1) it satisfies the pre-white criteria as to the validity of supernatural power; it defines the relationship of man to the spirit world in accordance with the aboriginal pattern of belief; (2) continuity with familial guardian spirits is provided; (3) the distinction between priest and layman does not occur; (4) supernatural means of curing and killing are services offered by both; (5) the same sanctions are offered: the fear of illness and death and the promise of reward on earth, in addition to Christian sanctions—the fear of punishment after death and the promise of reward in heaven [410-11].

5. The religious manifestations of the Indians must receive at least the tacit approval of the dominant white population, as expressed by toleration. The Shaker church received such approval because of the belief in God and Christ, the moral precepts, and the structure of the organization [411].

6. The church has continued because it has allowed scope both to those who wished to emphasize the aboriginal basis of religion and those who wanted to imitate the whites. The new offshoot of the Shaker church may be regarded as a further step in the latter direction [411].

10. Collins, June McCormick. GROWTH OF CLASS DISTINCTIONS AND POLITICAL AUTHORITY AMONG THE SKAGIT INDIANS DURING THE CONTACT PERIOD. AA 52, 1950, 331-42.

Purpose or Problem. — The possibility that white contact affected the development of the class differences that appeared on the Northwest Coast in the middle of the last century [331].

Definitions, Assumptions, and Hypotheses. — 1. In a society where wealth affected social position, an influx which was unequally distributed permitted greater differentiation along class lines [341].

2. Leadership emerged in response to the contingencies of the contact situation, when men were needed to deal with the whites, to direct warfare and defense, and to take charge of the new religious sects [341-42].

Methods and Techniques. — Field work August to September, 1946. Historical reconstruction.

Data. — While the kinship system was the primary matrix of social relations in pre-white times, an incipient class structure did exist, with the siap, distinguished by wealth and descent at one end of the scale, and the slave at the other. There were few of both classes. Both intra-areal and extra-areal warfare were much rarer before than after the arrival of the whites. The limitations of the economy were such that destruction of food or artifacts was not present in the Skagit potlatch. The first trading posts were several days' journey from Skagit country, but they played an important part in altering the economy of the Indians, encouraging a shift in their hunting habits. Formerly the people had been hard-pressed to secure enough food throughout the year; they could now place some reliance on food supplies obtained from the whites. It was this factor of dependability that encouraged the Indians to enter into trade.

New sources of food and new techniques for obtaining food which they learned from the traders tended to stabilize the economy and to make possible more frequent public displays. Other exchange commodities, such as blankets, also made it possible to have more potlatches, and more elaborate ones, than ever before. An accompanying development during this period was an increase in warfare, due to the introduction of the gun, and the breakdown of the old social controls. It is important to note that contact with other Indians as well as whites was important in shaping the direction of change; there were new incentives to visit and form alliances with others at some distances.

The effects of these changes upon Skagit social organization were pronounced. Distinctions in social rank began to be more marked, since new sources of wealth were now available. There were differentials in the way the new resources were distributed, such as nearness to the white settlements, etc. An increase in the number of siap persons thus occurred, and with this a parallel one in the number of slaves who were obtained by capture and purchase-- both of which were facilitated during this period. These changes in rank were accompanied by the development of the institution of chieftainship, men who distinguished themselves as leaders in war, religion (e.g., new cults combining native and Christian beliefs and practices), trading, or a combination of these. The office of chief soon became firmly established.

Conclusions. — 1. Distinctions in class which already existed in this society became greatly emphasized under conditions of white contact [341].

2. Leadership emerged in response to the contingencies of the contact situation. It was based on types present in the old pre-white society, although both continuity from pre-white times and changes due to new conditions are apparent. The whites, in their insistence on setting up the office of chief, gave formal structure to what had been informal [341-42].

3. Attention to the effect of white contact on the political structure of other American Indian tribes would enlighten us as to how such structure

comes to receive formal recognition and as to how the old types of leadership alter under new conditions [342].

11. Dozier, Edward P. RESISTANCE TO ACCULTURATION AND ASSIMILATION IN AN INDIAN PUEBLO. AA 53, 1951, 56-66.

Purpose or Problem. — Some of the cultural manifestations which seem to have been accommodating devices fostering or maintaining the distinctive minority group (i.e., the Tewa of First Mesa, Hopi) are presented and examined and a working hypothesis concerning the possible cause of this situation is presented. Investigation of this phenomenon promises to reveal significant information on the dynamics of culture change [56].

Definitions, Assumptions, and Hypotheses. — 1. The Tewa migrant group resisted acculturation and assimilation through several accommodating devices. These were implicit cultural mechanisms which successfully turned a subordinate position into a dominant one while maintaining tribal distinctiveness [59].

2. Merton's "Self-Fulfilling Prophecy" is of relevance: by means of an unrealistic belief in their own cultural and psychic superiority, the Tewa have maintained a cultural uniqueness and turned a subordinate status into a respected and favored position [63].

Methods and Techniques. — A preliminary report on one aspect of a research project on culture change now in progress at Tewa Village. It is based on four months' field work on a predoctoral fellowship and will continue for another eight months.

Data. — The Tewa have lived with the Hopi of First Mesa for about 250 years. Biologically they are completely mixed; however, the matrilineal and matrilocal emphasis has enabled them to preserve their distinctiveness. Among the many myths and migration legends there is agreement that the Tewa came to assist the Hopi against the ravages of the Utes and to serve thereafter as protectors of the Hopi. Other groups also aided them, but none but the Tewa have survived as a distinct group.

Important cultural mechanisms for maintaining Tewa self-esteem are: (1) the curse which is supposed to have sealed knowledge of the Tewa language and manner of life away from the Hopi mind; (2) early prohibition of marriage with the Hopi. Elements which could be incorporated within the Tewa pattern without endangering cultural aloofness have been borrowed. Both the clan and the current kinship systems are in this category and have fostered the preservation of their distinctive way of life. Tewa ceremonial practices are carefully guarded from the Hopi; conversely, their ceremonies are believed to have efficacy only to the extent that they are not polluted by borrowings from the Hopi. There is also a difference in religious orientation — a greater concern with illness and physical well-being.

The Tewa are at present attempting to identify themselves as descendants of the Rio Grande Tewa—a recognized, respected pueblo tribe of New Mexico, and to ignore their Tano ancestry. This has significant implications [62]. The Tewa are always more friendly to strangers since they still consider themselves as such in an alien land—and have thus become closely attached to the Navaho, and liaison agents frequently between Americans and Hopi. This has further served to increase their dominance.

Conclusions.— 1. The cultural mechanisms developed by the Hopi Tewa to maintain distinctiveness and to secure a respected and favored position were successful [62].

2. Both the mechanism of the "self-fulfilling prophecy" and fortuitous circumstances were important in this transition.

3. Most significant among these fortuitous circumstances seems to have been the organization and the basic psychological orientation of the two cultures involved (e.g., the extreme anxiety of the Hopi on which the Tewa capitalized).

12. Eaton, Joseph W. CONTROLLED ACCULTURATION: A SURVIVAL TECHNIQUE OF THE HUTTERITES. ASR 17, 1952, 331-40.

Purpose or Problem.— A study of some of the factors related to the survival of ethnic minorities in America, in a community where in-group cohesion and cultural autonomy are preserved to a high degree [331].

Definitions, Assumptions, and Hypotheses.— 1. The Hutterite community is unusual at least with respect to its effectiveness in maintaining a social system relatively free of individuals who are neglected or who engage in severely antisocial acts against their own group or the larger American society [332].

2. Controlled acculturation is the process by which one culture accepts a practice from another culture but integrates the new practice into its own existing value system. It does not surrender its autonomy or separate identity although the change may involve a modification of the degree of autonomy. Controlled acculturation can be practiced only by a well-organized social structure. There must be recognized sources of authority. The presence of this practice is evidence that the culture has considerable vitality for growth and continuity despite the pressures for change to which it is making an adjustment [338]. The process of controlled acculturation cannot be continued indefinitely without ultimately resulting in more assimilation. In time, the changes may accumulate to bring about a major shift in values which could destroy the group's existence as a separate ethnic entity [339].

Methods and Techniques.— A multiprofessional research team under the direction of the writer, investigating the Hutterite reputation for social cohesion and peace of mind.

Data. — 8,700 Hutterites live in 93 communal hamlets in western United States and Canada, the descendants of about 50 families who settled there between 1874 and 1877. The variations in belief and practice between individuals, families, and colonies are not great, but are currently increasing; however, by comparison with American culture, they can be characterized as relatively uniform. Religion is a major cohesive force in this folk culture, which is an Anabaptist sect. Homogeneity is further enhanced by the high rate of in-group marriage. In their social life and value system they are much more resistant to change than, for example, in acceptance of up-to-date machinery; they are trying to preserve many of American rural reformation-period values and yet become part of the twentieth century.

The Hutterites have unusual features, some of which are of considerable current scientific and political interest: (1) A family with little more than procreative and affectional functions. Economic support, preparation of food, etc., are community responsibilities. (2) A communal system of sharing property and products of labor. (3) A high degree of security, both economic and spiritual. (4) A predominance of the primary-group type of social relationships. (5) Fertility is high, coming close to the theoretical level of fecundity. (6) There is a narrow range of prestige variations, leaving virtually "a classless society." (7) Integration around an absolute value system; the culture is "totalitarian" in that no major deviations from central beliefs and socially approved practices are tolerated.

Although the Hutterites have maintained such a social system for many generations, at present the pressure for change and assimilation is strong and growing. First, there is pressure from the outside from such persons as salesmen, government officials, teachers, and doctors; second, there is pressure also from the "inside." Hutterites, especially the younger age groups, are internalizing some of the values of their American neighbors; they want more individual initiative and they consider things regarded as luxuries by their elders to be necessities. The principles of communal property, of austere simplicity, and of self-sufficiency are slowly undergoing change; in the long view of history these changes may accumulate into a lot. Discriminatory practices from outside function to increase their in-group orientation. No pronounced tendency of individual demoralization is observed among the Hutterites; they are generally self-confident about their group membership.

New rules are usually proposed at an intercolony meeting of elected lay preachers and are intended to combat a specific innovation of some members, which some of the preachers regard as a violation of the unwritten mores. Adoption or rejection of the formal rule is by majority vote of all baptized males in all the colonies; what started as a violation may, thus, in time become a law.

Conclusions. — 1. What is distinctive about social change in this culture is its gradual nature and the institutionalized techniques that have been developed to deal with pressure for change in an organized fashion. Hutterites tend to accept cultural innovations before the pressure for them becomes so great as to threaten the basic cohesiveness of the social system [334].

2. The largest number of austerity rules are concerned with clothing, which is the visible symbol of their autonomy. The forces of assimilation are most easily brought to bear against this form of symbolic segregation. Changes in dress often symbolize the beginning of a major break with the past [336].

3. The factors responsible are no doubt numerous, but controlled acculturation is one of them. This controlled process of adjustment to social change gives group support to the Hutterite individual who must adjust his way of life within the conflict of his own sixteenth-century Anabaptist peasant traditions and the twentieth-century American values of his environment. Hutterites are making the adjustment both as a total culture and as individuals while maintaining a considerable measure of functional adequacy and self-respect [340].

4. Their voluntary isolation from outside social influences has been all the more effective because their way of life is well integrated around a strong value system [333].

5. While the Hutterites differ in many important respects from their American neighbors, they are sufficiently Euro-American to make cross-cultural comparisons with predominant patterns in the United States and Canada somewhat more directly relevant than are the studies of American Indians. The Hutterites also show us telescopically how much we have changed and reveal some of the possible consequences of these changes for personality [333].

13. Gillin, John, and Raimy, Victor. ACCULTURATION AND PERSONALITY. ASR 5, 1940, 371-80.

Purpose or Problem. — In the present paper our interest is centered primarily on that type of acculturation found among preliterate peoples of non-European culture who are subject to the impingement of European or Western civilization. We wish to direct attention to two aspects of the study of such situations which have received scanty attention to date, namely, the effects of acculturation upon certain aspects of personality organization and upon the patterns of social participation of individuals [371]. Likewise, we wish to offer a few suggestions looking to the formulation of the results of such investigations in a manner which lends itself to ready and accurate comparison with all types of acculturation situations, regardless of the specific character of their respective components. The principal object of these suggestions is to indicate some means for the more precise statement or measurement of what we may call the "degree of acculturation" [371].

Definitions, Assumptions, and Hypotheses. — 1. Acculturation may be regarded as referring to those processes whereby the culture of a society is modified as the result of contact with the culture of one or more other societies [371].

2. The theoretical necessity of studies of the individual in acculturation situations is implicit in the view that culture does not exist apart from human beings and that neither the individual personality structure nor the cultural configuration can be meaningfully understood except by reference to the other [372].

3. Three outstanding manifestations of acculturation are usually apparent in all situations: (1) changes in cultural equipment or "material culture"; (2) changes in social organization and in the patterns and incidence of the participation of individuals in group life; and (3) changes in personality structure and organization [372].

4. Despite the limitations inherent in a mere listing of organized groups introduced into cultural life, it appears that such a listing, followed up by an analysis of the degree of integration of these introduced groups into the total social system, is an important lead to an understanding of acculturation [374-75].

5. With respect to personality changes under acculturation, it seems plausible to us that a quantitative, reliable, and meaningful method may be found by focusing attention on one of the subjective aspects of the personality, "the concept of the self," and using objective case-study methods to corroborate or revise the investigator's estimate of the degree to which acculturation has progressed in several significant differentials of personality [375].

6. The differentials selected in this study might be quite inapplicable in another study of different cultures, yet we feel that the quantitative results using other differentials would be quite comparable [377].

7. Since we are attempting to arrive at a quantitative method for appraising acculturation, it is necessary to consider the importance of statistical significance. This method of obtaining a "typical individual" should not necessarily be considered as representative of the group, but rather as a statistical referent to be used in comparing one acculturating society with another or in comparing the same society with itself at different periods of time [379].

Methods and Techniques. — Field work with the Lac du Flambeau Band of Chippewa in northern Wisconsin using historical materials, etc. The organized groups were studied and separated into three categories depending on whether they were introduced in recent times from other Indian tribes or whether they were introduced from white society. A sample of individuals was studied and their participation in the various categories tabulated. Judgment was subjective, and checked against opinions of well-informed members of the community. A five-point rating scale on each of the three differentials provided an acculturation index by adding together the arbitrary value assigned to each point on the scale.

Graphs and Charts. -- Number and Percentage of Indian Adults Participating in Nonaboriginal Groups (Illustrative) [376]. Acculturation Index for the Two Individuals [380].

Data. — The objections and limitations in the use of other manifestations of acculturation as indices are pointed out. In the work with the Flambeau Band, three differentials were distinguished: (1) The concept of the self as Indian or white. (2) The concept of self as Christian or Midewiwin. (3) The concept of the self as a regular wage earner or as a hunter and fisherman.

Conclusions. — 1. The appraisal of acculturation by the above method may have several advantages over the usual descriptions of changes which have taken place in a society. (1) The general approach and specific methodology is directed at persons, the carriers of culture, and not at constructs of culture in the abstract. (2) Quantitative descriptions may be arrived at which are always relative to the two cultures under consideration. Thus, the quantitative results may be used in comparing any two studies regardless of the specific culture or specific behaviors involved. Also, the same society may be studied at different periods of time and compared on the same basis regardless of changes in the dominant society. (3) The method provides a fair lead to acculturation without long-continued observation of the individual [380].

14. Gillin, John. ACQUIRED DRIVES IN CULTURE CONTACT. AA 44, 1942, 545-54.

Purpose or Problem. — To present an example of the way in which a combination of psychological and anthropological approaches may be utilized in the explanation of the results of acculturation [546].

Definitions, Assumptions, and Hypotheses. — 1. Anxiety: anticipation of punishment, aroused by stimulus situations of punishment, which have been productive of punishment. Any aroused drive is punishing until it is relieved. Anxieties may be based on this sort of punishment. Anxieties are specific to certain drives, innate and acquired [545].

2. A stable society in the period before intensive acculturation begins usually possesses patterns which on the whole are adjusted to its conditions [546]. Every culture contains certain "normal" anxieties which are inculcated in the members of its society and which motivate certain customs necessary for social control and for religious behavior. Two types of customs reduce anxiety: (1) positive (action); (2) negative (refraining from action).

Methods and Techniques. — Field work: 1938 to 1939. Attempt to expand Hull learning principles to a cultural level. General parallels are cited and specific reference is made to the Chippewa of Northern Wisconsin.

Data. — Hull learning theory postulates anxiety as an acquired drive which plays a role in habit formation and behavior. A change of conditions in any particular of culture may produce a situation in which performance of the old patterns is either no longer rewarding or actually becomes punishing. Conditions which may be changed as a result of continued contact with a society possessing a different culture are as follows: (1) natural environment (affects methods of exploitation); (2) social conditions (fluctuation in size of population; changes in education, etc.); (3) cultural conditions (introduction of new artifacts, buildings, means of communication, etc.) [547].

All or any of such changes as the above may lead to the development of new acquired drives. This period of adjustment to new patterns and a different sort of integration or configuration is characterized by confusion and instability. Constantly recurring changes of conditions will result in random behavior, cultural disorganization, and apathy and withdrawal, since no positive ways of reducing anxiety are available.

Chippewa cases in point are noted. Life-history materials indicate that not only anxieties related to the basic economic necessities of life were experienced by this group, but status anxieties as well.

Conclusion. — (Implicit.) There is great value in combining psychological and anthropological techniques with respect to analysis of acculturative situations. Particularly helpful are certain concepts which have grown out of Hull's learning experiments at Yale. It is possible to expand these concepts so as to render them applicable to the broader panorama of culture as a whole, even though they were arrived at in experiments dealing with individual subjects.

15. Goldfrank, Esther S.   HISTORIC CHANGE AND SOCIAL CHARACTER: STUDY OF THE TETON DAKOTA.   AA 45, 1943, 67-83.

Purpose or Problem. — (Not made explicit.) A brief explanation of the fluctuation of in-group and out-group violence among the Teton Dakota in the nineteenth century.

Definitions, Assumptions, and Hypotheses. — 1. The social character comprises only a selection of traits— the essential nucleus of the character structure of most of the members of the group which has developed as the result of basic experiences and a mode of life common to that group [67].

2. To understand the changes that have occurred in the Teton social character over the last century and a quarter, it is necessary to examine the structure of the society at different periods of time [68].

3. In-group violence is a useful criterion for evaluating tensions [68].

Methods and Techniques. — Historical reconstruction (based on inadequate materials, according to the author).

Data. — Today (1943) the Teton Dakota (population 14,000) live on reserves in an inhospitable physical environment. Poverty is prevalent. Ambition is considered a threat to the community, with the past sanctioning the inertia of the present. The advent of the horse revolutionized Plains Indian life. It created a surplus economy in which the horse became the object of highest value. Social advantage was a direct result of wealth although, theoretically, opportunity was open to all. The Oglala, with the most horses, also had the most in-group violence. Motivations noted for in-group violence are: (1) jealousy, (2) suspicion, (3) personal rivalry, (4) use of liquor (cf. Bunzel and Zingg and reinforcement of the pattern of social behavior), (5) introduction of the horse, (6) fur trade.

After 1850 tribal solidarity seems to have resulted in a diminution of in-group violence and a great increase in out-group violence. Nevertheless, competitive elements within the culture remained. (Examples: (1) child-beloved, (2) Huka, (3) buffalo ceremony, marked by competitive gift-giving, (4) entrance into men's societies, based on wealth, (5) purchase and sale of society paraphernalia.) Group solidarity reasserted the co-operative trends present in Teton culture. (Examples: (1) favorite-child rivalry muted, (2) gift compensation for life-taking, (3) confederation, (4) extensive expansion of kinship ties.) The tribe was broken in 1877 and immediately in-group violence broke out once more.

Conclusions. — 1. The tribal solidarity of the Teton, demonstrated in 1860 to 1870, grew from political necessity. Today's solidarity derives from economic scarcity.

2. The church has been the greatest solace to the tribe. The Teton eagerly accepted the "golden rule" holy days, gift exchange (Christmas), feasting, hospitality, etc. These features parallel aboriginal values. Competition now finds its place only in the rodeo.

16. Goldfrank, Esther S. THE DIFFERENT PATTERNS OF BLACKFOOT AND PUEBLO ADAPTATION TO WHITE AUTHORITY. ICAP 29th, 1952, 74-79.

Purpose or Problem. — To indicate how the imposition of white authority affected two very differently structured American societies: the Blackfoot—more particularly, the Blood of Alberta, Canada—and the Pueblos of the Southwest—more particularly, the Zuni of New Mexico [74].

Definitions, Assumptions, and Hypotheses. — 1. The acculturative process is a continuing one, and an understanding of its dynamics is equally important in any of these situations. It is necessary to define the basic structures as accurately as we can, not only at the moment of study—a method that has led to some highly questionable generalizations—but through time. Due consideration should also be given to the natural environment, the technological levels, and the organizational devices influenced by all these factors [74].

2. Comparative study of Oriental civilization has shown that large-scale water control, which demands co-operative effort, requires a directing center outside the family and local community [75].

Methods and Techniques. — (Not indicated.) A comparative study of two societies affected by white contact.

Data. — Until 1877, when the Blood were put on a reservation, they had been buffalo hunters and horse raiders, traveling in bands. Stability depended essentially on the personality of the band leader and on his ability to satisfy his followers' need for security and, to a lesser extent, for prestige. There was little in this fluid and fragmented social structure to encourage the development of a stable and learned hierarchy of power, an agency to maintain tribal tradition and to enforce law. The disappearance of the buffalo increased the Blood's dependence and made the Canadian government their only reliable "generous giver." Under white pressure, native authority became more stable and more centralized than it had ever been before. Due to their familiarity with techniques of large-scale wheat farming and stock breeding, they were not pressed to enlist by the Canadian government. Increasingly here the trend seems to be toward more democratic forms of organization.

Pueblo society was very different. The Spaniards found the Pueblo peoples living in permanent villages and depending on agriculture with well-defined theocracies. It was the priests or their official representatives who organized public co-operation and maintained discipline. The Pueblos have always been called "conservative." In effect, this means that where new patterns have been accepted either freely or under pressure, they have been fitted into the old theocratic frame. On the surface the modifications in living seemed significant. Actually, the centers of power were essentially unchanged. The constant pressure of recent events seems to have deepened hierarchic schisms. Zuni G.I.'s found Army life a welcome release from the strict controls of Pueblo society. On their return, while they no longer behaved like traditional Zunis, the old method of control worked. The hostility against the whites hardened as white influence became stronger and their programs more attractive. The story of the veterans of the Blood is a short one.

Conclusions. — 1. Whatever the area of activity among the Pueblos, community co-operation is not left to chance. It is therefore not surprising to find the Pueblo system of child training, taken as a whole, the most coercive, and the Pueblo system of adult control the most pervasive and severe, of all North American tribes [75].

2. Such different histories of contact have significant implications for practical policy makers and theoretical anthropologists [79].

3. In a world where the advance of civilization has meant the harsh and ruthless treatment of native peoples, the theory of cultural relativism has much to recommend it. But it should be asked, can we underwrite two sets of values, one for the so-called "higher" civilizations and another for the primitive societies? Should we accept and at times even bolster authoritarian trends when they appear in native communities? True, such trends may be completely indigenous and, as is frequently the case, the communities under these conditions may be well-ordered. But cultural integration has its negative as well as its positive aspects [79].

17. Hallowell, A. Irving. ACCULTURATION PROCESSES AND PERSONALITY CHANGES AS INDICATED BY THE RORSCHACH TECHNIQUE. Rorschach Research Exchange, VI, 1942, 42-50.

Purpose or Problem. — To report some results obtained by the Rorschach technique which show the effects of acculturation upon the personality of the Berens River Saulteaux, comparing samples of the general run of individuals in two locales where the population shows marked differences in acculturation [42].

Definitions, Assumptions, and Hypotheses. — 1. If there are intimate connections between the organization of personality and culture patterns, it follows that changes in culture might be expected to produce changes in personality. Consequently, one of the problems in the study of acculturation concerns the relation between acculturation processes and personality changes [42].

2. The assumption that the group differences revealed in the Rorschach results are connected with the difference in the degree of acculturation in these two locales [42].

Methods and Techniques. — Use of Rorschach test. Statistical techniques.

Graphs and Charts. — (1) Average number of Determinants; (2) Average Time per Response of Inland and Lakeside Subjects.

Data. — The Rorschach samples represent two intermediate segments of a cultural gradient that, at one extreme, can be thought of in terms of Indians who have given up practically all their native culture (Lakeside group) and, at the other extreme, of those who have been even less affected by acculturation than the Inland group.

Conclusions. — 1. Since 81 percent of the best-adjusted individuals come from the Lakeside locale, as well as 75 percent of the maladjusted individuals, this seems to indicate that the conditions set up by the acculturation process precipitate vital problems of personal and social adjustment for the individual. Some individuals make excellent, even superior adjustments, others fail to make as good adjustments as under the old regime, where the range of adjustment as represented by the Inland group is more restricted [47].

2. We must conclude that acculturation has proved a more favorable matrix for the personality development of Saulteaux women than for Saulteaux men, temporarily at least [48].

3. Some of these deductions might be made without the benefit of the Rorschach technique, but it would be difficult to demonstrate them without a method of investigation through which the actual personal adjustment of concrete individuals could be evaluated. This should indicate some of the possibilities offered by the Rorschach technique as a tool in the investigation of personality changes in relation to acculturation processes [48].

18. Hallowell, A. Irving. VALUES, ACCULTURATION, AND MENTAL HEALTH. AJO 20, 1950, 732-43.

Purpose or Problem. — 1. To show how the modifications of the personality structure of the Ojibwa Indians under the very acute pressures and frustrations of acculturation highlight the integrative role of the value system of their native culture in relation to the functioning of the total personality [733].

2. The crucial question remains: Are there, or are there not, any significant differences in personal adjustment to be observed if, by using an optimum concept of integrative behavior as a measure, we examine the consequences of one set of culturally embedded value systems as compared with another [733]?

Definitions, Assumptions, and Hypotheses. — 1. We should not close our minds to the possibility that, from the standpoint of the psychodynamics of human adjustment, the value systems of different societies may vary significantly as more or less efficient instruments in the molding of personalities that are fully capable of functioning at a level of mental health. We may ask: What is the role of different systems of value with reference to the general level of personality adjustment which is found in different groups [732]?

2. It is possible that some light may be thrown on this question by the anthropologist. First, by studying systems of value in different societies from the standpoint of total personality integration and functioning viewed in the perspective of our knowledge of mental health. Second, by studying more closely the psychological aspects of acculturation, particularly the effects of the social readjustment involved with reference to personality structure and value systems. One of the questions that arises here is how far and under what conditions the value system of one culture is transferable to individuals in the process of acculturation in order for it to become an integral part of their life adjustment [733].

Methods and Techniques. — Accounts of seventeenth- and eighteenth-century observers, to obtain a psychological base line; field work among levels 2 and 3 of acculturated groups, including comparison of Rorschach records; Rorschach and TAT samples of the most acculturated groups (level 4).

Data. — A general description of the values held by individuals of the four levels of acculturation (see article by Caudill). It can be said that the main binding force of aboriginal Ojibwa institutions was to permit individuals seeking a common central value to achieve it without too much human interference from without; no one could ultimately escape moral responsibility for his conduct since departure from approved behavior provoked withdrawal of supernatural support in achieving the Good Life. Other individuals, however, could interfere with its achievement through sorcery. Consequently, there was a general suppression of overt hostility accompanied by a surface amiability between people who were actually wary of one another. This was especially true among men, since women ordinarily did not practice sorcery. But covert hostility, especially in the form of gossip and slander, was rife. The relationship to nature was essentially passive; a basic principle was the obligation to preserve the equilibrium of nature.

Conclusions. — 1. The acculturation process at Flambeau has reached a level which presents a situation in which we find the personality structure of the Ojibwa in the process of breaking down rather than undergoing reintegration in any new or positive form. Overt aggression appears to have replaced the covert aggression that formerly existed in the form of sorcery. The inner core of their nonintegrative adjustment may be characterized as regression in the sense of a kind of primitivation, not literally falling back upon actual modes of earlier behavior, but a frustration of maturity. Thus the Flambeau Indian represents what is, in effect, a regressive version of the personality structure of the Northern Ojibwa [742-43].

2. It would appear that the role of values as a factor in an integrative level of adjustment has implications beyond this particular instance. Values have an important significance with reference to the whole problem of mental health and the conditions necessary for its fulfillment [743].

19. Hallowell, A. Irving. OJIBWA PERSONALITY AND ACCULTURATION. ICAP 29th, 1952, 105-12.

Purpose or Problem. — If contact between peoples with different modes of life may sometimes be the source of basic cultural changes, it seems reasonable to inquire whether, as a result of the same set of readjustments, a parallel reconstellation occurs in the typical psychological characteristics of the people so affected. In other words, are changes in the modal or typical personality organization of the individuals of a society a necessary and intrinsic part of the readjustments that acculturation implies, or can acculturation take place under certain conditions without radical changes in personality structure [105]?

Definitions, Assumptions, and Hypotheses. — 1. If there were no personal readjustments in the lives of the people concerned, there would be no subsequent changes observable in the culture pattern of any group. Consequently, one of the crucial questions is the nature, character, and psychological depth of such readjustments. A comprehensive understanding of the acculturation process, therefore, demands an approach that is psychologically, as well as culturally, oriented [105].

2. It seems reasonable to conclude that personality structure, once established, is highly resistant to change. If this is so, then one of our fundamental hypotheses might be that the modal personality structure of a society would be expected to persist until conditions arose that enforced some change. Thus, while all acculturation may be said to involve some psychological readjustment in the sense that new habits must be learned or new attitudes or values acquired, there is no reason to assume that such readjustments in themselves involve the psychological core of the personality. The crucial question is how far one language can displace another, a new world view or new religion be acquired, moral values be reconstituted, and sweeping changes in technological and material culture take place without deep and penetrating psychological effects [106]?

Methods and Techniques. — Use of projective tests such as the Rorschach and TAT. Establishing of a psychological base line, from the accounts of early observers. Field work among the Ojibwa of the Berens River and among the Ojibwa of Lac du Flambeau.

Data. — The Ojibwa Indians represent an ethnic group with a common cultural background now exhibiting varying levels of acculturation. None live in a purely aboriginal state and few if any have been completely assimilated to Western culture. In between these extremes, four levels of acculturation can be distinguished on a more or less impressionistic basis. Level 1: The Ojibwa of certain parts of Western Ontario; they represent the least acculturated groups, whom no one has studied. Level 2: The Inland Ojibwa (Saulteaux) of the Berens River; some are not Christianized and speak no English. Level 3: The Lakeside Indians of the Berens River. These people are Christianized, use no aboriginal dwellings, and no former rites or ceremonies persist. Some speak English; about 20 percent are mixed white and Indian. Level 4: The Lac du Flambeau Ojibwa (Northern Wisconsin). About 80 percent are mixed white and Indian. Practically all speak English; the children attend an excellent government school; some have radios, etc. This group was in close contact with whites during the summer tourist season. Nevertheless, a small group still cling to the Midewiwin.

The generalized characterological picture that emerged from the accounts of observers in the seventeenth and eighteenth centuries was that of a people whose typical characteristics were: emotional restraint, stoicism, fortitude under torture, the inhibition of all expression of aggression in interpersonal relations, a culturally demanded amiability and mildness. This pattern of inhibition and anxiety was coexistent with an absence of superordinate authority; but despite the minimal power of chiefs, open conflicts were rare. However, covert slander was a constant expression of the inhibited aggressive impulses. There was also an institutionalized means of covert aggression—sorcery. Since there were no highly institutionalized agencies of reward and punishment, individuals functioned in terms of a highly internalized conscience.

Comparison of the Rorschach protocols of levels 2 and 3 indicate that no radical psychological shift had occurred; there is an essential continuity in personality organization, with some modifications indicating that some serious, if not actually neurotic, strains were developing within the personality structure. If we compare the Indians of level 2 with those of level 4, we obtain a psychological picture in which the latter represent a regressive version; many psychological characteristics which in the north bear a positive relation to the adjustment of the individual have been exaggerated to the point where they assume a negative role at Flambeau. Apparently the acculturation process at Flambeau has generated a situation in which the personality structure is breaking down rather than undergoing reintegration on any new or positive level.

There has been no real substitute for the aboriginal type of religious belief in a superficially acquired Christianity; thus, even now a few Indians at Flambeau cling to the Midewiwin, which epitomizes this aboriginal outlook. In actual behavior, the tremendous incidence of drunkenness and juvenile delinquency on the Flambeau reservation may be interpreted as a sign of the psychological struggle which many individuals are experiencing in reacting to the apathy which the paucity of inner resources, brought about by this regression, produces. They are attempting to survive in a situation which as yet offers them no culturally defined values and goals that they have really made their own and which have become psychologically significant for them. Their advanced stage of acculturation as externally viewed is thus deceptive.

Conclusions.—1. It seems reasonable to infer: (1) that the personality structure of the Berens River Indians, considered as a whole, approximates an aboriginal type of modal personality structure which was characteristic not only of the Ojibwa but of other Indians of the Eastern Woodlands; (2) that a considerable degree of acculturation could occur (i.e., up through level 3) without any radical change in this personality structure; (3) that in level 3 the readjustment demanded in the acculturation process did produce stresses and strains that were leading to certain modifications in the modal personality structure; and (4) that, while some individuals, especially women, were making an excellent social and psychological adjustment, there were other individuals, men in particular, who were much less successful [109].

2. There is a considerable body of evidence that all points in the same direction—a persistent core of psychological characteristics sufficient to identify an Ojibwa personality constellation, aboriginal in origin, that is clearly discernible through all levels of personality yet studied. For this reason all the Ojibwa referred to are still Indians in a psychological sense. While, culturally speaking, they appear more and more like whites at "higher" levels of acculturation, there is no evidence at all for a basic psychological shift in a parallel direction. Thus, terms like "borrowing" and "diffusion," which are entirely appropriate to describe the acculturation process in a cultural frame of reference, are misleading and inappropriate if the acculturation process is viewed from the standpoint of a psychological frame of reference.

3. All the evidence points to far more complicated psychological processes than those which have led to the acquisition of the culture traits which were used as empirical guides to different levels of acculturation. Consequently, descriptive facts of this order are no direct index to facts pertaining to personality adjustment and personality organization [111].

4. From a psychological point of view the Flambeau Ojibwa are not yet acculturated enough, in the sense that while contact with the version of Western civilization available has enabled them to acquire innumerable culture traits, so far at least it has not provided the psychological means that might implement a satisfactory basis for personal adjustment [112].

20. Hawley, Florence, and Senter, Donovan. GROUP-DESIGNED BEHAVIOR PATTERNS IN TWO ACCULTURATING GROUPS. SJA 2, 1946, 133-51.

Purpose or Problem. — In an area such as New Mexico, where three large culture groups meet, the daily problem of their misunderstandings throws into relief the differences of group-designed behavior patterns [133].

Definitions, Assumptions, and Hypotheses. — The continuity of personal reactions throughout the life of the individual depends fundamentally upon integrative systems which are built up during his period of growth and provide the value concepts typical of his own culture. As long as minority peoples can remain relatively isolated and self-supporting, the patterns of thought and reaction learned in childhood will meet the background requirements of adult life. But when persons trained in one culture move into a social and economic position dominated by persons of another, the differences between the two generalized basic personality structures or reaction patterns create conflict and confusion for both groups [134].

Methods and Techniques. — Presentation of a general problem, based on considerable field data.

Data. — The Spanish Americans, or Manitos, most of whose ancestors settled in New Mexico in the seventeenth and eighteenth centuries, readily accepted American citizenship in 1847, but have remained isolated in mountain settlements until recently.

Among both Pueblos and Manitos, disciplines are lenient during infancy and childhood, but severe during later youth. This early permissiveness fosters development of an initially sound nervous system, but anxiety concerning witchcraft, economics, and occasional difficult situations of acculturation appears during youth and adulthood. Manito culture invites the rise of the individual, yet controls it through relationships of dependency within the extended family and social approval within the village; the modern Manito's thinking reflects the medieval Catholic background of his culture. In contrast, the Keresan social system, even under a dictatorial religious hierarchy, is fundamentally democratic in operation.

The surprising similarity in degree of standardization of Spanish-American village customs to those of the Pueblos results from the original transfer of the stabilized social system of feudal Europe to the isolated area of New Mexico, an isolation that continued for 250 years. The position, duties, and customs of a Spanish-American individual depended upon tradition, within which was incorporated an emphasis upon class stratification and the personal leadership of outstanding individuals from the prominent families. The pueblos, however, were small units which maintained a precarious existence within a hostile world by means of close integration of the individual into the group, democracy within the group, and subservience of all tendencies toward personal individuation in favor of group conformity and a united front.

Conclusions. — The condition of acculturation of Spanish Americans and of Indians in the present period sets both in a new environment, one in which geographic and cultural isolation are continually being reduced and in which, consequently, security and even self-preservation depend upon a new orientation of the individual into the larger generalized American pattern. In this process superficial change of language, habits, and economics may appear to take place with relative ease, but lingering beneath these, as basis for a long period of transcultural confusion and resistance, remain the ancestral modal group-designed behavior patterns transmitted at home by precept and by example during the primary childhood period of each individual's orientation [150-51].

21. Hawley, Florence. AN EXAMINATION OF PROBLEMS BASIC TO ACCULTURATION IN THE RIO GRANDE PUEBLOS. AA 50, 1948, 612-24.

Purpose or Problem. — To point out that the most confusing problem to an individual involved in an acculturation situation is the difference between the relative position of institutions in his own culture and in the new, plus the changed orientation of his position in relation to the institutions of that new culture [613].

Definitions, Assumptions, and Hypotheses. — The position of any institution in relation to degree and type of integration with the other institutions is a paramount factor in its effect upon the whole culture construct and upon the basic personality of the culture bearers [613].

Methods and Techniques. — Exposition by means of a series of constructs.

Graphs and Charts. — Five diagrams in which the social systems of Keresan, Tewan, Spanish-American, and American towns are presented schematically.

Data. — The author describes, and represents diagrammatically, the differences between configurations of two Pueblo social systems (Keresan and Tewa) and those of the Spanish-American villages and Anglo towns in which the Indian attempts to establish himself when he renounces native life. In the eastern Keresan village, the individual is peripheral to the structure, but has close interdependent relationships to clans and societies. In the Tewa system, the individual makes a more direct approach to his universe through the moiety. As in the Keresan system, all institutions are closely bound into a whole. In Spanish-American or Anglo towns, the individual is represented as at the center of the system. In the latter, he is faced with the problem of orienting himself directly to a number of unrelated institutions, unfortified by the extended family of the former. An Indian who moves into this system experiences a constriction of his universe and a feeling of aloneness.

Conclusions. — The Pueblo Indian finds acculturation in the larger society difficult because of a contrast to his customary orientation toward institutions. Since the Tewan is more directly related to his central institution, the moiety, than the Keresan is to his complex institutional system, the former is able more easily to comprehend the American situation.

22. Heinrich, Albert. SOME PRESENT-DAY ACCULTURATIVE INNOVATIONS IN A NONLITERATE SOCIETY. AA 52, 1950, 235-42.

Purpose or Problem. — An account of the genesis, among a group of rather isolated Eskimos, of several innovations that depart widely from anything that existed previously in the culture of these people. The field of interest is the local ivory-carving industry, carried on for the purpose of sale to the tourists and not for home consumption [235].

Definitions, Assumptions, and Hypotheses. — All the types of art form under discussion have resulted from the impact of recent borrowing on stable, long-established patterns of Eskimo art and technology. No really new type of art object has been taught to the Eskimos of Diomede, nor have any innovations been made that are not foreshadowed by previous designs and techniques. On the other hand, no type of ivory carving carried on by the Diomeders before the coming of the white man has been incorporated unaltered into the modern carving industry [236].

Methods and Techniques. — The data were obtained while in the employ of the Alaska Native Service during 1944 to 1948. Details of the various objects (innovations) are presented. Three figures.

Data. — Unlike most other regions of Alaska, the island of Diomede does not produce any cash crop that can be sold to the outside world in a relatively unfinished form. But they have an abundant supply of ivory and, with the encouragement of middlemen interested in profits, Diomede has developed ivory carving into the industry that supplies it with most of its cash income. The objects, in the carving of which the Eskimos have achieved a very high degree of skill, are of five main types, with two classes of figurines. Three of these innovations came recently enough to enable their beginnings to be discovered. A series of circumstances is listed which may constitute the chain of cultural borrowing which led the innovator to conceive of the idea of producing the inlay bracelet by incorporating the well-established bracelet-making trait with the similarly well-established Eskimo geometric design. Its survival is shown to be due to its economic value.

Conclusions. — The present ivory-carving industry of Diomede is radically different and much more highly developed than the ivory carving that existed there twenty-five years ago. This is a response to the stimulus provided by the prestige value of money in the contemporary American culture; it was brought about apparently by gradual and consistent refinement of techniques and also by a series of innovations, none of which sprang out of a void. Each was a conspicuous new development of a previously existing trait, a regrouping of traits, a synthesis of existing traits with borrowed traits, a readaptation of a trait, or a combination of two or more of these. For each innovation there was a demand, even though it was only vaguely defined, before it occurred; and each invention was accepted and achieved significance, or was rejected and neglected, not on the basis of its intrinsic value, but on the basis of whether or not it met with public approval.

23. Herskovits, Melville J. THE SIGNIFICANCE OF THE STUDY OF ACCULTURATION FOR ANTHROPOLOGY. AA 39, 1937, 259-64.

Purpose or Problem. — (Implicit.) To trace the historical development of anthropological research and theory antedating acculturation studies and to offer the view that acculturation studies serve in the study of cultural dynamics and cultural interaction as well.

Definitions, Assumptions, and Hypotheses. — Acculturation comprehends those phenomena which result when groups of individuals having different cultures come into continuous firsthand contact, with subsequent changes in the cultural patterns of either or both of the groups [259].

Methods and Techniques. — Traces the development of anthropological theory and demonstrates how acculturation studies fit into two major disciplinary emphases.

Data. — The historical background of anthropological theory out of which acculturation studies have grown is presented: (1) Reaction against evolutionism. (2) Period of overgeneralization in Europe and historical reconstruction in the United States. Both ignored relationship between culture and its "human carriers." (3) Reaction to historicalism. These studies concentrate on interrelationships and integration in culture, with the time depth ignored [260].

Herskovits points out that the interests of some researchers engaging in work among the American Indians and New World Negroes as well as those of some European Colonial administrators foreshadowed acculturation studies. He stresses that culture change should be studied from a cultural base line. The student of acculturation has at his disposal materials of historical documentation [262]. The anthropological "purist" need not object to culture-contact studies merely because they may be confused with "applied" anthropology [264].

Conclusions. — 1. Acculturation studies bridge the gap between cultural dynamics of historicalism and functional studies [261].

2. For a basic understanding of the problems which concern the nature and mechanisms of culture and the relationship between a culture and its carriers, the approach through studies in acculturation, by permitting greater control over data under analysis and by allowing the anthropologist to employ the laboratory of history, must play a role of ever-increasing importance in anthropological research.

24. Herzog, George. PLAINS GHOST DANCE AND GREAT BASIN MUSIC. AA 37, 1935, 403-19.

Purpose or Problem. — An inquiry into the relation and stability of musical form and function in the Ghost Dance songs of the Plains Indians, where we have music associated with a movement definitely known to have arisen in a different setting [403].

Definitions, Assumptions, and Hypotheses. — Practically all songs found associated with the Plains Ghost Dance are so closely related to each other that they must be conceived as representing a distinct type, forming an integrated "style" of their own. This style can be traced to the Great Basin [403].

Methods and Techniques. — Based on transcriptions, some made by the author himself; analysis of various Plains and Great Basin songs.

Graphs and Charts. — Tabular analyses of the songs; eight examples of melodies.

Data. — Comparison of all the Plains Ghost Dance melodies available revealed in most of them a striking similarity amounting to a uniformity of style. The prevailing structural patterns on the Plains are different from that of the Ghost Dance. That the merging of patterns (of Plains with Ghost Dance patterns) did not progress further may be due in part to the exceedingly quick spread of the Ghost Dance movement and to its brief life in many places. In a few tribes, hand-game music became permeated with the new pattern (bearing out Dr. Lesser's suggestion that the Ghost Dance represented a revivifying and reintegrating force in Pawnee life).

Conclusions. — 1. The music of the Plains Ghost Dance represents a case in which what may be called a tribal or regional style became diffused, as the style of a special ceremonial complex, with continuous distribution, through processes which we know from historical evidence to have been exclusively those of culture contact. While this illustrates the great persistence with which music can adhere to a ceremonial or other complex, it also indicates that similarities of style between two disconnected regions would not necessarily imply that some elements of the population itself were to be considered related. Nor would they necessarily prove long and very intimate culture contacts [417].

2. The Ghost Dance songs may also have a bearing on the question whether, and how far, formal features of a musical style can be explained or derived from their function in social life. The present finding is negative [417]. The example under discussion suggests that musical form can weather amazingly well the vicissitudes to which it is exposed, although if it comes from a fundamentally different cultural setting, or from a bygone age, it may receive in the new setting a new life and meaning.

25. Hill, W. W. THE NAVAHO INDIANS AND THE GHOST DANCE OF 1890. AA 46, 1944, 523-27.

Purpose or Problem. — The question of why the Navaho failed to embrace a doctrine found palatable by so many Indian peoples of North America [524].

Definitions, Assumptions, and Hypotheses. — An alternative possibility for the rejection of the 1890 Ghost Dance by the Navaho other than Barber's "life was integrated around a stable culture pattern" (or lack of social and spiritual "deprivation") is that a covert pattern or configuration, deep-seated in the unconscious psychology of the people, acted as a barrier to the diffusion of a complex embraced by most of the tribes in western United States [524-25].

Methods and Techniques. — A short deductive essay based on re-examination of data gained in earlier field work; includes an appendix of statements by various Navaho about the 1890 Ghost Dance.

Data. — While no direct participation did occur, this messianic development reached the Navaho and the impact registered profoundly on the minds of the individuals of the period. It is clear that they were thoroughly cognizant of all the essential elements of the Ghost Dance of 1890. Accounts appended to the article show Navaho attitudes toward the Ghost Dance to have been ones of extreme ambivalence and not based on benefits which the movement promised. The idea of acceptance or rejection was of minimum importance; the Navaho interest in the movement was a manifestation of anxiety concerning the return of the dead. The Navaho were frightened for fear this major tenet of the movement were true, in view of their extreme fear of all connected with death and the dead.

Conclusions. — 1. The lack of acceptance of the 1890 Ghost Dance among the Navaho resulted from the covert pattern (or configuration) of Navaho culture, and not from a lack of social and spiritual "deprivation" (as suggested by Barber).

2. Had the "economic" or "social integration" factors been compulsive, a selective element could have been expected to operate; the Navaho might gladly have embraced parts of the complex, while rejecting the tidings that the dead were to return. However, the compelling element for them was clearly their fear of the dead, so much so that all other tenets were infected by it, hence suspect and to be rejected [525].

26. Humphreys, Norman D. THE CHANGING STRUCTURE OF THE DETROIT MEXICAN FAMILY: AN INDEX OF ACCULTURATION. ASR 9, 1944, 622-26.

Purpose or Problem. — To indicate changes in the Mexican family in the United States.

Definitions, Assumptions, and Hypotheses. — 1. It is the contention of this paper that the changes in the structure of the family, under the impact of a new social and cultural environment, constitute a highly sensitized index of the process of acculturation [622].

2. A social structure is a system of culturally defined status roles which form a relatively stable nexus of subordinate and superordinate selves.

Changes in the structure will index what happens in the merging of cultures. However, adjustments of social structures to changes in the total culture do not occur automatically. When there is agreement as to the definitions of status roles in a culture, a social structure is stable, since duties and obligations accord with the roles which individuals must act out. Since we regard the family as the one in which the self-conceptions of those who occupy roles are most intimately related to one another, we believe it will reflect most truly the changing meanings generated by the larger culture [622].

Methods and Techniques. —Source of material not indicated; case material excerpts from various publications.

Data. — In general, the decline in status of the Mexican father, due to his failure to provide adequately for the family, has been so gradual that a lessening of respect was not accompanied by overt family conflict. The extent to which the father has continued to command respect is largely determined by the degree of assimilation of the nonpatriarchal American culture by the wife and children. A second facet of the father's role which has undergone change in Detroit is that concerned with the exercise of moral protection over the wife and female children. Most women accept this role; however, if the wife has assimilated American culture more rapidly than has her husband, she may use her knowledge to effect a reversal, from subordination to superordination, in family roles. This was most possible when the wife was considerably younger than the husband or was American-born. No distinct pattern is evident in a man's treatment of his wife's illegitimate children; the duty to care for aged relatives in some cases breaks down, largely a consequence of the wage system, which precludes such burdens. The less the assimilation of American culture, the greater the probability of the maintenance of the compadre role. Many things which for the parental generation were values of peasant Mexico, lie for the children in the realm of utilitarian symbols, concerning which choice may be exercised. The main recreational outlet of these people is the movies, and their main goal is the husband's regular employment in the "shop": in short, they have become functionally a young American working-class family.

Conclusions. — 1. As a result of the differing degrees to which they have acquired American culture and retained Mexican culture, the members of the Mexican family have changed positions relative to another within that unit. In general, the structure of the peon family in Detroit has changed in three ways: the status role and corresponding conception of self of the father has declined relative to that of the women and children; the wife has tended to retain her previous status-role position through the greater retention of Mexican meanings and understandings, although in some instances the wife has come to occupy a position of social superordination; the status role of the children has largely reversed itself, and this is particularly true for the oldest boy, who plays an entirely new role [625]. In Mexico, the status hierarchy in the family runs father, mother, son, and daughter, in that order, from high to low position. Four fairly distinct levels are apparent. In Detroit the positioning is decisively altered. The son has assumed a position about equal with the father, while the daughter has climbed at least onto the same level with the mother. Also it appears that the possible over-all range of status has been distinctly narrowed: this may be interpreted as a phenomenon of leveling out, or democratizing within the family [625-26]. Reorganization on a new level has not sufficiently advanced in the second generation to allow for the empiric construction of emergent and stabilized status roles.

2. It is evident that the dissimilar symbols and values possessed by each member of the family is largely a consequence of differential association of family members with Americans, of unlike participation in American culture, and of the dissimilar store of meanings originally carried by these individuals. These factors have given rise to discordant conceptions of self [625].

27. Kinietz, Vernon. EUROPEAN CIVILIZATION AS A DETERMINANT OF NATIVE INDIAN CUSTOMS: THE DELAWARE INDIAN BIG HOUSE CEREMONY. AA 42, 1940, 116-21.

Purpose or Problem. — To give approximate dates to the addition or subtraction of the various elements in the Big House Ceremony and to show the activating force and directional factor to have been in contact with European civilization [117].

Definitions, Assumptions, and Hypotheses. — 1. The effect of European civilization on native Indian customs has not always been disastrous. In many cases it has even contributed or been responsible for features of Indian life which the Indians have considered as their own [116].

2. Many of the religious revivals and the militant programs of champions of Indian rights were coincident; both were the result of a feeling of resentment against white aggressions (particularly marked in the case of the Delaware).

3. The fact that there are many vestiges of the Delawares' original culture remaining is due in no small measure to the effect of recurrent revivals. The nature of the revivals was determined by the sort of influences that European civilization was exerting. With the Delaware, the effect of contact with European civilization was a stabilization of native customs [116].

Methods and Techniques. — Based on contemporary written documents and the writings of Harrington and Speck. Otherwise, sources are not indicated.

Data. — Encroachments of the whites on the domain of the related Delaware groups drove them farther west and contributed to their union for mutual protection. The efforts of the missionaries kept the attention of the Indians on religious subjects, forming separate communities of their converts, and thus engendering the opposition of the unconverted, who were fighting for the tribe's existence. One of the most effective methods of opposition was that of the native teachers, who preached a message similar to that of the missionaries but made it more attractive by incorporating the feasting and dancing customs instead of attempting to supplant them. Many of these restrictions and admonitions were later mentioned as being expounded in the Big House. Trends after 1762, the date of the religious revival led by the Delaware Prophet, indicate a formalization of the Big House Ceremony, modification of the length and frequency of the ceremony in recent times, and show its comparatively recent growth in importance. The last performance was held about 1924.

Conclusions. — 1. European civilization in contact with that of the Delaware was unconsciously responsible for the integration of the Big House ceremony, the dropping and addition of many features, and then with continued contact the probable swan song of the ceremony [121].

2. While there were changes in early historic times, the greatest changes did not occur until evidences of treachery on the part of the whites. Their conservatism seems to have developed as a united front and shield against all aspects of European civilization. The two facts — that the Delaware received more than their fair share of abuse at the hands of the whites and that they are the only people to have developed the Big House — seem to be related [121].

3. By the mere act of introducing substitutes for native implements, the whites exerted an influence on the concepts of the Indians. The wooden bowls and fire drills used in the Big House now have a religious significance, and are supposed to represent the old ways.

28. Kraus, Bertram S. ACCULTURATION, A NEW APPROACH TO THE IROQUOIAN PROBLEM. AAq 9, 1944, 302-18.

Purpose or Problem. — To suggest a way of approaching culture from a diachronic instead of the usual synchronic point of view, and to illustrate the initial step in this approach [305]. A plea for the complete reworking of the Iroquoian material, archaeological and historical, from the point of view of acculturation (cf. Fenton) [302].

Definitions, Assumptions, and Hypotheses. — We can reasonably hope to know something about: (1) the native culture at the precontact level; (2) the surrounding contemporary aboriginal cultures and their influence on our particular native culture; (3) the various elements of the contact continuum; (4) the "noncultural" results of contact; (5) the changes in culture through acceptance of new, or elimination of old, culture elements; and (6) the total effect on the group of contact and resultant change. Without this minimum of data, we can hardly hope to accomplish much in studying acculturation [303-4].

Methods and Techniques. — A theoretical paper, concerned with establishing the possibility of acculturation studies of Iroquoian material, suggesting the methods by which this can be done.

Data. — Survey of the material indicates that the evidence that is essential for an analysis of the effects of white contact is incomplete. We have a fair knowledge of the precontact culture; documentary sources provide us with a good description of the historic culture, but they are not supplemented by reliable archaeological material. The documentary data are predominantly of a nonmaterial nature and hence cannot be compared with the prehistoric archaeological data which are largely of a material nature. There is evidence that the contact continuum was neither of a long duration nor intense; it was spasmodic and not really a continuum at all.

The gaps in our knowledge can, however, be filled. Reworking of the written records combined with careful archaeology will eventually reveal the material contents of the culture of the historic Neutrals, and the effects of white contact, such as it was, will then be observed. History has already recorded the fate of the Neutrals as a political entity; to what extent white contact was a factor in bringing it about is a question that must await further archaeological research.

Conclusions. — The possibilities for observing acculturation phenomena in the development of Neutral culture are by no means far beyond the grasp of the scholar. Other Iroquoian tribes offer much more evidence for the student of acculturation, having been much more fully documented, both archaeologically and historically (cf. Fenton's suggestion of the Seneca) [316].

29. Lee, D. D.　THE LINGUISTIC ASPECT OF WINTU ACCULTURATION. AA 45, 1943, 435-40.

Purpose or Problem. — To present some material bearing upon the falling into disuse of terms and grammatical forms as a result of white contact with the Wintu [435].

Definitions, Assumptions, and Hypotheses. — None stated.

Methods and Techniques. — Recorded ethnographic texts and conversations based on one informant exclusively. The data are admittedly meager. Many examples are included.

Data. — The focus of this paper has been little dealt with previously, as pertinent materials are often obscure. When a new trait was introduced to the Wintu, the language responded in one of three ways: (1) gave it a new

name; (2) gave it a name which had been previously applied to a similar trait; or (3) accepted the English name which went along with the trait [435].
Examples are offered, as well as a list of obsolescent words.

Conclusions. — 1. White culture has affected two types of change on the Wintu language: (a) It has caused the introduction of new words. (b) It has caused the loss of old words.

2. Under the influence of white culture, action in words is stressed to the detriment of observation, indicating that there has been a systematic change of attitude [438, 440].

30. Malouf, Carling, and Arline A. THE EFFECTS OF SPANISH SLAVERY ON THE INDIANS OF THE INTERMOUNTAIN WEST. SJA 1, 1945, 378-91.

Purpose or Problem. — To present reasonably detailed historical information dealing with the circumstances in which a particular system of slavery arose in sympathy with Spanish colonial practices [378]. Slavery as an institution was unknown to precaucasoid Ute. What, then, were the circumstances and conditions which encouraged slavery [380]?

Definitions, Assumptions, and Hypotheses. — Ethnological data indicate that the aboriginal Ute, untouched by the white man, was living on a low cultural level, restricted by a very rigorous and parsimonious environment. Human life had a low value and cannibalism was not unknown in times of dire stress. When Spaniards indicated their willingness to purchase or trade for slaves, the Indian, with little emotional aversion, was willing to provide the supply [380].

Methods and Techniques. (Implicit.) Library work. Historical study.

Data. — Slavery among the intermountain Ute, Paiute, and Shoshone was stimulated by a market opened by the Spaniards. There were many intermediaries between the ultimate household and the band from which the captives were seized. These included native Ute and Navaho, as well as Spanish Mexicans. The entrance of the Mormons into Salt Lake valley endangered the flourishing slave traffic. Slave sources were divided generally into two categories: those acquired in more peaceful pursuits, such as barter or exchange or in gambling bouts, and those acquired by force, such as capture or in warfare. Girls were especially desirable as they could be more readily conditioned to the domestic life of their masters. Values had already been established by the Spaniards when the Mormon pioneers arrived. Hunger seems to have been a very stimulating drive in the sale of children to whites or to the more prosperous Indians, such as Ute and Navaho. Children who were captives of the Indians were treated in a most cruel manner and were starved and beaten. The physical condition and appearance of the captive evidently played but a minor part in the bargaining between Indians and Spaniards. Both Mormons and Spaniards felt that they were improving the lot of the Indians by imposing their brand of religious ideology and moral values upon the captives. The Mormons, however, had the advantage of occupying the same territory as the bands which supplied the captives. Their military power was likewise greater than the Spaniards'. What is most important, however, is that the Mormons did not intend to perpetuate slavery. With this policy in mind, together with a superiority of military power, slavery in the intermountain West was doomed. The most striking result of Spanish slavery was the development of bands of raiders which preyed upon the weaker bands in their vicinity. In Walker's band there was introduced human sacrifice and the burial of humans with the bodies of notables. While the practice was extremely brief in the history of the Utes, it does give some indication of the extent of changes wrought upon Ute society after the Spaniards entered the area [389-90: Summary].

Conclusions. — 1. Two points of general anthropological interest develop in this material: first, the imitation (diffusion) of this trait of Spanish colonial culture was subjected to a re-evaluation and adaptation to native culture; and, in consequence, slave labor among the Indians never assumed industrial proportions, slaves remaining chattels to be used in trade [378].

2. Slavery, to which Ute culture was already compatible, rendered it possible for those Indians with more effective accouterments (e.g., newly introduced horses, weapons, utensils) and organization to enhance their advantages while other groups became the hunted and tended to pass into obscurity [382].

31. Mekeel, Scudder. A DISCUSSION OF CULTURAL CHANGE AS ILLUSTRATED BY MATERIAL FROM A TETON-DAKOTA COMMUNITY; AA 34, 1932, 274-85.

Purpose or Problem. — To illustrate the kinds of problem involved in a study of culture from the viewpoint of processes [274-75].

Definitions, Assumptions, and Hypotheses. — A study of change as a process of culture inevitably leads to a consideration of the transformations in concepts, attitudes, values, surrounding those culture traits which are in flux. For people react not to object-in-itself reality, but to its symbolic derivatives. Therefore, only by an investigation of meanings current within a group can one approach an etiology of alterations in specific culture products [274].

Methods and Techniques. — Based on field work among the Oglala Teton-Dakota in the summer of 1930.

Data. — A concrete situation is presented showing the political organization of the present-day nomadic camps of a "fullblood" and "backward"

Teton-Dakota community. The differences with the past, that is, in the character of the group (it is now completely voluntary and therefore selective) and in its objective (today it is to attend a rodeo, while in former times it was to hunt), have to be kept in mind when making any comparison between the present and the past.

Some of the problems arising when culture is viewed from this angle of interest are: (1) Could this nomadic, restless tendency be called a culture trait which has been passed on from generation to generation? The question resolves itself into whether sufficient stimulus now exists to account for the nomadism, or whether these stimuli are merely re-enforcing some deep-set cultural tendency. (2) What forces are at work for and against the continuance of this nomadic summer life? Here, a division is made between exoteric and esoteric forces. (3) If the government enforces its ruling against Indians attending such rodeos, what form or outlet for summer restlessness would the Indians adopt, taking into consideration their contemporary culture patterns? (4) What can be postulated for the future change in organization on the basis of the present, should such group traveling persist? This involves (a) a study of existing variations and their etiology; (b) a study of the ancient organization in relation to the present; (c) a survey of the attitudes, concepts, and values held now by various factions and individuals toward specific traits. (5) If techniques be devised for answering this type of problem for the whole cultural content of a people, and be applied to many ethnographical areas, what would be the possibility of formulating laws of culture processes?

Conclusions. — In conclusion it may be wise to defend a study of culture process — especially from the viewpoint of change.

32. Mekeel, Scudder. THE ECONOMY OF A MODERN TETON DAKOTA COMMUNITY. YUPA 6, 1936, 3-14.

Purpose or Problem. — The study of the economy of a modern Teton Dakota community, that of the White Clay District on Pine Ridge Reservation, South Dakota [5].

Definitions, Assumptions, and Hypotheses. -- In order to evaluate the present-day economic behavior of a Dakota community it is necessary first to find out what master ideals were expressed in the ancient economy and what force they exert today [3]. Each culture holds and imbues its participants with a set of prime values which are expressed symbolically in the overt behavior of a community. The values upheld by a culture may be discovered by its conception of the Good Man.

Methods and Techniques. — Part of the material was gathered on field trips from 1929 to 1932, and from 1932 to 1933. The community studied is considered to be the most backward and to have the least admixture of white blood on the reservation. It contains about 930 Indians.

Graphs and Charts. — Map of White Clay Community, Pine Ridge Reservation [4].

Data. — The Teton were supposed to have had four virtues: Bravery and Generosity, Fortitude and Moral Integrity (the last two not so explicit in general application). These four virtues can be traced as ideals for all social institutions, ideals which were striven for in every context of the culture under any pretext. When first known to white men in the eighteenth century, the Teton were exclusively a hunting people, the buffalo being the main source of food supply and entering into every part of the culture. The loss of this animal proved to be a death blow to the culture. A hunting economy gave way to a parasitic existence dependent on United States government rations; native religion weakened and intertribal warfare ceased. As a result, the Teton men lost their traditional activities and along with them their chief paths to glory and prestige— warfare and hunting.

Three different strata exist in the present-day community: (1) those who lived the hunting life from the age of at least ten (all born before about 1865); (2) those who grew up during rationing by the United States government (those born between 1870-1900); (3) those who have grown up during the period of the relatively recent government policy of forcing the bodily able to provide for themselves. In this latter group, there is no genuinely eager anticipation of manhood; whatever adjustment is reached in the present reservation environment will be at best of a passive, listless sort. Farming has never appealed to the Teton Dakota, whereas the life of the cowboy caught their imaginations, and the transition to a farming existence is far from complete. This is due both to the quality of the land and to the lack of cultural interest in farming.

The leveling operation of certain social customs is very strong. Whatever money does come into the community is quite evenly divided by the functioning of many customs which, in their totality, virtually prescribe a state of socialism. This is one of the most characteristic features of Dakota culture. This society has founded its cardinal values on the release of wealth. The major configurations which express Generosity as an ideal and which make for an even distribution of goods are discussed under the headings of (a) hospitality, (b) give-away, and (c) giving of honor. The result of all this is that no man, however industrious, can get very far ahead of those about him and still remain an active member of the community. By the custom of hospitality, however, many families are kept alive. The most despised man, in the past, was he who was rich but did not give out his riches to those about him. The fact that this is as true today may possibly be in large measure due to extreme poverty. Farming remains an economic necessity but hardly a social asset. There are no institutions which create or uphold value in the act of getting a living. Remnants of old institutions still exist which maintained value in the hunting economy, but they were not picked up and given new form and new motivation. The farming pattern has never been grafted upon any of the native institutions such as the "bands," which today form "natural" communities, and as a result there is, with few exceptions, little enthusiasm for farming and little pride in being known as a successful farmer.

Conclusions. — 1. Economic activity within a well-integrated society exists not only for the mere perpetuation of its members but is inextricably woven into the social fabric. Insofar as the Teton Dakota raise gardens, they have made a change of vocation, yet if one examines their institutions one finds how little farming has entered into the social context [14].

2. Agriculture is apparently not securely rooted, since it does not enter the social patterns deeply; since the Indians feel that there is a last ditch—the government—for support; and since their patterns oppose economic accumulation. It is not an integral part of the social whole, coalesced by sentiment, reinforced by value, and maintained by prestige [14].

33. Opler, Marvin K. THE INTEGRATION OF THE SUN DANCE IN UTE RELIGION. AA 43, 1941, 550-72.

Purpose or Problem. — To provide a thoroughgoing treatment of the Sun Dance among the Ute.

Definitions, Assumptions, and Hypotheses. — 1. The Sun Dance is central in Ute religious organization [550].

2. Of a number of dances and rituals which functioned formerly, only the Bear and Sun Dances persist with anything like their original force. Since the latter is a borrowed complex, coming originally from Plains Indian sources, the modifications of this rite by the Ute must throw light upon the integration of their religion and upon its distinctive features [551].

Methods and Techniques. — Includes a typical and generalized account of the purpose and emotionalized religious effects of the Sun Dance; a fairly detailed picture of the entire ceremonial.

Data. — The ceremonial reached the Norther Ute from the Shoshoni around 1890, and in all probability originated with the Arapaho and Cheyenne. It arrived late in the reservation period, and there are many differences between the Ute ceremony and that practiced by many of the Plains tribes. The dream feature added to the fasting, thirsting, gazing complex was the most characteristic Ute trait. The individuality of shamanistic and semishamanistic behavior corresponded closely to the uniqueness of individual supernatural power among these people. From this point of view, unification of the performance was achieved by virtue of the fact that all the dancers sought rapport with the supernatural at the same time. The training of shamanistic powers under a medicine man is an old established method of attaining the ranks of a practitioner. Here the tutelary functions of the Sun Dance leader emerge as the main point of correspondence to the ordinary, everyday shamanistic guidance. In various other central religious doctrines of the Sun Dance we find solid agreement with older aboriginal beliefs. Further congruity with ancient Ute lore can be found in such rites as those associated with the Ute Round Dance and the Deer-Hoof Rattle Dance; the modern prayers for health and for crops and cattle, so prominent in the Sun Dance of 1937, may be viewed, therefore, as having ancient prototypes deeply rooted in the past.

Conclusions. — 1. When we have subtracted the ancient prototypes from the Ute Sun Dance of the present, little is left of formal elements beyond the spectacular trappings of a Plains ritual, and nothing remains in ideology which was not already there. In a real sense, the Ute never borrowed the Sun Dance of the Plains at all. Rather, they seized upon its existence, hastening to reinterpret it in the light of their own religious experience. Readapted to fit their own needs the ritual swung out of its Plains orbit and was reinvented to meet the needs of a Basin culture.

2. The introduction of the Sun Dance coincides with the lessening of interest in other dances to which there was an amazing correspondence. Because of this, the spectacular Plains rite provided suitable instrumentalities for the reaffirmation of essential ideological features in Ute religious organization with very little shift required in formal elements of the Plains pattern to effect the substitution [571]. The reason that this substitution of new dances for old was made at all may be that the Sun Dance welded together a number of former Ute conceptions and merged them together into a unified whole. Its introduction coincided with disease and disillusionment, threatening the very existence of this society; revivalistic cults were finding fertile soil.

3. Today, the Sun Dance's great success is in centralizing the more important aspects of religious life against the destructive tides of cultural oblivion.

34. Pritchett, John Perry. HISTORICAL ASPECTS OF THE CANADIAN MÉTIS. ICAP 29th, 1952, 249-55.

Purpose or Problem. — (Not explicitly indicated. Presumably as stated in the title.)

Definitions, Assumptions, and Hypotheses. — Métis is the term preferred for "half-breed." It does not imply contempt, that only the non-Indian part of one's parentage is of any value. It is also inaccurate, since after the first generation the proportion is likely to be anything but a half [249].

Methods and Techniques. — Historical.

Data. — The métis population of Canada was for a long time, especially in the region lying between Lake Superior and the Rocky Mountains, comparatively large and autonomous. This was due mainly to the character of the Canadian fur trade. Since these men went, unaccompanied by women, into a remote wilderness, where they remained in close contact with native tribes for long periods of time, it was inevitable that mixture of the two races should occur on a large scale. The historical circumstances were such that the French who entered into these relations, and their consequent offspring, were vastly in the majority. The peculiar needs of the fur trade made it practicable for the voyageur to settle down permanently in the Northwest; the rich soil and teeming game of the country made it quite easy, and for many years the scanty population and the isolation of the region put no barriers in its way. As long as the country in which they lived remained comparatively isolated, the métis continued to multiply and to become more race-conscious and autonomous. Arrival in 1818 of Catholic priests from Quebec made them more docile, but also strengthened their position as a group by infusing into them a unified culture and attaching them to the soil and to parish life more closely.

By the middle of the nineteenth, the métis were at the height of their prosperity and power; however, the coming of the settlers, the elimination of the buffalo, the railroad, etc., all helped to destroy the characteristic métis ways of life. In adjusting themselves to the new order these people of mixed ancestry were in many cases handicapped by their cultural background. Those who had largely adopted agriculture and a settled parish life continued to prosper, and many in time merged with the white population. Others, who had emphasized hunting or carting, tended to sink into comparative poverty. The purely nomadic groups, too, failed to adapt themselves to a changing world.

Conclusions. — (None made explicit. Might be assumed to be the differential adjustment of the métis.)

35. Quimby, George I., and Spoehr, Alexander. ACCULTURATION AND MATERIAL CULTURE. FA 36, 1951, 107-47.

Purpose or Problem. — An approach to the study of the complexities of culture contact by means of analyses of museum collections [107]. An analysis of a series of museum specimens reflecting the contact of the native cultures of North America and Oceania with Western civilization. This study deals with culture contact and diffusion not by plotting the distributions of culture traits, but by examining a series of specimens to determine the regular changes in form, material, use, and technological principles expressed in such specimens in the contact situation [107].

Definitions, Assumptions, and Hypotheses. — 1. A complete inventory of a primitive people's material culture from the time of initial contact with the West to the time of assimilation would provide an enlightening record of acculturation [107].

2. Any artifact can be described from several different points of view: form, the three-dimensional proportions of an object; the material of which it is made; the use or purpose to which it is put; and the technological prin-

ciples involved in its design and manufacturing. Meaning is significant, but difficult to ascertain [108].

Methods and Techniques. — Examination of museum collections, with photographic illustrations of "nonacculturated" and "acculturated" specimens.

Data. — The following categories of change (with illustrations of each) are suggested: A. New types of artifacts introduced through contact: (1) Objects imported through trade or other contact channels. (2) Forms copied from introduced models, but reproduced locally of native materials. (3) Introduced forms manufactured or decorated locally, partly from native materials and partly from imported trade materials. (4) Introduced forms manufactured locally from imported materials through the use of an introduced one. B. Native types of artifacts modified by contact: (1) Native artifacts modified by the substitution of an imported material for a local material that is inferior in physical properties or lacking in prestige. (2) Native artifacts modified by the substitution of an imported material whose use involves a different technological principle although the same end is achieved. (3) Native types of artifacts modified by the introduction of a new element of subject matter.

Conclusions. — 1. In the earliest stages of culture contact the cultural changes involve material things — artifacts. Most of the examples belong to the B-1 category (e.g., metal for stone or bone tools). In such modifications, utility, convenience, and prestige may be involved, in combination or separately [146].

2. In both major categories the form tends to show very considerable stability. Aboriginal forms tend to persist although imported materials may be substituted for native materials. Also, forms once introduced likewise show stability though local materials may be used. As long as the tool or weapon has the same use the form will naturally tend to remain stable. However, this does not explain why relatively nonfunctional aspects of form also exhibit stability. Culturally patterned motor habits also make for stability of form. The effect here is, first of all, the retention of tool types that fit the motor habits in question. In culture generally, form seems to be more stable than material or content. The question arises whether three-dimensional "form" is more stable than two-dimensional "form." We suspect that pottery shapes are generally more resistant to change than decoration [147].

3. We have not considered the particular stage in the acculturation process of the societies from which we have drawn our material. By and large our impression is that the time level from which our material comes is one generally prior to large-scale disintegration even though a long period of contact has been involved [147].

36. Ransom, Jay Ellis. WRITING AS A MEDIUM OF ACCULTURATION AMONG THE ALEUT. SJA 1, 1945, 333-44.

Purpose or Problem. — (Implicit.) Presumed to be the study of writing "as a medium through which acculturation may modify behavior" [338].

Definitions, Assumptions, and Hypotheses. — As a medium through which acculturation may modify behavior, writing tends to exert a restricting influence, though without doubt a powerful one. Because of its religious origins and the intensive use made of written Aleut by the Russian churches, it would logically be expected that the dominant effect which writing would contribute to the culture would be of a religious nature [338].

Methods and Techniques. — Ethnologic and linguistic material secured from 1936 to 1937, based on contact with the Umnak and Unalaska Aleut; supplemented by informant's data. Includes a bibliography of Aleut publications [344].

Data. — Aleut was transcribed into Russian phonetics in the nineteenth century and was used at first mainly in connection with the Russian Orthodox Church; it spread over considerable geographic area, to be taken up and used by thousands of native Aleut speakers. The attitude toward transcribing Aleut today is half-ceremonial, with writing being basically male property. Today, since use of the Russian language is dying out, a considerable distinction is made between the writing of Russian and Aleut, and writing English, which is the business language, the language forced upon the children in the village school, and the only language permitted within the government buildings. It is taught equally to boys and girls so that there is no particular prestige attached to the ability to utilize written English. The only background of printed literature readily available in Aleut consists of translations from Biblical works; this is thoroughly familiar to every adult male.

The complete abstraction of the written word as a symbol standing for a substantive or an act does not appear to be entirely clear to the Aleut writer. It seems to be a civilized manifestation of a dimly remembered Eskimo belief that every inanimate object possesses a spirit capable of performing acts detrimental or beneficial to himself. In this way he feels that he is able to control the external object to a greater extent than by physical manipulation [338].

Correspondence has been a unique development among the scattered Aleuts, and among many of them it has become highly developed. Private diaries are also common. Writing has also served as a medium of communication by flag signaling. The ability to write their native language has injected into the family of almost every native an atmosphere of study and a delight in the realm of the mind. Preoccupation with writing materials and books has caused the more pedantic of the Aleut men to set aside a corner, a chest, etc., as a "study" where such materials may be kept; around this revolves the circle of religious life, correspondence, and daily records.

Conclusions. — 1. Writing has had a profound psychological influence on the daily life of the inhabitants of the Aleutian Islands, wholly apart from contact with the whites. It is as if a new invention, acquired by cultural diffusion, had awakened a nonliterate people to a realization of what the wealth of their own culture could be made to mean to them and to their descendants [334].

2. It is the symbolic and mystical attraction of writing that has been the contributing factor in its spread throughout the region and the principal cause of its perpetuation throughout an ever-increasingly dominant American overlordship [334].

3. If one considers the frequent reference to the printed religious works in the daily writings of present-day natives, divorced from Russian rule more than two generations, it becomes evident that the whole acculturation process resulting from the introduction of writing and its acceptance by the populace must have been severely restricted for a long time to this field. The Christian religion then appears to have been the primary acculturation product directly due to the introduction of writing. This has curiously affected the aboriginal beliefs and customs in that present-day natives attempt to rationalize their beliefs by Biblical references concerned with what, to them, are similar cultural factors [339].

4. When the writing of Aleut diverged from the Church to include all community activities, and several organizations had their hands in formulating ukases and posting bulletins, opportunity was presented for the passage of the reading and writing concept out of pure religion to the field of generalized human activity. Once the idea of writing has been divorced from a restricted adherence to one field, the common man can make use of its potentialities. This the Aleut men have done [341].

5. If the first product of acculturation is religious furtherance, the second is social intercourse [341].

37. Reichard, Gladys A. THE NAVAHO AND CHRISTIANITY. AA 51, 1949, 66-71.

Purpose or Problem. — The lack of understanding which the Navaho Indians have of Christianity, constitutes a summary of cultural resistance.

Definitions, Assumptions, and Hypotheses. — 1. A religion should allay the individual's fears, give him courage, and, if he needs it, some hope of immortality. Navaho religion fulfills the first two of these requirements and leaves the last so abstract as to be neither a solace nor a fear [67].

2. Fear of the dead among the Navaho is the most universal of all reactions. This is a great stumbling block in the acceptance of Christianity,

whose divine hero is a man become god because he is risen from the dead.

Methods and Techniques. A discursive essay based on the author's considerable experience with the Navaho.

Data. — There are various Navaho beliefs (in addition to the two above) which are in opposition to those of Christianity. To the Navaho, reproduction is the ultimate human and supernatural purpose—a man cannot, therefore, be conceived in sin. Man is the greatest thing in the universal scheme, seeking to identify himself with the deity rather than humiliating himself through mortification, penance, or sacrifice. When he has disobeyed the rules he is faced with misfortune; this he sets straight by ritualistic correction. The test of wrongdoing is the way life runs; it is not concerned with life after death. Reciprocity, rather than "giving," is a value, as must be manifested in practice; none is theoretical; thus, co-operation and reciprocity are practical means of obtaining security. Other stumbling blocks to conversion have been the missionaries' denouncing of polygyny (which to the Navaho was a proof of economic success, of increased sense of obligation, and enhanced position through many offspring); bigotry and proselytism; sectarianism among the Christian missions; the attitude of reverence required by the Church—as opposed to the primarily enjoyable religion of the Navaho.

Conclusions.— 1. (Implicit.) The Navaho and Christian religions are antithetical in many basic factors. This has retarded Navaho religious acculturation.

2. The native wants only the material and not the spiritual part of "civilization." Thus any compromise must be made in the direction from "civilized" to native [71].

3. The white man, instead of ordering, must suggest, counsel, and advise, to make the Navaho understand (while adopting cultural gifts which, without understanding, are becoming lethal), by emphasizing good will, give and take—behavior quite easy for the Navaho to understand since it is the basis of his own system of life [71].

38. Rhodes, Willard. ACCULTURATION IN NORTH AMERICAN INDIAN MUSIC. ICAP 29th, 1952, 127-32.

Purpose or Problem.— To see what impression Western European music may have made on the native pattern [128].

Definitions, Assumptions, and Hypotheses.— 1. It seems reasonably sound to postulate the uniformity of musical styles as the end result of a long period of culture contact between tribes, sometimes related but ofttimes unrelated, within a given geographic area [128].

2. It is in the field of social dances that one must look for the phe-

nomena of musical acculturation. Since the esoteric music of sacred ceremonials must be perpetuated and performed with the strictest accuracy and fidelity and may be participated in only by those whose rights have been validated, there is little opportunity for individuality of expression [130].

Methods and Techniques. — Written during a field trip (not further indicated).

Graphs and Charts. — (1) Buffalo Dance Song; (2) Social Dance Song [131].

Data. — The contacts of North American tribes with Western European culture have varied in kind, duration, extent, and strength of impact, producing divergent results. The two institutions of white culture which have impinged most strongly and consistently upon the music of native Indian cultures are the church and the school with music functioning actively in both these institutions. During the past three or four decades there has developed a sizable repertory of social dance songs which have passed from tribe to tribe. Once they have achieved popularity and acceptance in the new environment, they become models for the making of more new songs. These songs show little or no evidence of the influence of Western European musical culture beyond a somewhat refined vocal technique, with some singers, and a tendency to regularize the rhythmic pattern and phrases. They remain distinctly Indian in style. The proportion of songs with English texts remains a small fraction of the native song literature. In the Southwest, where social and ceremonial institutions function comparatively undisturbed by the impact of white culture, cult music has perpetuated itself with a nice regard for its own individual style or type. In the Plains area, where social and ceremonial life function rather weakly in an acculturated pattern, there is to be observed a trend toward uniformization of musical style. Since the secular social dance song remains the focal point of musical activity for this area, the musical style is to be found in the song type.

Conclusions. — 1. The material presented here substantiates the theories of our American anthropologists (that individuals are the dynamic centers of this process of interaction) rather than that of Malinowski, who emphasized and exaggerated the role of the institution as an agent of culture change [132].

2. Primitive music is so inextricably bound up in a larger complex that it is practically nonexistent out of its functional context. This is one reason why the Ghost Dance, etc. disappeared without having wrought any change on Plains music. This confirms a conclusion made by Herzog that song types, especially with regard to form, are more rigidly and clearly defined than the so-called musical style of a tribe [132].

3. We are led to believe that the amount and extent of acculturation in North American Indian music are remarkably small in relation to that

which has taken place in other fields of native culture, both material and psychological. This reaffirms an observation made by Sachs that music is one of the most persistent culture elements to be found in primitive societies and the most resistant to change [132].

4. Regarding the influence of North American Indian music on our Western European musical culture, though this category of music is small in proportion to the total literature, it is large enough to give the impression that we have accepted more from the Indian than he has accepted from us [132].

39. Richardson, Stephen A. TECHNOLOGICAL CHANGE: SOME EFFECTS ON THREE CANADIAN FISHING VILLAGES. HO 11, No. 3, 1952, 17-27.

Purpose or Problem. — 1. To investigate some isolated communities which may in the near future experience rapid technological change. 2. To analyze the reasons for the local fishermen's hostility toward a particular technological change, namely, the introduction of the dragger for fishing. 3. To consider the process and effects of past technological change on the islands. 4. To predict the process and effects of the possible introduction to and adoption of the dragger by the islands' fishing industry [17].

Definitions, Assumptions, and Hypotheses. — (None made explicit.)

Methods and Techniques. — Descriptive paper, apparently summarizing a considerable amount of material collected with reference to the fishing industry and community relations on the islands. Otherwise not stated.

Graphs and Charts. — Number of persons in different occupations; number of persons in different fishing techniques; organizations processing fish; summary of some of the main technological changes on the islands, with results and reaction to the change reported by respondents.

Data. — The predominant form of subsistence on the islands is fishing. Some of the common characteristics of the fishing methods used on the islands are listed, as are the factors determining what type of fishing technique a fisherman will use. There is a strong tradition of co-operation in times of danger and loss which does much to mitigate the risks and dangers inherent in fishing. The success of the co-operative is largely attributed to the fact that the founder and leader is a trusted minister; other attempts to start unions for marketing have failed. Forms of organization satisfying other than subsistence needs are: a few associations (e.g., Masons); the church (Baptist and Church of Christ); government (trend away from local toward centralized). Education beyond the compulsory age generally results in boys settling away from the islands. Attainment of leadership positions is handicapped by the irregularity of working hours and the lack of contacts outside the islands.

During the last century, there has been a shift from a subsistence to an import-export type of economy, with a resulting decrease in the use of local resources and an increase in the use of imported finished goods bought for cash. The increase in what islanders feel are their material needs has been far greater than their ability to make and earn sufficient to cover these needs; they are now more dependent on the economy of North America. There has been increased mechanization and capital investment in gear per fisherman; an important consequence has been the technological displacement of manpower which has been compensated for by emigration and having smaller families. More money is leaving the islands in the form of taxes and there has been an increasing dependence on government payments; this has had important consequences for local leadership. Profits during the World War II period permitted a very rapid rise in the standard of living, and this period lasted long enough for the high standards of living to become well established.

Conclusions. — 1. Other consequences of the wartime prosperity were: (a) Increased concentration on fishing as a livelihood and an accelerated trend away from traditional activities, such as growing vegetables, which were a safeguard against economic depression in the larger economy. (b) There was an increase in education and training for occupations other than fishing, the children thus leaving the islands for good. (c) Workers in the small fish plants have had a relatively small increase in income, probably reinforcing the fisherman's dislike of becoming a wageworker [23].

2. The evidence summarized in this article supports the hypothesis that economic co-operation on the islands is carried out most frequently by the primary family and with close relatives, and that, outside of family co-operation, fishermen have little experience or skill in economic co-operation [21].

40. Rousseau, Madeleine and Jacques. LE DUALISME RELIGIEUX DES PEUPLADES DE LA FORÊT BORÉALE. ICAP 29th, 1952, 118-26.

Purpose or Problem. — (Implicit.) To explain the mixture of Christianity and paganism that exists among the American Indian tribes of Quebec [118].

Definitions, Assumptions, and Hypotheses. — There is room for another theory which better corresponds with the facts, that of a religious dualism: the two religions go alongside each other without intermingling, in the same individual [118].

Methods and Techniques. — Prolonged personal contact with the Mistassini Indians (Anglicans) and the Montagnais (Catholics). Otherwise not further indicated. Paper theoretical in orientation.

Data. — The Indian tribes in Quebec have been subject to white influence for three hundred years, but the contact seems to have been much more tenuous than previously thought. Most of the natives have retained their language; their relations with the traders are brief and purely of an economic nature; their stay in places where they meet missionaries lasts hardly a few weeks. For the most part, they remain isolated in their hunting territory ten months a year and have retained intact their ancient culture.

However, it cannot be maintained that the Christianity of these natives is purely a veneer; one finds, for example, Christian practices at great distances inside the forest where there are no missionaries. The Mistassini are attracted mainly in terms of ritual and daily practice; their motives for the acceptance of many of the trappings of Catholicism may well be esthetic rather than religious. These seem to have more attraction for them than the Anglican ceremonies; for many, Catholicism and Anglicanism appear as the same religion with minor variations. Pagan persistences are found less among the Catholic missions since the Catholic missionaries learn the language of the Indians and spend their lives with them.

Conclusions. — 1. The absence of more perfect contacts between missionary and population does not entirely explain the dualism that exists.

2. The rituals of shamanism and Christianity differ profoundly, but the primitive morality of the American Indian hunters is basically similar to that of Christianity — isolation in a hostile environment, independence, etc. [124].

3. The hierarchy of Christianity has certain similarities with the world of the spirits of the forest; while the fundamental dogmas hardly touched them [125].

4. Certain new elements of Christianity were advantageous, e.g., resignation, plus the promise of happiness after death [125].

5. There was no pagan hierarchy to oppose the invasion of the white religion [125]; their religion was individual and hence without weapons for combating a strange one.

6. Religious eclecticism does not go contrary to the spirit of the American Indian forest dweller [126]. Because of his difficult environment and the traditional philosophy resulting, the forest Indian is ready to accept a religious dualism that gives him a double assurance for the future.

41. Senter, Donovan. ACCULTURATION AMONG NEW MEXICAN VILLAGERS IN COMPARISON TO ADJUSTMENT PATTERNS OF OTHER SPANISH-SPEAKING AMERICANS. RS 10, 1945, 31-47.

Purpose or Problem. — To contrast the adjustment processes of three different groups of Spanish-speaking peoples within the United States [31].

Definitions, Assumptions, and Hypotheses. — 1. The gradient of stress is a major determinant in selection of adjustment mechanisms, even though the process of selection be unconscious [33].

2. Minority groups face three possibilities of adjustment: (1) They may attempt to maintain their original culture. (2) They may attempt quick acceptance of the new culture, the situation leading to eventual assimilation, although the path would be made rough by prejudice. (3) They may develop something foreign to both their ancestral culture and that of the present majority group [33].

3. It is through understanding the class system that one can predict today whether certain groups of Manitos will attempt to maintain their original culture or to accept the new as quickly as possible [35].

Methods and Techniques. — Part of a detailed study of Spanish-American villagers of New Mexico; comparative study with only sketchy information on the other two groups.

Graphs and Charts. — Fig. 1: Map showing location of the three groups [32]. Fig. 2: Relationship of Status Systems in New Mexico [36]. Table 1: Important Characteristics Delineating Manito Social Classes [45-47].

Data. — All three possibilities have been tried by different groups of Spanish-speaking peoples within the United States: the Manitos (or Spanish Americans of New Mexico), dividing themselves between the first and second possibilities; the border Mexicans, contenting themselves with the first; and the "Mexicans" or Pochos of southern California, attempting something of all three.

The personnel of the Spanish settlers of New Mexico included three broad classes: the upper class perpetuated what they could of the European background culture of their group; the middle and lower classes adapted the old culture to the exigencies of frontier life, satisfying most of their religious needs through the Penitente cult. After food and shelter, religion and family ties remained the two most important considerations for all classes. At present, three class systems exist in New Mexico: the system of the Anglo populace, the system of the Manitos within the state as a whole, and that of the Manito villagers.

The socialization of a Manito child during infancy and childhood is accomplished with less stress than for Anglo children; the adolescent, however, comes into full collision with the stress of changes necessary to acculturation, plus the frustrations and adaptations necessary because of intercultural prejudice. So far, such overt aggression toward the majority group, as zoot-suit gangs, has not occurred among the Manitos because actual power in the affairs of the state rests in the hands of their elders. For upper-class young people, accustomed to Anglo mores through long contact, adjustments are much easier than for the other status groups.

The Pochos of California look to Mexico for their cultural cues. The distinctions which they make within their own people are primarily those of class status. California offers less opportunity for the "Mexican" to rise; the significant cultural expression which arises from the feeling of oppression and frustration is seen in the defiance of the zoot-suit gangs.

The border Mexicans, or Tejanos, are not as frustrated by inequalities as the other groups. The pattern of the patrón system is common, with Mexican laborers considering orders given by the Anglos as entirely legitimate, while resenting orders by other Mexicans. In this they are expressing an objection to class distinctions among themselves but acceding to class difference between the two ethnic groups; theirs might be characterized as the peon attitude. The upward-striving individuals in this group are the ones who suffer especially from the inequalities in their position.

Conclusions. — 1. The sociological problem of the Manitos might be summed up as that of two racially and culturally opposed groups, each feeling itself to be actually the dominant group. The Anglo is looking at his position from the point of national and international power, the Manito from the viewpoint of former state control, now descended merely to small regional dominance. The point primarily is that of confusion between concepts of "dominant group" and large "majority group." The approximate equality in present population and consequently in political power of the two groups within the state itself aggravates the tendency toward friction but allows the minority group enough power, especially in politics, to compensate to a large extent for other stresses [40].

2. Among the California pochos, discrimination and segregation, coupled with the large proportion of individuals of Mexican descent within the area, is responsible for the tendency to place a high value upon their Mexican and racial characteristics [42]. The gang movement is based upon psychological problems and is an attempt to achieve distinction by refusing to copy the ways of either the Mexican or the English-speaking groups, a nonadaptive trend of definite anarchistic tones. This is the extreme result of the minority paranoid complex. The trend is Dionysian [42].

3. The war situation will do more for acculturation than otherwise could have been accomplished in many years. Returning soldiers who have seen the opportunities of the outside world will not all be content to settle on a strip of poor land, and their standards of living will have raised beyond those of the old subsistence level. Their experience with Anglo language and customs will provide them with a new advantage in competing with their fellow citizens. Fewer will attempt to maintain their original culture intact when the stresses of change have been eased [44].

42. Shimkin, D. B. DYNAMICS OF RECENT WIND RIVER SHOSHONE HISTORY. AA 44, 1942, 451-61.

Purpose or Problem. — To record the achievements of the Wind River Shoshone who, lacking any one guiding genius, still gained a decent adjust-

Definitions, Assumptions, and Hypotheses. — It is the ordinary, intelligent people who saw the problems besetting their folk and solved them as best they knew how, who have woven the basic threads of history [451].

Methods and Techniques. — Historical reconstruction.

Data. — Direct relations between French trappers and the eastern Shoshone, which began in 1801, changed completely the tribal contacts of the Shoshone as well as supplied them with goods. In addition, the mixed-bloods were to become extremely influential in the future. Peace with the whites continued as a result of the increasing importance of the leadership of Washakie after 1842; this coincided with the decline of the fur trade and the entry of an agricultural population. Following this period of Shoshone power, prosperity, and independence, there was a good deal of misery, with the Arapaho entering their reservation, the buffalo decreasing, etc. Marked cultural changes coincided with this period.

The elements of such change originated from three sources: the whites, other Indians, and the Shoshone themselves. The whites introduced education and religious influences. The loans from other Indian groups came in part through introduction by outsiders, but largely as the result of deliberate quests for new values and new institutions on the part of the Shoshone themselves. Unfriendliness with the Arapaho did not prevent contacts and borrowing. The Ghost Dance and Peyotism were introduced at about this time. Internal modifications among the Shoshone were numerous and important, with new societies founded on the Crow pattern; the dances characterizing the new societies were mixtures of old Shoshone, Crow, and new features. In their relations to Christianity, the Wind River Shoshone very generally adopted much of the essential moral outlook of that religion, stressing worship, humility, good will to men. This permeation of Christian ideology led not only to participation in the church but to profound reorientation of the Sun Dance. A differentiation, however, arose between Christian ideals and forms. Personal dislike of missionary leadership and the desire to maintain their worship themselves led to an early turning of the emotions from church worship principally to Peyote, with formal Episcopal membership rarely relinquished. The immaterial nature of Christian deities also led occasionally to complete rejection.

It is important to note that no elaborations took place in the Shoshone Ghost Dance. Within this period of change the roles of needs and personalities seem very clear; it is probable, too, that factors of personal animosity were weighty in excluding the Ghost Dance as a mechanism of change. The stress upon psychic unity and good will in the Sun Dance and Peyote cult of today, as well as the excessive concern with illness in all of the modern institutions, seem to be the result of the bringing together of a heterogeneous group of people which tended to split into bitter factions once evil days fell on them.

Conclusions. — 1. The geographical position of the Wind River Shoshone, which exposed them to many streams of influence, contributed to a great fluidity of culture and the choice of many cultural alternatives. As a result, the possible roles of individuals and the drives animating them have always been great [461].

2. The openness of the Shoshone to innovation after 1875 seems to have been the result, partially at least, of the collapse of their values and of their great physical distress. After 1906, when a new culture had recrystallized, new elements were not so readily accepted. Consequently, it appears that, with the increasing total adjustment of the community, the creative role of the individual in Wind River Shoshone culture has declined once more [461].

43. Siegel, Bernard J. SOME OBSERVATIONS ON THE PUEBLO PATTERN AT TAOS. AA 51, 1949, 562-77.

Purpose or Problem. — In analyzing the strong valuation of collectivism combined with a strain toward individualism at Taos, the writer proposes to examine four variables as they have continuously operated in the more recent culture history of the pueblo and as they continue to operate today [565].

Definitions, Assumptions, and Hypotheses. — 1. Four conditioning and interdependent factors are most germane to assessing culture change at Taos: (a) Communications; (b) population increase; (c) subsistence economy with respect to land and agriculture, wage earning, and property rights; (d) patterns of authority and leadership.

2. There is considerable evidence to support the hypothesis that the dominant form of interaction in any one of the primary institutions tends to be generalized through the others [575].

Methods and Techniques. — The data were gathered from informants at Taos. The author notes that Lasswell and Parsons have studied ceremonialism as a source of information on the strength of individualistic tendencies; he himself pays greater attention to demographic and economic facts, using as an index of behavior the amount of time persons spend at various kinds of activities [564].

Data. — 1. Communication with white culture has been frequent and easy; most members of the pueblo speak Tanoan, English, and Spanish. 2. Population has increased 125 percent since 1890. 3. The amount of irrigated land has remained fairly constant. The population makes little more than half its living from agriculture, and engages in an increasing variety of occupations for wages or profit. Private ownership of land and houses exists side by side with common, pueblo-owned property. 4. Five case histories reveal strong individual drives toward economic enterprise; the fact that these are largely "plans" reveals the inhibiting effect of patterns of collectiveness and of the authority of the Taos elite (the elders).

Conclusions. — 1. (a), (b), and (c) (Definitions, Assumptions, and Hypotheses) are factors conducive to the development of individualism at Taos; these are counteracted because (d) the patterns of dominance and submission prevail: old over young, males over females, and guardians of sacerdotal knowledge over novitiates. Few direct inroads have been made in this institutional configuration, and the authoritative ideology which supports it continues to educate the young in those habits of nonassertiveness so characteristic of the Pueblo world view [575].

2. The incipient factionalism noted at Taos might be used as the starting point for a comparative study of emergent factionalism [577].

44. Slotkin, J. S. JAZZ AND ITS FORERUNNERS AS AN EXAMPLE OF ACCULTURATION. ASR 8, 1943, 570-75.

Purpose or Problem. — To provide an illustration of R. E. Park's thesis (that continued contact between two groups leads to eventual assimilation) in the development of jazz, which reflects the increasing contact between Negroes and whites in the United States [570].

Definitions, Assumptions, and Hypotheses. — (None are made explicit other than as stated in purpose.)

Methods and Techniques. — Discursive; historical tracing of the problem.

Data. — An historical outline of the development of jazz is presented. First, a stereotype of Negro music which had little relation to the real thing was developed in the coon song of the minstrel show (1830-90); the simpler aspects of Negro musical rhythm were then taken over in ragtime (1891-1914), followed by the diffusion of Negro harmonies to produce the blues (1914-17). Finally, as a result of more intimate contact, most of the features of Negro music were taken over through the medium of hot jazz, which, in turn, has now been modified by white music. Thus, in the nineteenth century, white musicians took over a few characteristics of Negro music which they adapted to the tastes of the whites, but in the post-World War I period, not only had whites developed an understanding of Negro popular music which they adopted but, conversely, the Negro idiom has been affected by West European music through the influence of white jazz musicians.

Conclusions. — (Implicit.) In this instance, continued contact between the two groups has led to eventual assimilation, both groups being affected.

45. Speck, F. G. ALGONKIAN INFLUENCE UPON IROQUOIS SOCIAL ORGANIZATION. AA 25, 1923, 219-27.

Purpose or Problem. — To describe an instance where the actual process of change from one type of economic life was accompanied by a corresponding social alteration [219].

Definitions, Assumptions, and Hypotheses. — Tribal groups living side by side will influence each other according to the environmental situation, not necessarily according to their respective levels of development.

Methods and Techniques. — Information gathered from elderly Iroquois informants. Data on Algonquin custom apparently of a general nature, from the literature.

Data. — After 1720 a band of Iroquois (Mohawk) and an assortment of Algonquin Indians were in residence together on a mission at Oka; each group retained its own language and social identity. The Oka Iroquois, until recently, practiced hunting and trapping in addition to agriculture (the traditional basis of Iroquois subsistence). Iroquois men owned both hunting and agricultural lands (matrilineal inheritance of land characterizes Iroquois bands). These exceptional traits are commonly found among Algonkian tribes and, in addition, specific customs relating to punishment of trespass and game conservation, practised by the Oka Iroquois, closely parallel those of the Algonquin.

Conclusions. — Specific similarities between Iroquois and Algonquin customs relating to subsistence technique and social organization indicate that at Oka the former group modified their traditional ways in borrowing from the latter group.

46. Spindler, George Dearborn. PERSONALITY AND PEYOTISM IN MENOMINI INDIAN ACCULTURATION. Ps 15, 1952, 151-59.

Purpose or Problem. — To summarily discuss selected aspects of the social and psychological functions of the Peyote cult in the processes of Menomini culture change, and to define a close relationship between cult-defined behaviors and psychological process that appears to suggest the identity, under certain conditions, of what have been called personality and culture [151]. The interest has been in the relationship between adaptations in personality structure and adaptations in the overt objective aspects of social life [151].

Definitions, Assumptions, and Hypotheses. — 1. Membership in the Peyote cult is a special variant of a transitional acculturative type [151]. Members share with all Menomini in transition the common experience of loss of group identity, conflict between cultural directives and the roles patterned by them, and deep disturbance of the self, but despite this the cult represents a systematic deviation that distinguishes its members from the amorphous and unorganized mass of transitionals that have few, if any, clear-cut group identifications [156].

2. The Peyote cult should represent, psychologically, a systematized and narrowly defined species of transitional type. In short, the systematic deviation apparent in overt aspects of behavior within this group may be expected to appear, likewise, as a systematic deviation in personality type. This, it is suggested, will be true, regardless of variability in other life experience, including early child training. The intensity of the shared and symbolically supported systematic deviation, it appears, may be such that all other factors, past or present, tend to be overridden [156].

Methods and Techniques. — Use of a schedule of sociocultural indices to isolate and define the sociocultural variable, and the Rorschach to define the psychological variable. Statistical techniques; participant observation; interview materials and personal documents. Based on fifteen adult male members of the Peyote cult.

Data. — The four acculturative categories are as follows: (1) the least acculturated Medicine Lodge and Dream Dance group; (2) the acculturationally transitional levels (including the Peyote cult); (3) the most acculturated level with lower socioeconomic status; and (4) the most acculturated level, with elite socioeconomic status.

Christian symbols are apparent in the material structure and paraphernalia of the cult, but the basic conceptions and premises are native-oriented. The ultimate declared purpose in taking peyote is to acquire the power with which it has been invested by the "Holy Spirit." In order to attain this power, humility and concentration are required in keeping with the traditional Menomini approach. They are accompanied, however, by feelings and declarations of guilt; another difference is that the intense concentration during the Peyote meeting is not only concentration upon the nature of the power to come to the individual, but also upon the personal self and its conflicts. Curing and visions occur, the latter only infrequently in full-blown form — with detailed imagery and content particularly significant to the person. Usually this happens at the time of conversion; in it are always a sense of guilt, conflict, and deep anxiety— the sinner being saved.

Every one of the fifteen most active male members, during childhood at least, had experience with a way of life turned toward the old culture as well as extensive experience with Western culture.

Conclusions. — 1. To the individual, the cohesive in-group support of the Peyote cult is attractive because it gives him a social body with which he can identify. It not only gives him personal security but resolves for him the intense conflict he feels between the internalized compulsives of the old way of life and the values and modes of satisfaction in Western culture— for in ritual, premise, and in-group position in the reservation's social structure, the Peyote cult is a unique rationalization of the two culture complexes [155].

2. There are fewer differentiations between the least acculturated and the most acculturated levels than between the least acculturated and the Peyote group, despite a unity of cultural experience during the early years of life shared by the persons in the last two categories. There is also less intragroup variability among the Peyote members than within any other group excepting that of the least acculturated [156-57]. (Based on Rorschach data.)

3. All of the transitional Menomini tend to be differentiated by virtue of the degree to which the less-form-controlled responses using color tend to dominate. This represents the breakdown of rational control over the outward-oriented emotional responses. Social disorganization reflected in individuation and dislocation is most logically accompanied by psychological disintegration and regressive tendencies, and this is the case here [158].

4. The Peyote cult members represent, as a group, a systematic deviation socially and psychologically, and this is so irrespective of variation in early childhood experience. The implications are significant for the relationship between what have been called personality and culture, for here the two seem practically identical [158].

47. Stewart, Omer C. SOUTHERN UTE ADJUSTMENT TO MODERN LIVING. ICAP 29th, 1952, 80-87.

Purpose or Problem. — A preliminary report on the adjustment of the Ignacio group as it has progressed since Opler's study [80].

Definitions, Assumptions, and Hypotheses. — Indian adjustment is conditioned as much, if not more, by the attitudes and behavior of the majority group as it is by their own efforts [80].

Methods and Techniques. — (Not indicated. Presumably field work done in the area.)

Graphs and Charts. — Map of Southern Ute Indian Reservation, 1942 [81].

Data. — The community of Ignacio has a population of approximately 1,500 people, including about an equal number of Southern Ute, Spanish Americans, and Anglo-Americans. In spite of a birth rate twice as high as the national average, the Ute population has increased only slightly since 1920; the Spanish Americans in Ignacio have had by comparison a large and steady natural increase during this period, even though their general economic position has been considerably lower. This is felt to be a sign of the incomplete adjustment of the Southern Ute to modern American culture, as is also their economic position and their political participation. The Ute apparently lack the motivation to strive more diligently on the land. Although the Indians trade in the town and go there frequently, they do not participate in the political life of the town. While Ute children seem to be able to get along well in the public school, the majority of the Indians prefer to avoid active association with Anglos and Spanish; thus, they vigorously opposed and succeeded in stopping the consolidation of the Indian school with the public school.

Various objections to Opler's statements are made, as for instance that the average family displays a good deal of co-operation in agricultural labor; that the majority of families are rooted to the farms; that the Ignacio Ute show a better economic adjustment to modern living that the Ute Mountain Indians. Stewart states in this connection that the Towaoc Ute, in spite of their opposition to all government aid and direction, have learned cattle raising, which fits their environment, whereas the Ignacio Ute have been unsuccessful. He points out that one obvious difference between the two groups is the amount of governmental assistance offered and accepted.

Conclusions. — 1. There exists a cultural pattern among these Indians of getting by as easily as possible [83]. A number of people believe that Ute lack of energetic drive to "get ahead" results from the old ration system and the policy of a paternalistic federal administration. One other possible cause of Southern Ute apathy is the insidious belief held by many non-Indian government employees and by the local white population that the Ute Indians are incompletely evolved and are therefore biologically incapable of successful participation in American culture [86].

2. The preservation of aboriginal marital behavior in the face of constant and strong pressure from Agency officials for Indians to marry legally suggests that other more subtle and less obvious old Ute patterns may survive to condition present-day life [85].

3. In summary, it might be stated that the incomplete adjustment of Southern Ute to modern American culture is evident from an analysis of (1) their vital statistics, (2) their economic position, and (3) their political participation. Some factors contributing to their maladjustment are (1) persistence of old cultural values and practices, (2) discouragement resulting from exploitation and discrimination, and (3) paternalistic administration by the Indian Service.

48. Thompson, Laura. ATTITUDES AND ACCULTURATION. AA 50, 1948, 200-215.

Purpose or Problem. — To investigate certain basic orientations among various tribes (Sioux, Ojibwa, Navajo, Papago, and Hopi) with relation to the concept of "immanent justice" [200].

Definitions, Assumptions, and Hypotheses. — The results of a Piaget-type guided interview revealed the presence of certain attitude patterns differing from those of the white children tested and persisting in the acculturation situation [200].

Methods and Techniques. — Based on guided interviews of the Piaget-type, administered by the Indian Education Research Staff, to 1,000 selected Indian children (aged 6 to 18). Theoretical exposition.

Data. — The results indicated that in no Indian community studied, regardless of degree of acculturation, was there a statistically significant decrease in the number of responses indicating belief in immanent justice. The author relates this fact to other attitudes characterizing members of the five tribes. She develops the thesis that we can isolate a "predomestic animal" world view, involving an attitude of helpless dependence upon the supernatural; this is observed among the Ojibwa and Dakota Sioux. At the other end of a continuum of progressive change in the concept of the form and dynamics of the power source [211] she places the Hopi, whose concept of man changed to that of a power entity in a correlative system. The shift from supplication to coercion as techniques for dealing with the supernatural corresponds with a shift from hunting to agriculture. The Navajo, with a composite mosaic of localized but unrelated and unreliable personal-power entities (whom men coerced and propitiated), and the Papago, who juxtaposed individual and communal techniques for control of nature, represent transitional cases.

Conclusions. — 1. Although differences in attitude are marked among these tribes, they share belief in immanent justice even among the more acculturated. Thus, basic orientations regarding the nature of the universe are major psychocultural structures, deep-rooted in the tribal past and persisting through millennia, despite far-reaching changes in the group's ecology, economy, sociology, and ritual expressions [212].

2. Certain popular hypotheses, e.g., that religion is a projection of child-training patterns, or is a rationalization of the social system, are inadequate to explain this persistence, which is a central problem in social science.

3. Understanding of these attitudes, and their tendency to endure, is essential to the satisfactory administration of Indian affairs.

49. Tschopik, Harry. NAVAHO BASKETRY: A STUDY OF CULTURE CHANGE. AA 42, 1940, 444-62.

Purpose or Problem. — An attempt to combine the "functional" and "historical" approaches with reference to a particular problem — Navaho basketry. (1) Why does Navaho basketry survive at all as a functioning craft and as a relatively common article of material culture in the Ramah Navaho community, since most articles of aboriginal material culture have disappeared? Is basketry a survival without function? (2) Have the present attitudes toward baskets and the present functions prevailed in the recent past? (3) If there have been changes in these attitudes and functions, what are some of the processes which seem to have brought about these changes [444-45]?

Definitions, Assumptions, and Hypotheses. -- The difference in approach between the "culture historian" and the "functionalist" is not to be maintained on the theoretical level.

Methods and Techniques. -- An attempt to depict the relationships of the basketry craft to its context of Navaho culture at two points in the time continuum: (1) at the present day and (2) at the close of the nineteenth century. The data relating to the present time consist of (1) observed behaviors; (2) anecdotal accounts by informants; (3) statements of the beliefs of these informants.

Data. -- The use of basketry at the present time is wholly ceremonial; the attitudes toward baskets today are virtually identical with those manifested toward articles of ritual paraphernalia. Recently, there has been a tendency on the part of some of the younger Navaho women to take up the manufacture of baskets and to ignore completely the institutional procedures; since they lack formal training, this would seem to signalize the breakdown of the traditional basketry craft. Their motivation—that of making money—does not coincide with the cultural goal, the production of baskets for ceremonial usage.

At the close of the Bosque Redondo era (1868), a range of forms were manufactured by Navaho basket makers, and the craft was pursued by a proportionately larger number of women than is true at the present time. Baskets were then used for a far greater variety of purposes than they are today. A duality of attitudes toward basketry existed, ranging from the "sacred" ceremonial baskets, on the one hand, to the "profane" culinary and gathering baskets, on the other. The manufacture of all baskets seems to have been surrounded by fewer ritual restrictions than at present. Whereas little may be said of the function of basketry in the past, it is to be suspected that the "economic" functions—and possibly also the "social" functions—were formerly of less importance than they are today.

Conclusions. -- 1. Fear of the external sanctions, coupled with the identification of basketry with ritual, has in large measure produced the restrictions on basket makers as a specialized group, and the processes may still be observed as operative [453].

2. With the passing of the utilitarian needs (through contact with Western material culture), baskets became rarity objects. This fact, coupled with the initial association of basketry with ritual, seems to have caused the coiled basketry tray alone to survive for ceremonial purposes. Further-

more, in recent years there appears to have risen in the Ramah area an almost hysterical emphasis on the ceremonial aspects of Navaho life. The identification of basketry with ritual, and the emphasis on ritual per se, seems to have led to the ritualization of the Navaho basketry craft to an unparalleled extent. This fact, in turn, has enhanced the value of basketry to the degree where it is enabled to perform certain "economic" and "social" functions [461].

3. We must agree most wholeheartedly with Linton's proposition that "use" and "meaning" are more closely related to one another than either is to "form"; that "function" seems to derive particularly from "meaning." While "form" has remained stable, "use," "meaning," and (in part) "function" have changed [461].

50. Voget, Fred. INDIVIDUAL MOTIVATION IN THE DIFFUSION OF THE WIND RIVER SHOSHONE SUN DANCE TO THE CROW INDIANS. AA 50, 1948, 634-46.

Purpose or Problem. — To present a brief history of the diffusion and a description of the roles and motives of the individuals directly responsible for the transmission of the Shoshone ceremonial [634].

Definitions, Assumptions, and Hypotheses. — (Implicit.) An examination of the motivation of individual innovators is of primary significance in the study of diffusion.

Methods and Techniques. — Observations made during field study at the reservation in 1941 and 1946.

Graphs and Charts. — Sketch Map of the Crow Indian and Wind River Shoshone Reservations [635].

Data. — In June 1941, friendly Shoshone Sun Dance leaders supervised the production of the Shoshone Sun Dance on the Crow Indian Reservation of Montana. Since that time they have been given repeatedly by Crow leaders.

Three Crow men and one Shoshone man have been especially instrumental in the dissemination of the Sun Dance (which originally spread from the Crow to the Shoshone). These men vary greatly in degree of acculturation, but are all middle-aged and show general cultural dissatisfaction. They are marginal or nonmembers of Christian churches, and have abandoned or rejected an economic life according to the American pattern. The Crow leaders lack faith in modern medical practices and believe education to be of little use to the Indian as race discrimination prevents effective use of it.

The occasions on which these Crow leaders gave Sun Dances were determined by crisis situations, the illness of a relative, or anxiety about sons at war.

A fourth Crow leader responsible for dissemination of the Sun Dance on the Reservation is a highly acculturated man who is superintendent. He encouraged the Sun Dance acceptance, but did not participate in the dancing.

Conclusions. — The three Crow leaders reveal that both cultural and individual factors were operative in their attitudes toward and participation in the Sun Dance. Each shared the following: (1) a dissatisfaction with the cultural situation; (2) a reorientation of values around the native culture; (3) life crises which demanded solution; (4) a progressive reinforcement which confirmed them in the native direction which they had taken [646].

51. Voget, Fred.   A SHOSHONE INNOVATOR.   AA 52, 1950, 53-63.

Purpose or Problem. — An adequate understanding of the diffusion of culture requires a full consideration of the special circumstances obtaining in the donor society as well as the cultural and social conditions favoring adoption by the receptor society [53].

Assumptions, Definitions, and Hypotheses. — 1. No reservation today can be treated as if but one "native" culture were represented there. The contact of cultures of differential complexity has produced not only social and cultural disintegration of the less complex, but new social categories and cultural integrations also, which, until a relatively stable situation arises through their establishment as a part of the total configuration, germinate problems of adjustment [53].

2. We may have to deal with individuals who are social isolates in that they do not share in sufficient degree a common sociocultural background, but share certain basic dissatisfactions which serve to unite them into a functional group. We may have to deal with functional groups possessing a special culture which may be classified as native, native-modified, white-modified, and white.

3. An investigation of the dynamic relationship of the individual, motivated by self-perceived needs and desires, and the culture which makes certain solutions available to him, is essential to an understanding of specific cultural modifications [54].

Methods and Techniques. — Biographical data obtained in the summer of 1948.

Data. — A description of the motivation and role of John Truhujo in the diffusion of the Wind River Shoshone Sun Dance to the Crow Indians, illustrates the function of dissatisfaction (manifest in a socially and culturally marginal individual) in the stimulation of activity leading to intercultural borrowing and to changes attempted within the culture of origin. Biographical data reveal the informant to have developed his reactions to his setting in a well-defined series of stages. (1) Witnessed his attempt to identify himself with the dominant white group; (2) was in the nature of a "crisis" — the social and cultural situation became increasingly defined in terms of participation in a Shoshone group rather than in a white group; (3) is marked by Truhujo's efforts to participate to the full in that part of Shoshone society which may be classified culturally as native-modified. The significant characteristic of this group was a cultural integration, based on nativistic forms of worship, the most important of which was the Sun Dance.

The partial realization of his ambitions to become a ceremonial leader has been possible for Truhujo only by achieving distinction in a society outside his own. In 1941, he played a paramount role in the diffusion of the Shoshone Sun Dance to the Crow, and since that time he has been disseminating his deviant form of the dance among that group. He has attempted subsequently to realize his status ambitions in his own group by establishing his innovations as a part of the Shoshone performance. He has been aided by a situation in which leadership control is now well established in the Sun Dance owing to the death of the old leaders, but complete success has not been achieved.

Conclusions. — 1. Spectacular "cures," genealogical relationship, and personality were the primary factors in Crow acceptance of Truhujo [59].

2. Complete success cannot be predicted for Truhujo for two reasons: (1) his innovations represent nativisms inconsistent with current trends in the Shoshone Sun Dance, and (2) his personality structure is inconsistent with the ideal status-personality of the Sun Dance leader as it is defined by the Shoshone [61].

3. A knowledge of sociocultural conditions in both the donor and receptor societies is essential to a full understanding of diffusion [62].

4. Culture change among such groups (native societies in North America) may be studied to advantage by investigation of the dynamics of adjustment manifest by those undergoing it vis-à-vis the dominant white and the subordinate native sociocultural groups.

52. Voget, Fred. ACCULTURATION AT CAUGHNAWAGA: A NOTE ON THE NATIVE-MODIFIED GROUP. AA 53, 1951, 220-31.

Purpose or Problem. — Investigation of the native-modified group at Caughnawaga — structure of the group, the basic premises by which the membership operates, and the type of social and cultural organization which is supported [222].

Definitions, Assumptions, and Hypotheses. — 1. One may not treat native societies in the process of change as homogeneous units, but must direct attention to sociocultural groups, the basis for whose emergence lies in certain conceptions of self and of the social and cultural situation rather than in simple political or religious factionalism.

2. Three sociocultural groups may be identified at Caughnawaga: native-modified, Euro-American-modified, Euro-American marginal [222].

Methods and Techniques. — Preliminary report on a field study of the three sociocultural groups on the reservation.

Data. — At Caughnawaga Iroquois Reserve (Canada), Indians have been undergoing acculturation for 300 years. At present, the native-modified group is divided into two parts: those following the religion of the Seneca prophet, Handsome Lake, and adhering to the constitution of the Five Nations Confederacy, and those with a marginal interest in Christian churches and functioning under the political organization established by the Canadian Indian Act. Both groups share conceptions of themselves as Indians, dispossessed by whites who seek to submerge them in the population at large. The more conservative subgroup stresses sib membership and allegiance to life chiefs. They do not take part in community elections as provided for by the Indian Act. The others, who are politically active, oppose every move which would end the isolation of the reserve. Those following the religion of Handsome Lake constitute the core of the native-modified membership. They stress repudiation of Christianity; they relate the Mohawk to God as his "chosen people," whose rights he will protect. The Catholic Church is seen as threatening these rights, as clergy and Agency appear to be working toward the dreaded enfranchisement.

Conclusions. — The Caughnawaga data seem to confirm the relationship of the basic values held by a group and the type of culture which is supported [230]. Emergent nativism is developing in the face of increasing threat to the social and cultural identity of the group. The data also suggest that as conflicts arise and intensify, the assumptions by which a people order their life are increasingly verbalized and objectified, and thus assume a greater role for the individual and the group.

53. Voget, Fred. CROW SOCIO-CULTURAL GROUPS. ICAP 29th, 1952, 88-93.

Purpose or Problem. — In the course of prolonged contact and directed change new social categories possessing a rather distinctive subculture appear to have been generated. It is maintained that these emerging groups are significant for the understanding of contemporary culture change for new problems of adjustment have arisen which have brought the emerging sociocultural groups into conflict on some issues, while on others they may be in agreement or in accommodation [88].

Definitions, Assumptions, and Hypotheses. — 1. Reservation populations in the United States can be treated no longer as socially and culturally homogeneous. It is here suggested that a definition of the native sociocultural groups in terms of numerical proportion, cultural integration and content, and interaction is now particularly essential to a full understanding of contemporary culture change among reservation populations.

2. Four sociocultural groupings appear to be distinguishable among the Crow at the present time: (1) native, (2) native-modified, (3) American-modified, (4) American-marginal.

Methods and Techniques. — (Not indicated.) The paper is theoretically oriented.

Data. — (1) The native group comprises a minority of the population whose significant integration is in the unchanged native values. While membership is mostly confined to the aged, of greater significance are the occasional individuals of middle age who identify themselves with this group and not only seek to perpetuate the aboriginal social values but also strive to revive aboriginal religious practices and meanings. Membership in this sociocultural category is assumed to consist mainly of those of pure descent. (2) The native-modified grouping constitutes the majority of the population; culturally it finds its primary values in native Crow culture, but some adjustments have been made to changed conditions. The principal factors in the adjustment of this category are: (a) nonparticipation in the functioning aboriginal culture; (b) childhood training by parents who were basically native in thought and action; and (c) intensive formal socialization within the institutional framework of the dominant society, viz., education and religion. Members of this group may be said to be the purveyors of contemporary Crow culture; a major emphasis is laid upon the social solidarity of the Crow, and criticism is leveled against those who do not participate in the cultural activities of the group. They share with the native group a basic belief in the necessity for maintaining the reservation system, since it contributes much to their security; changes tend to be conceived in terms of administrative reform. The majority are interested basically in a worship which is nativistic in form, function, and principle, the meaning being fundamentally Christian. It is this acceptance which allows the facile participation in a Christian or nativistic religious expression—a duality which points up their ambivalent tendencies. (3) The significant criterion for the American-modified group is a cultural integration based upon the fundamental values of American culture without relinquishing membership in the subordinate society. This category is characterized by an active participation in a Christian church and an exploitation of the land in a manner conforming to the American economic tradition; there is fuller appreciation of the American ideal of improving oneself: education is emphasized, property is accumulated and protected from deterioration. There is a marked tendency to exploit a marginal position vis-à-vis the white and the native-modified societies, possible in large part because of their skillful command of English. They are the representatives in the tribe's official relations with the administration; indeed, the political activity of this group tends to give a number of its members a special function and status in the total reservation configuration. (4) American-marginal, those whose cultural integration and identification is thoroughly American. They constitute a segment of the dominant society inasmuch as they do not participate with the sociocultural groups of the Crow but, on the contrary, strive to identify themselves with the white group; this is hindered by local social discrimination based on a recognition of their partial Indian ancestry. They thus tend to be social isolates.

Conclusions. — 1. From the viewpoint of culture change, the four sociocultural groupings described are significant because of the problems of adjustment which are posed for individuals singly and collectively. Each sociocultural category includes individuals whose orientation developmentally has been in two or more subcultures [92]. In some instances, an ambivalent response pattern results. Some, frustrated in their attempts to participate fully in a particular sociocultural group, withdraw and devote themselves to another of lesser status. Frequently such attempts involve leadership and the introduction of innovations. Examples are the American-modified group, where the bar to participation in American society intensifies the problem. A proportion of such "marginal" individuals develop an exaggerated emphasis upon aboriginal values and attempt to perpetuate them as innovations in the native-modified ceremonials or to introduce nativistic forms of worship. Others may separate themselves and attempt to function in semi-isolation as a segment of the dominant society [92].

2. It is suggested that the sociocultural groups described for the Crow typify a recurrent development in a contact situation involving cultures of differential complexity [92].

3. An initial investigation of differentially acculturated societies which originally possessed a similar culture, and which were subjected to similar cultural influences, followed by a comprehensive regional comparison should produce significant over-all trends in the acculturation picture [92].

4. It is reasonable to assume that at the time the aboriginal culture of the Crow ceased to function a greater proportion of the population would have been classifiable as "native" than is currently indicated. Numerically, then, the groups may be conceived to shift through time as acculturation proceeds. A statement of the numerical proportions of the sociocultural groups would thus serve as an index of acculturation [92].

54. Wallace, Anthony F. C. SOME PSYCHOLOGICAL DETERMINANTS OF CULTURE CHANGE IN AN IROQUOIAN COMMUNITY. Symposium on Local Diversity in Iroquois Culture, Smithsonian Institution, BAEB 149, 1951, 55-76.

Purpose or Problem. — (Implicit.) To study the complementary functions of culture and modal personality structure of any society in terms of four psychological traits exhibited by a community of Iroquois Indians [59, 63].

Definitions, Assumptions, and Hypotheses. — 1. The psychological characteristics (primarily modal personality structure and its derivatives) of the individuals who compose a society act as a screen tending to accept as new culture elements forms of behavior which are psychologically congenial, and tending to exclude forms of behavior which are psychologically uncongenial. The term "psychic conservatism" may be applied to any occasion in which culture change is not accompanied by significant psychological change.

2. There are important conceptual differences between cultural pattern and psychological screen as determinants of culture change. There are really two questions in the pattern formula: (1) What is the relation between cultural innovations and existing culture? (2) What is the relation between cultural innovations and psychological structure [62-63]?

Methods and Techniques. — Observations of John Lawson between 1701 and 1709 are the source for the Tuscarora psychological past; Wallace's observations, for the present. Not a sketch of Tuscarora modal personality structure: only a few traits are presented [64].

Data. — The following psychological traits of the Tuscarora Indians are discussed: (1) The absence of a fear of heights; (2) the chronic longing for alcoholic intoxication; (3) the lack (relative to white norms) of anal-reactive character formations; (4) and an oral type of personality. (1) has been an important determinant of culture change in that the Tuscarora have entered the highly paid construction work, markedly reducing the number of men engaged in agricultural work and working closely with white men. In connection with (2), certain cultural techniques have been developed to solve the moral problem of a people who disapprove of intrafamily and intracommunity brawls; thus, certain institutions exist which set up cultural mechanisms of defense against an unwanted drive. In connection with (3), fundamental personality changes would have to be effected before the Tuscarora could ever become a people with an ethical system that demands frugality, punctuality, systematic neatness, etc. This is an example of a group of possible cultural changes which did not occur in spite of pressure on their behalf, partly because they implied behavior for which the Indians were not psychologically prepared. With reference to (4), while all persons have dependency wishes, it is conceivable that one people may, because of the prevailing mode of formative experience, characteristically be more dependent in their impulses than another. In aboriginal times, when the kinship organization was stronger, such dependency impulses presumably had more effective intracommunity implementation than the reservation culture provides today. For over 150 years, institutionalized, "official" dependency relationships have been fostered, the Indians putting themselves into the position of a corporate child.

Conclusions. — 1. If we grant that all peoples have a definable modal personality structure, that this structure is inflexible within one generation, and that this structure (in conjunction with other factors) determines what cultural forms can be implemented in behavior — then we may conclude that no cultural form can be successfully introduced, within the space of one generation, which requires behavior which is uncongenial to that personality structure. The Iroquoian community reported upon in this study represents a case in point. The psychological characteristics of the Tuscarora have permitted some innovations in behavior which were psychologically feasible, and excluded other suggested patterns which would have been psychologically incongruous [75].

2. The far-reaching cultural changes (e.g., entrance into construction work and other white industries) are based partly upon the maintenance of at least one element of the old personality structure [65].

55. Waterman, Richard Alan. AFRICAN INFLUENCE ON THE MUSIC OF THE AMERICAS. ICAP 29th, 1952, 207-18.

Purpose or Problem. — (Not indicated more explicitly than the title would suggest.)

Definitions, Assumptions, and Hypotheses. — There are two reasons why African musical elements have influenced the musical styles of the Americas: (1) American Negro groups have remained relatively homogeneous with regard to culture patterns and remarkably so with respect to in-group solidarity. (2) There is enough similarity between African and European music to permit musical syncretism [207].

Methods and Techniques. — Field work in Cuba, summers of 1946 and 1948; much library work.

Data. — In some respects, the western one-third of the Old World land mass is musically homogeneous, for it is set off from the other major musical areas by the extent of its reliance on the diatonic scale and by its use of harmony which latter appears nowhere else in aboriginal music. Dominance of percussion, polymeter, off-beat phrasing of melodic accents, overlapping call-and-response patterns, and the metronome sense, account for the major differences between tribal African and European folk and popular music.

The use of song as a device for social control and for the venting of aggression and the traditional contests of virtuosity in singing and playing are functioning elements of West African culture today, as they are of such musical styles as the Trinidad "calypso" in the New World. There is also in West Africa little difference, in purely musical terms, between sacred and secular usage; this is mirrored in all the areas of Negro settlement in the Americas.

There are two aspects of the problem of African influence on the music of the Americas. One concerns the music of predominantly Negro populations, the other the spread of stylistic elements from American Negro music to the music of New World populations in general. Also, two distinct geographical areas—North American and Latin American—must be considered separately since they have had different acculturation histories. It becomes evident that in the regions mentioned (e.g., Brazil, Haiti, the United States) which span the habitat of the Negro in the Americas, music associated with Negroes is, in terms of the five dominant values listed, predominantly African. The music of these same areas which is not specifically identified with Negro populations likewise shows, in many instances, the same African traits. While jazz is an intricate blend of musical idioms and has also had its own evolution as an art form, those elements that mark off any kind of jazz from the rest of the popular music of the United States are precisely those we have cited as diagnostic of West African music.

Conclusions. — 1. Both of the criteria offered above (Definitions, Assumptions, and Hypotheses) for the persistence of a tradition in an acculturative situation have been fulfilled in the case of the African musical style in the Americas [210] —contrast the rarity of examples of genuine syncretization between American Indian music and the music of either Europe or Africa [209].

2. Because it amounts to an unverbalized point of view concerning all music, this traditional value (the "metronome sense") which differentiates African from "pure" European systems of musical appreciation is a typical example of the variety of subliminal culture pattern most immune to the pressures of an acculturative situation [211].

3. In areas where the official European religion permitted the syncretism of deities with the saints of the Church, African religious music has persisted almost unchanged, and African influence upon secular music has been strong. In Protestant areas where such syncretism has not been possible, the influence of African musical patterns on both religious and secular music has hinged upon a more extensive process of reinterpretation but is nonetheless considerable, in that fundamental characteristics of West African music have been retained [217].

4. In the case of the music of the Negro in the New World, we have an ideal situation for the study of musical change. We know, in general, the African side of the equation. We also know the European side, and we are in a position to study the American results of musical acculturation. Furthermore, among the less tangible aspects of culture, music is unique in that it can be readily quantified and submitted to rigid statistical analysis. It may be expected to have relevance for the study of other cultural intangibles which, while not so easily subjected to quantitative treatment, are, like musical patterns, carried largely below the level of consciousness [218].